Our Elders Lived It

Our Elders Lived It

AMERICAN INDIAN IDENTITY IN THE CITY

▼ ▼ ▼

Deborah Davis Jackson

NORTHERN

ILLINOIS

UNIVERSITY

PRESS

DEKALB

© 2002 by Northern Illinois University Press
Published by the Northern Illinois University Press, DeKalb, Illinois 60115
Manufactured in the United States using acid-free paper
All Rights Reserved
Design by Julia Fauci

Library of Congress Cataloging-in-Publication Data
Jackson, Deborah Davis.
Our elders lived it : American Indian identity in the city / Deborah Davis Jackson.
    p.   cm.
Includes bibliographical references and index.
ISBN 0-87580-281-8 (clothbound: alk. paper)
ISBN 0-87580-591-4 (pbk: alk. paper)
1. Indians of North America—Urban residence. 2. Indians of North America—
Ethnic identity. 3. Indians of North America—Urban residence—Great Lakes
Region. I. Title.
E98.U72 J33 2002
305.897'3077'091732—dc21
2001044520

The illustrations in this volume are from various collections of the Bentley
Historical Library, University of Michigan, used with permission.

Substantial portions of Chapter 4 first appeared in *American Indians and the
Urban Experience*, a special edition of the *American Indian Culture and Research
Journal* 22, no. 4 (1998): 227–54, and is used here with permission.

for Michael

Contents

Preface

"Identity" is not something you design a research project to find; it is something that finds you when you've gone looking for something else.

—*Roy A. Rappaport*

This book analyzes the dynamics of ethnic identity as they occur within a particular American Indian community in a particular urban center of the United States. In order to ensure the privacy of those who so generously allowed me entry into their community and into their lives, I have chosen to keep the location anonymous. I use the fictitious name "Riverton" for the city in which I conducted my fieldwork, and "Birmingham" for the county in which Riverton is located. I refer to the small state university there as "Riverton University," and to the corporation that has loomed largest in Riverton's economy throughout most of the twentieth century as "American Automotive Corporation." I have also, of course, changed the names of all the individuals quoted or referred to in the course of describing the community, as well as information concerning tribal affiliation, occupation, and other such personal data that might compromise their anonymity. Having made these changes, I am reasonably reassured that I will not inadvertently repay the kindnesses of my American Indian friends, coworkers, consultants, and interviewees by bringing upon them unwanted attention or publicity.

Riverton is located in the region of North America that might best be designated the Upper Great Lakes. As shown on the map, the exact borders of this region are rather arbitrary. It encompasses the state in which Riverton is located and several nearby states with similar demographics and political-economic histories; furthermore, the portions of Ontario shown are relevant especially for their Indian reserves, from which many urban migrants in Riverton and similar cities originated. This area of North America constitutes a reasonable context within which to consider Riverton's American

Indian community, and the Upper Great Lakes region, as defined by this map, is what the reader should keep in mind when thinking about where Riverton is located.

The largest urban centers of the region—Cleveland, Detroit, Indianapolis, Chicago, Milwaukee, Minneapolis/St. Paul, Des Moines—are shown for orientation. However, it is the midsized cities—such places as Toledo, Ohio; Saginaw, Michigan; South Bend, Indiana; Rockford, Illinois; Kenosha, Wisconsin; Duluth, Minnesota; and Waterloo, Iowa—that one ought to think about when considering the demographics, economy, and history of Riverton. Like many of these midsized cities, Riverton has been dependent on industry—in particular, the automotive industry—throughout the twentieth century. As one historian put it, "[t]here were two midwestern auto industries: the famous and visible one clustered around Detroit, and the less well-known industry of parts makers [including steel and sheet metal, glass, tires, and engines], concentrated . . . [on and near] the shores of Lake Michigan and Lake Erie" (Nelson 1995: 75). I use the term automotive industry to encompass both the "visible" and the "invisible" auto industries. As that industry shifted its manufacturing operations out of the region during the later part of the twentieth century, Riverton and other automotive cities suffered.

Riverton's position in the local economy of the Upper Great Lakes region, throughout the twentieth century and in the present day, provides a vitally significant context within which to consider the American Indian community there. Most of the members of that community are *Anishinaabe*—the Native-language term for the closely related Chippewa/Ojibwa, Ottawa/Odawa, Potawatomi, Menominee, Miami, and other Algonquian-speaking peoples of the Upper Great Lakes region. The plural form is *Anishinaabeg*.

With regard to that community, a few comments on terminology are in order. While the terms "Native American" and "American Indian" both appear throughout this book, I use American Indian considerably more often, reserving Native American for relatively formal contexts. This is due to a change among Native Americans themselves in recent years—a change I became aware of while conducting research in Riverton. The most often-used term among Native Americans there was "Indian" (used here in some contexts, as well as simply "Native"), with the second most common being "American Indian," while "Native American" was hardly used at all. In fact, during my fieldwork, the group at Riverton University's campus that had been calling itself the Native American Student Organization changed its name to the American Indian Student Organization.

Fieldwork proceeded from the spring of 1993 through the fall of 1995. There are no distinct American Indian neighborhoods in Riverton, and my primary point of entry into the community was the Indian Center operated by Riverton's largest and most prominent Native American organization, the Birmingham County Indian Association. I worked there as a volunteer, spending one day per week providing a variety of services from cleaning the office and watering the plants, to running errands and performing secretarial duties such as filing, typing, and computer work. I also got involved in Riverton University's American Indian Student Organization, helping out with their events, as well as events sponsored by the Indian Education Program in Riverton's public school system. During two and a half years there, I attended virtually every public American Indian event that took place in Riverton, and was often involved in the work of planning or producing the event. This involvement in the activities of the community allowed me to meet and get to know many American Indian people in Riverton.

My primary research method was participant observation. I also conducted life-historical interviews with twenty-four adult individuals of varying ages and backgrounds—half of them men, the other half women, but all of whom had some degree of American Indian ancestry, in most cases Anishinaabe. I designed loosely structured interviews to elicit information on certain topics concerning the interviewee's life experience, such as family life during childhood, schooling, interactions with other American Indians as well as with non-Native people, types of work done and conditions on the job, and so on. The interviews took place in locations comfortable for the interviewee—usually either in a restaurant or in the interviewee's home. I then supplemented the knowledge gained from the tape-recorded life-historical interviews with hundreds of informal conversations with a great variety of American Indian people in Riverton; I recorded the main points of these conversations afterward, along with general observations, in the form of fieldnotes. Finally, I drew on available statistical and archival resources and contemporary publications such as the local newspaper and minutes of Birmingham County Indian Association board meetings to provide a larger context within which to evaluate my findings.

During my research, I was also involved in an oral history project with a tribe whose headquarters are in a small city about sixty miles north of Riverton. The project was sponsored by the Kellogg Foundation, and I served as director and primary interviewer. Since there was some overlap between the interviewees in the Riverton area and tribal members who participated in the Kellogg project, I donated some of my Riverton interview transcripts to the Kellogg project—with permission of the interviewees. All participants in the oral history project were personally known to me. Thus, some of the project interviews served to support both my dissertation and this book. (I have indicated their origin at the end of the quote by showing "Jackson" in parentheses, along with the page number on which the quoted material appears in the edited collection of Kellogg transcripts.)

While in some ways a general ethnography of a particular urban ethnic community, this work is primarily concerned with a specific aspect of community life—issues of ethnic identity. I did not set out to study this phenomenon. In fact, when I designed my field research proposal in the early 1990s, I had decided not to pursue ethnic identity as a topic; not only is it an elusive phenomenon, but the very popularity of the topic made me reluctant to add yet another study to the ever burgeoning ethnic identity literature. I set out instead to determine the role that home communities (reservations and off-reservation rural communities) play in the lives of American Indians in the urban Indian community of Riverton. However, in order to learn anything about a particular ethnic group—whatever the specific topic of interest might be—one must first determine who is in that group. And the more I learned during my first year of fieldwork, the more confused I became as to who the American Indian people of Riverton were.

Based on early research, I had initially assumed that most people in the urban Indian community came from a home reservation themselves, or were the children of people who had migrated from such communities. Yet many of the people I met in Riverton had to go back several generations to find an ancestor who had grown up on a reservation or in an off-reservation American Indian community. This not only thwarted my efforts to learn about the significance of such home communities; it also raised some troubling questions. Who might reasonably be considered American Indian, and in what sense were they American Indian—that is, what constituted their "Indianness"? Was it simply a matter of recognizing those who self-identified as American Indian, or was there more to it than that? If the former, what would be the consequences of such a position for my research? If the latter, what other criteria lay beyond self-identification? Physical appearance, or "phenotype"? Genetic lineage? Cultural traits such as speaking a Native language or adhering to indigenous beliefs and practices? Such issues eventually became the central focus of my research.

As these questions begged ever more insistently for answers, I had the sense of becoming less, not more, knowledgeable about American Indians in Riverton. Then, I observed an incident that dramatically illustrated how the same questions I had been asking myself—who is American Indian and by what criteria—were also vitally important for the people involved with Riverton's Native American community. The incident also provided hints as to how to make sense out of the ambiguous, conflicting, and contested identities I had been observing. My account of Riverton's American Indian community and my exploration of ethnic identity issues there begins with a description of that incident.

Acknowledgments

The research and writing that led to this book could not have been sustained without material, intellectual, and emotional support from many sources. Starting with the material, I wish to acknowledge the assistance of the following institutions, each of which funded a portion of the work: the Margaret Wray French Scholarship Fund at the University of Michigan; the Wallenberg Foundation at the University of Michigan; the Phillips Fund for Native American Studies of the American Philosophical Society; and the Horace H. Rackham School of Graduate Studies at the University of Michigan. Finally, I received funding during the initial stages of writing the book from the National Institute on Aging's Grant T32-AG0017.

Intellectual influences are more difficult to identify with absolute accuracy and completeness, but I can certainly begin with E. Valentine Daniel, who served as my adviser and has been my most important mentor and intellectual role model since I took his Semeiotic Anthropology class and found my identity as an anthropologist. His written work, along with intense conversations about specific theoretical issues, have inspired me and given me direction. Crisca Bierwert and Frithjof Bergmann have also assisted me at crucial junctures along the way with their commentary on my written work and in conversations and collaborations of various kinds. Regna Darnell, of the University of Western Ontario, provided intellectual guidance during early stages of the writing through her published works. She gave an early draft an extraordinarily close reading and made extensive comments—from pointing out typos to suggesting alternative interpretations of substantive points and steering me toward additional relevant sources. I appreciate all her help, as well as Timothy Bisha's active role in introducing me to Regna and facilitating our working together. Finally, I wish to express my deep gratitude for Roy A. Rappaport's guidance. He aided me until the illness that eventually took his life made it impossible for him to continue. Skip never failed to amaze me with his ability to see immediately the core issue of every conceptual problem and to offer terse advice that was right on target. In addition to his intellectual gifts, Skip was an extraordinarily humane and generous man. I am honored to have known him.

Others at the University of Michigan who have significantly influenced my academic development both in the classroom and through their writings are: Sergei Kan; Alton Becker (in linguistics); Bruce Mannheim; Sherry B. Ortner; and George C. Rosenwald (in psychology). I owe them each an intellectual debt. Finally, there are those professors who have become such friends that it is difficult to determine where one role leaves off and the other begins: Robbins Burling was a lively interlocutor as we met periodically over lunch or tea to discuss the merits of scientific vs. humanistic anthropology—Rob kept me honest with his challenging questions; James McDonald was extraordinarily generous with his time, making useful suggestions, putting me in touch with people important to my research, and serving as my most engaged and informed conversational partner as I attempted to unravel the complexities of American Indian identity in "Riverton"; and Holly Peters-Golden, whom I first met when I served as her teaching assistant, has been an important mentor, role model, and friend, offering unlimited encouragement and support throughout every stage of my work.

Another professor at the University of Michigan who played a key role in this project was Roger Rouse. During my early research, I was fortunate to be able to participate in monthly meetings of an interdisciplinary discussion group on the cultural politics of class—founded and facilitated by Roger as a means of generating cross-fertilization of ideas and sharing of information among social scientists (anthropologists, sociologists, political scientists, economists, historians) working in the Upper Great Lakes region. The readings and discussions offered by the group provided the key impetus for the global perspective present in this book. I am grateful not only to Roger Rouse, but also to Andrea Sankar of Wayne State University for her role in helping to keep the group going, and to all the members of the group for sharing their work and making suggestions regarding my own research plans.

Transcription of my field interview tapes was provided, with technical expertise and anthropological insight, by Paul G. Davis. Heather Eisenhart of Eastern Michigan University used greatly appreciated technical expertise and conscientiousness to assist in the creation of the map that appears at the start of this book. Sian Chivers provided invaluable assistance in compiling the index. I am also grateful for the assistance provided by the staff of the Bentley Historical Library at the University of Michigan in Ann Arbor, who helped locate the photos reproduced in this book, duplicated those photos, and made sure that permission to publish had been given by the individuals who had donated the photos to the library.

While working on an early stage of my work I was greatly assisted, both intellectually and emotionally, by graduate students in the group that met regularly during 1996. Additionally, I was blessed with two readers who were very much a part of the process: Katherine Zirbel and Deborah Freedman Lustig each saw most of my early work and made extensive, thoughtful comments and suggestions. Deborah came to my assistance again at a later stage of the production. Two additional readers, Kate Hitchcock and Susan Miller, both offered guidance during the preparation of this book.

At Northern Illinois University Press, my first contact was with Robert Anthony, the acquisitions editor who encouraged me to strive toward a publishable manuscript even as I was just beginning to work on my dissertation. His successor, Martin Johnson, was supportive and patient as I struggled to complete the revision amid many competing obligations. I am grateful to both Robert and Martin and other members of the Press for their assistance in preparing the final manuscript for publication. Finally, I wish to thank Northern Illinois University Press's two anonymous reviewers, both of whom offered encouragement and excellent suggestions for improvement, many of which I have incorporated into this final version.

This study could not have been completed without the help and cooperation of the American Indian people in Riverton who comprise its subject matter. I was constantly surprised and touched by the willingness with which the staff and board of the Birmingham County Indian Association, and officials and members of other organizations as well, allowed me access to their world and accepted my participation in their activities. Providing anonymity for all participants in this study prevents me from naming names, but I want to express my deep and heartfelt gratitude to all interviewees for having shared their lives with me so generously. I also wish to acknowledge the many people who, both in the context of formal interviews and informal conversations, helped me sort out the complexities of American Indian identity and community in Riverton. As I tried out various theories, they patiently explained to me what I had gotten wrong, and how things *really* were. The final analysis owes much to these discussions and to the contributions of my American Indian consultants, friends, acquaintances, and coworkers. Anything I still may not have gotten quite right is, of course, my own fault.

Finally, I wish to express thanks to all my family members— husband, son, parents, siblings, in-laws, "steps," aunts, and uncles— and friends old and new, who over the years have encouraged and supported me in various ways. Most notably, my mother, Anne S. Davis, has been there for me as role model, having completed her own college degree at age forty-six. Her constant pride in my achievements, as well as financial support at certain crucial junctures, made all the difference. Finally, my deepest gratitude goes to Michael R. Jackson, my life partner, intellectual mentor, challenging interlocutor, and insightful and provocative commentator on nearly every page of the various stages of this book. Without Michael's unflagging faith in me, his willingness and ability to engage in long and intense discussions on every important idea that has guided my graduate and postdoctoral work, and his unstinting support throughout the process, this book quite literally could not have been written. It is to him that I dedicate this work.

Our Elders Lived It

Introduction

The Question of Identity

▼ ▼ ▼

Who *are* the Indians? *What* are the Indians?!
—a member of Riverton's Indian community

In the fall of 1994, I attended the annual business meeting of the Birmingham County Indian Association (BCIA)—the primary organization serving Riverton's American Indian population. While including people from many different tribal backgrounds, the Association predominantly comprises people of Anishinaabe descent from around the Upper Great Lakes area. Membership in the BCIA is open, and announcements of its annual business meeting are disseminated widely throughout the Birmingham County area, well in advance of the event. At the meeting, board members are nominated and elected, and other matters of concern to the community are taken up. The BCIA rents a banquet facility for the event, the meeting is preceded by a potluck dinner, and all interested parties are welcome to attend, enjoy the meal, offer their input, and cast their votes for board members.

THE 1994 ANNUAL MEETING OF THE BCIA

At this particular annual meeting about seventy-five people turned out—families, couples, and single people of all ages. I had become aware during the months preceding the meeting, from people at the BCIA's Indian Center where I volunteered, that there might be "trouble" at the gathering due to growing discontent among some segments of the American Indian community about policies the BCIA had recently adopted, and about the personal behavior of some recently elected board members and powwow committee members regarding their handling of the annual powwow the previous July.

When I arrived, however, everyone seemed to be in good spirits and a number of the long cafeteria-type tables were already filling up with families and groups of friends. The BCIA had provided turkeys and hams for the dinner, and everyone had brought a side dish to share; the buffet table was laden with such American Indian regional favorites as corn soup, wild rice, venison stew, and Indian fry bread, as well as more mainstream salads, casseroles, breads, and desserts of every description. During dinner, I circulated around the room, sitting for a time with each of a number of groups and individuals I had come to know during the past year. The atmosphere was festive, and most people seemed to be enjoying themselves. Then, after everyone had finished eating and the paper plates and cups had been cleared away, the business meeting began.

The director gave a brief report, and the moderator asked if there were any comments from the floor before nominations for new board members began. For the first time, I noticed a slight tension in the air. After a brief but uncomfortable pause, a woman in her forties wearing a long, brightly colored skirt and a tee shirt bearing a Chippewa tribal insignia stood up. She said she was concerned that the board of directors was not in compliance with its own bylaws, because the bylaws called for a majority of board members to be Native American, and that was clearly not the case. Next, a slightly older man in a denim work shirt, his gray hair cut short, expressed support for her position. He also expressed concern about voter eligibility—he felt that only Indians should be able to vote. He ended by asking rhetorically: "Who *are* the Indians?" "*What* are the Indians?!"

Then others joined in, saying the BCIA was no longer truly an Indian organization, and that it ought to get back to promoting Anishinaabe language and customs. When a woman claiming a Cherokee heritage protested, saying, "This is an *urban* organization of *all* nations, not just Chippewa!" she was summarily dismissed by one of the previous speakers, who silenced her with the epithet: "Cherokee Princess!"

At this point I realized for the first time that the room had become spatially polarized. About thirty people, mostly in family groupings, were sitting at tables on the left side of the room. Those who were voicing increasingly emotional concerns about the present composition and actions of the BCIA's board of directors and who advocated for more Indian, and specifically more Anishinaabe, involvement were all among this group. Meanwhile, on the right side of the room, there were about twenty people—mostly couples and single individuals—of whom a group of some ten people seated together at the end of one table were members of the powwow committee. The woman who had just spoken out in support of a more pan-tribal approach was sitting with this powwow committee group. In most cases, the individuals on the right traced their American Indian heritage to a Cherokee ancestor several generations back, whom they had not known.

In contrast, those on the left side were families whose heritage was Anishinaabe. They had not been active in the BCIA during the past year, but they represented the established families of the urban Indian community, those who had founded the BCIA and had been its primary constituency until quite recently. While younger adults in these families—people now in their thirties and forties—had grown up in Riverton, the elder generation had grown up on reservations and in off-reservation rural Indian communities throughout the Upper Great Lakes region, migrating to Riverton at midcentury to take factory jobs. It was the city-raised generation that was actively engaged in this heated exchange, with the elders for the most part sitting quietly by.[1]

The tension in the room had become palpable and continued to increase as people on each of the two sides took turns standing up and shouting accusations toward those on the opposite side. With emotions running high, a woman on the left—a member of one of the founding families of the BCIA who had served as a board member in the past—stood up and asserted with quiet dignity: "The BCIA shouldn't be putting on a *white* powwow. I think we should disband the powwow committee."

This provoked an angry response on the opposite side of the room from a man in his thirties who self-identified as Cherokee, but who had an Hispanic surname and who was considered by many in the Anishinaabe families to be "white." He was one of the most outspoken of the powwow committee members, and he retorted: "You have no right to disband our committee. Where were *you* when we were working hard to plan the powwow!?"

Immediately a reply came from the same woman on the left: "Where were *you* when it wasn't popular to be Indian?!"

At this, a woman on the right, her long blond hair held back in a beaded barrette, stood up and protested: "We *are* Indian! We have just as much right to be in the Association and to plan the powwow as you do. We know our culture, too!"

But she was silenced with a rejoinder from the left, "I'm sick of you self-proclaimed experts. You find some old Indian on your family tree and you think you know everything. Then you start telling other people what to do! *Our* elders *lived* it!"

As people talked heatedly among themselves, those on the right side of the room—the powwow committee people—huddled in what was no doubt a desperate effort to prepare an effective response. The moderator attempted to regain control of the proceedings, but without success. At this moment, amid all the confusion and chaos, someone on the left side of the room held a small rectangular piece of cardboard up in the air. Then another person on the left did the same, and one by one other members of this group followed suit—without any discussion among themselves, people were reaching into their wallets, taking out the cards, and holding them aloft. Within a couple of minutes, virtually everyone on the left side of the room—including both the younger and elder generations—was sitting silently, holding up one of these cards. As the others, on the right side of the room, became aware of this extraordinary demonstration, they fell silent as well, and a hush came over the crowd. It took a few moments before I realized what those on the left were doing: as their final rejoinder in the battle over who was Indian and who was not, the Anishinaabe people had no need for words—they simply held up their "Indian cards."[2]

This dramatic and spontaneous display of cards documenting enrollment in a federally recognized tribe convinced me that identity issues are of primary importance to the community. By using these cards as indexical[3] signs that pointed to a tribal background—and thereby indicating the inability of the others to make such a display—one group had achieved a decisive victory over the other, at least for the time being. Furthermore, my own understanding of the BCIA community had also begun a major transformation: *identity* had, as Roy Rappaport would say, "found me." Over the following weeks and months, as I considered what I had witnessed, my task became clear. I needed to find a way to make sense out of the complexity of the issues in such a way as to shed light on the diversity of identities I had observed, not only at that annual meeting of the BCIA, but in many other venues as well.

Identity, however, has a wide variety of usages and meanings in anthropology and related disciplines. This variety has increased dramatically during the veritable explosion of "identity studies" that has occurred over the past twenty years or so. It will be useful, therefore, to review the relevant literature before returning to reexamine the confrontation at the BCIA meeting.

IDENTITY AS ETHNICITY

In anthropology, the single most important work in establishing ethnicity in its contemporary sense is Frederik Barth's (1969) *Ethnic Groups and Boundaries: The Social Organization of Cultural Difference.* In his introduction to this slim volume—a collection of essays on the nature of ethnic groups by a variety of authors—Barth laid out his notion of what it is that makes ethnic groups significant to social science. He challenged the predominant presuppositions of the time— "the simplistic view that geographical and social isolation have been the critical factors in sustaining cultural diversity" (p. 10). He also questioned the closely related claim that ethnicity is determined by "the overt cultural forms which can be itemized as traits" (ibid.)— such features as language, religion, styles of dress and hair, and foods. These "content" items had traditionally been explained by a common origin, either in terms of a shared history in a particular territory, or genetically as "racial" heritage. Barth contended that such traits can be misleading because they do not allow for change (through both time and space), and thus are not good indicators of ethnicity.

In contrast to the prevailing view, Barth designated the *boundary* between ethnic groups, rather than "the cultural stuff that it enclosed," as "the critical focus of investigation" (Barth 1969, 15). Thus, Barth not only suggested a radically new approach to the study of ethnic groups; in a way, he invented the notion of "ethnic *identity"*—a term he used frequently, and which had not been used much, if at all, prior to 1969, by others who discussed ethnic groups or similar social entities. Barth's cogent formulation of ethnicity held that: 1) differences and conflicts between groups are at least as important as homogeneity and harmony within them; 2) "natives" play active roles in their own self-definition; and 3) ethnicity is more about social *action* than it is about cultural *content*. In all these aspects, Barth prefigured developments that have come to be of central importance in anthropological theory.

With his emphasis on the active construction of ethnic identity by agents, Barth introduced *subjectivity* into the analysis of ethnic groups. While he did not actually use the word in his seminal essay, Barth clearly intended a subjective orientation when he stated that the features taken into account (in determining ethnic differences) "are not the sum of 'objective' differences, but only those which the actors themselves regard as significant" (Barth 1969, 14). Likewise, he specified that "socially relevant factors alone become diagnostic for membership [in an ethnic group], not the overt, 'objective' differences which are generated by other factors" (ibid., 15). This subjective/objective split has continued to be a primary concern for ethnicity scholars such as Cohen (1974), Glazer and Moynihan (1975), and Romanucci-Ross and DeVos (1995), all of whom have elaborated on the distinction between subjective and objective aspects of ethnic identity. Those who focus on the ethnic

Minnesota Reservations

1. Bois Forte (Chippewa)
2. Deer Creek (Chippewa)
3. Fond du Lac (Chippewa)
4. Grand Portage (Chippewa)
5. Leech Lake (Chippewa)
6. Lower Sioux
7. Mille Lacs (Chippewa)
8. Shakopee (Sioux)
9. Prairie Island (Sioux)
10. Red Lake (Chippewa)
11. Sandy Lake (Sioux)
12. Upper Sioux
13. Vermillion Lake (Chippewa)
14. White Earth (Chippewa)

Wisconsin Reservations

15. Bad River (Chippewa)
16. Potawatomi Reservation
17. Lac Courte Oreilles (Chippewa)
18. Lac du Flambeau (Chippewa)
19. Menominee Reservation
20. Oneida (West) Reservation
21. Red Cliff Reservation (Chippewa)
22. St. Croix (Chippewa)
23. Sokaogon (Chippewa)
24. Stockbridge Reservation
25. Winnebago (Ho-Chunk)

Michigan Reservations

26. Bay Mills (Chippewa)
27. Grand Traverse (Chippewa and Ottawa)
28. Hannahville (Potawatomi)
29. Isabella (Chippewa)
30. Lac Vieux Desert (Chippewa)
31. L'Anse (Chippewa)
32. Little Traverse (Odawa)
33. Ontanogan (Chippewa)
34. Pine Creek (Potawatomi)
35. Potawatomi Reservation
36. Sault Ste. Marie (Chippewa)

Ontario Reserves

37. Batchewana (Ojibway)
38. Chapleau (Cree)
39. Fort William (Ojibway)
40. Garden River (Ojibway)
41. Kettle & Stony Point (Ojibway)
42. Mattagami (Ojibway)
43. Michipicoten (Ojibway)
44. Mississauge (Ojibway)
45. Pays Plat (Ojibway)
46. Pic Heron Bay (Ojibway)
47. Red Rock (Ojibway)
48. Rocky Bay (Ojibway)
49. Sarnia (Ojibway)
50. Temagami (Ojibway)
51. Walpole Island (Ojibway, Ottawa, Potawatomi)
52. Whitefish River Reserve (Ojibway)
53. Wikwemikong (Ojibway)

identity of American Indian societies have done so in terms of subjective versus objective approaches as well.

AMERICAN INDIAN ETHNIC IDENTITY STUDIES

The classic ethnography on American Indian identity is Karen Blu's *The Lumbee Problem: The Making of an American Indian People*, published in 1980. The Lumbee are a people in rural North Carolina of mixed Native American, African American, and European American ancestry, who claim an American Indian identity. Blu draws on Barth, as well as others, in exploring the nature of ethnicity generally, and of Lumbee identity in particular. She emphasizes relations between Lumbee and non-Lumbee, and the complexity of the Lumbee situation—historical disruptions, policies of forced assimilation, intermarriage with other groups, plus additional factors—and concludes with the decidedly subjectivist suggestion that the state of mind of Lumbee people, with regard to their own ethnic identity, is of central importance in untangling the many strands of competing and conflicting criteria. Other ethnographers of American Indian communities (e.g., Braroe 1975; Landsman 1988; Foley 1996; Hensel 1996) have, like Blu, focused on relations between Native groups and non-Natives—on the boundary that Barth emphasized so strongly.

These studies are important in drawing attention to Native peoples' definitions of their own identity. In some settings, however—especially urban contexts—a straightforward acceptance of the claims of groups and individuals to a Native American identity has become problematic in recent years due to changes in the sociopolitical context. The romanticized imagery that has always been present in some form in American popular culture (along with demonized images of blood-thirsty savages, benighted primitives, and lazy, drunken Indians that have coexisted with and usually eclipsed their more "positive" counterparts), has been enjoying a resurgence since the mid-1980s. At the same time, an ethic of multicultural diversity has been gathering momentum since the Civil Rights movement of the 1960s, ultimately encouraging people of all backgrounds to reclaim their ethnic heritage. Thus, increasing numbers of Americans are claiming an American Indian heritage, while at the same time a growing number of communities are seeking official federal recognition as Indian tribes. Some historical background on this issue may prove useful.

Although Indian tribes were deemed "dependent, sovereign nations" in 1832 by the Supreme Court of the United States in *Worcester v. Georgia*, later U.S. federal Indian policies largely ignored this special political status and even acted overtly to break up tribal communities through the allotment policies of the late nineteenth and early twentieth centuries. Then, in 1934, Congress passed the Indian Reorganization Act (IRA), which provided a mechanism for the reestablishment of tribal governments that would be officially "recognized" by the federal government. These federally recognized tribal governments would then qualify for such benefits as guaranteed hunting and fishing rights for tribal members, protection of the tribe's natural resources, and the right to make their own laws in governing tribal territory (reservations). Some tribes applied for federal recognition under the IRA during the 1930s, and many of these (though by no means all) were granted official tribal status by the government.

During the 1940s, the federal government reversed itself completely with its infamous "termination" policy, whose goal was to dissolve tribal governments and all the responsibilities and obligations the federal government had toward them. Since the beginning of the 1960s, after the termination policy was abandoned, the number of applications for tribal recognition has risen dramatically. The federal Indian policy that replaced termination and that remains in effect to the present is called "self-determination" and is based on the principle that tribes be allowed greater control over their own economic as well as political affairs. The policies of this period have given tribes the means to create their own business enterprises. These economic freedoms, along with the political freedom confirmed in the IRA, have resulted in the rise of casino gambling (among other endeavors) as lucrative tribal businesses.

The recent increase in Indian communities seeking federal recognition as tribes has been paralleled by an increase in individuals claiming a Native American heritage and seeking official membership in a tribe. In response to these two interrelated trends, some recent books on American Indian identity (e.g., Clifton 1990; Green 1995) focus generally on issues of authenticity. Rather than being ethnographically or culturally grounded in particular communities, these works provide general overviews of how American culture has responded to romanticized myths of Indianness, and what some of the repercussions of this response have been. The authors seek to debunk the myths, and thereby expose as frauds those groups and individuals who rely on such myths for their claim to an American Indian identity. These works are preoccupied with authenticity in a way that the ethnographic treatments of American Indian identity are not. One such work has been criticized by prominent Native American intellectual Ward Churchill as follows: "When the various authors actually get around to touching upon questions of identity at all—which is seldom—it is all but exclusively by way of analyzing and sometimes rebutting Euro-American conceptions of what Indians are, have been, or should be" (Churchill 1996, 207). The question of authenticity, however, hovers around the margins of virtually all American Indian ethnic identity studies (and most ethnicity studies generally), whether explicitly addressed or not. The notion of the "invention of tradition," treated at length by Hobsbawm and Ranger in their 1983 book by that name, has not only been influential, but has been liberally applied to questions of American Indian identity.

Works that focus on authenticity, with their attention to whether a specific cultural form is genuine or whether it ever historically belonged to a particular group or presently belongs to an individual, might be considered to take an objectivist, as opposed to a subjectivist, perspective. Whereas subjectivists (in the extreme) accept the "native's point of view" at face value—Native Americans are those who identify themselves as such—the authenticity scholars seek to establish a documentable, historical reality in which the Native American identity of an individual or group is seen as an empirical question to be determined by empirical (i.e., objective) means. These studies have made valuable contributions to an understanding of American Indian identity issues. However, the approaches taken in the objectivist studies are only partially helpful in sorting out the implications of what happened at the Birmingham County Indian Association annual meeting. They seek to establish authenticity by means of cultural content or, more often, to expose inauthenticity by revealing the lack of such content or the invalid nature of what content there is.

Looking back now on the incident that took place at the BCIA meeting that afternoon, one can see that from the strictly objectivist perspective, which considers the "cultural content" of the groups represented, it might be difficult to define anyone there as American Indian. After all, very few people spoke a Native American language, virtually all were Christians, and none made his or her living through the subsistence practices that had sustained American Indian people in pre-Columbian and early contact times. And while some assumed features of traditional—or to borrow a term from Nancy Lurie (1971), "contact-traditional"—dress and hairstyle, these markers were not necessarily consistent with the specific Native American group to which an individual traced his or her ancestry. For example, someone claiming a Cherokee ancestry might signal this identity by wearing Navajo-style jewelry. Furthermore, aside from a few token clothing or jewelry items worn by certain individuals, all were dressed primarily in the jeans, shirts, skirts, blouses, and tee shirts of the dominant culture, and most of the men wore their hair short. Finally, there was no common genetic heritage, since most people there had a number of European American, Hispanic, or African American ancestors, in addition to those who were American Indian (not to mention the variety of genetic heritages lumped into the category "American Indian"). Therefore, an objectivist view would lead one to conclude that there were no "real Indians" at the annual meeting of the BCIA—the assemblage was simply a group of individuals with a distant genetic link to an American Indian ancestor, claiming an ethnic identity based solely on a desire to be associated with a Native American heritage.

Conversely, a strictly subjectivist perspective would yield the opposite finding. Since everyone there claimed to be American Indian, and each felt that he or she had a valid reason to make that claim, there would be no need to look any further. The people at the meeting were members of the BCIA, they were active in its programs, they all had at least one American Indian ancestor they knew of, and each felt connected to that aspect of his or her ancestry in some way that was personally meaningful. Within the logic of a subjectivist perspective, it would be inappropriate for an outsider (such as an ethnographer) to pass judgment on these claims to an American Indian identity, because the very act of making such a claim would constitute sufficient proof of the claim.

Both these alternatives are equally unsatisfying. There was something happening at the annual meeting that hinted at a distinction among the factions, a distinction representing more than the mere subjective claim to Indian identity shared by both factions. And yet it certainly was not based on the straightforward criteria of cultural content and genetic heritage that strict objectivists would insist upon. Furthermore, the degree to which different individuals displayed features of American Indian cultural heritage (mainly through clothing, jewelry, and hairstyle) seemed to exist in an *inverse* relation (though by no means a perfect one) to their connection to an American Indian extended family or Indian community in which they might have grown up. That is, those who grew up on reservations or in off-reservation rural American Indian communities were least likely to display such identity markers, while those who had only recently discovered a Native American ancestor were most likely to do so. Finally, the effective use of the Indian cards—by those who possessed them—in silencing those who did not have such cards was particularly striking. It is deeply ironic that those cards, while issued by tribes, are ultimately based on European American definitions of race.

In pre-Columbian times, the indigenous peoples of North America had no notion of categorizing different groups by ancestry—rather, it was cultural differences that served to distinguish one group from another, and those who changed groups (usually because of capture or marriage) and fully accepted the customs of the new group were considered full members of their adopted group (cf. Clifton 1989, 11; Fogelson 1998, 44–48). The criterion of blood quantum (having a certain fraction of "Indian blood," or, more precisely, a degree of ancestry) now used by most American Indian tribes in determining their membership is based on the European American perspective in which genetic heritage is quantified and objectified into fractions of racial types. It was the colonizing policies of the American government that institutionalized this criterion of Indianness in such a way that it has become difficult—given the weight of history behind the policy and the complexity of the present-day situation—for contemporary tribal governments to find alternative means of determining their memberships.

Thus, the use of tribal membership cards—which in most cases certify that the bearer of the card is at least one-quarter American Indian—defines American Indian identity in terms of the white man's laws, the colonial legacy, rather than in terms of indigenous notions of community/group membership. Yet the demonstration at the BCIA meeting was so effective that I suspected there must be other criteria at work beneath the surface, and that the Indian cards simply served as a convenient symbol for those other criteria. Further research indeed confirmed such a suspicion. Before pursuing these hidden criteria, I wish to suggest an alternative approach to the thorny question of ethnic identity—one that is based on a set of underlying presuppositions that differ from those of the studies reviewed above.

THE SEMIOTIC SELF

The difficulties inherent in having to choose between subjective and objective approaches to ethnic identity can be resolved, I would suggest, by abandoning the Cartesian notion of self on which that dichotomy is based. In its place can be substituted a semiotic notion of self such as that developed by the American philosopher C. S. Peirce.[4] In explicit contrast to the Cartesian notion of the self—the notion of an individual subject that is separated from other selves and from an objective world and that is relatively static over time—Peirce proposed that the self is a *sign*.

For Peirce, signs are not representations of the "objective" world. Unlike the more influential notion of the sign developed by Saussure, in which each sign stands in dyadic relation to the object it represents, Peirce's sign has a triadic structure in which the sign relates to its object through an "interpretant." This interpretant is not to be equated with the unified rational subject of Cartesian dualism. Rather, it is the functioning of a semiotic *process* that can occur above or below—as well as at—the level of conscious awareness of the individual. It is primarily the interpretant, as distinct from a conscious, rational interpreter, that distinguishes Peirce's semiotic from that of Saussure, and from which all the other differences flow.[5]

In Peirce's system, signs are dynamic, mutable entities that constantly interact (via the interpretant) with other signs, and with the "objects" with which they relate, causing them to transform over time. To say that the self is a sign is to attribute these qualities to the set of ideas and representations that constitute the self. Thus, Peirce's account develops a notion of selves that are continuously defined by representational activity, and in Peirce's conception, these sign-selves additionally interact with other sign-selves and are transformed by such interaction over time. That is, selves are inherently *social* in nature, and a notion of the self entails a notion of *community*. Thus, Peirce's semiotic self is not a private subjective entity but, rather, is transparent, open, constantly constituting and being constituted by the whole spectrum of signing activity within a community of others in the prism-like process of semiosis. The individual self is, according to Peirce, a fiction, an illusion; the semiotic self is fully communal.

Furthermore, in addition to this *inter*subjective level of selfhood, there is also an *intra*subjective level at which semiosis (the process by which signs convey meaning) occurs in chains. Thus, while the classical subject of Cartesianism is unitary and static, the semiotic self is constantly being transformed by signing activity both above and below the level of the individual and is therefore inherently diverse and dynamic in nature.

Finally, for Peirce, signs are always grounded in material reality. Because they share some aspects of the objects they signify, signs are capable of representing those objects, even in their most static and inert manifestations; and they themselves can function not only as the leading edge of cultural transformation but also, when properly rooted in an enduring material social and historical context, as a force of cultural resistance and preservation. Thus, to say that the self is a sign in the Peircean sense is not to say that it exists only in the ideational, or subjective, realm—as a complex of ideas and thoughts that simply reflect or comment upon the objective world—rather, it is to say that the self exists in the material realm as well. The semiotic self, then, released from the prison of Cartesian subjectivity, is open to the flow of signing activity. It is a prism, reflecting, refracting, and reconfiguring the spectrum of meanings within a community of semiotically constituted others; but also, in certain circumstances, it is a powerful counterforce of resistance and preservation of identity and culture. This dynamic interplay of signification creates an intense interconnectedness, both emotionally and intellectually, among selves within the community, while at the same time anchoring them in the reality of the material world.

This semiotic notion of the self is one that I have found especially fruitful in attempting to understand certain expressions of ethnic identity observed in Riverton. By adopting a notion of the self that is neither strictly subjective (a matter of determining what is "in people's heads") nor objective (a matter of determining the "authenticity" of traits they display), it is possible to explore the dynamics of various American Indian identities as they are constructed, enacted, and transformed within the various communities in which Indian people live and work.[6] Furthermore, I would suggest that a generally semiotic approach to the self, or identity, is consistent with the traditional Anishinaabe worldview that shaped the identities of those who grew up in rural Indian communities of the Upper Great Lakes region during the first half of the twentieth century.

"OUR ELDERS LIVED IT!"

When the members of Riverton's established Anishinaabe families held up their Indian cards at the Indian Association's annual meeting, they were clearly attempting to demonstrate their authenticity as American Indians. But given the history of tribal enrollment policies and the complexities of contemporary U.S. society, the Indian card criterion ultimately was not of much help. This criterion, like so many others, proved unsuited to the task of resolving the complicated and troubling questions of Indian identity that plagued the community. Some people who were clearly Indian by common sense criteria had not been able to obtain tribal membership for one reason or another (usually related to the lack of official documentation of some crucial birth or marriage in their family history). On the other hand, some people whose American Indian ancestry was considered dubious or marginal by many in the community *had* managed to obtain Indian cards (usually through tribes with liberal enrollment policies). In light of these problems with the Indian card criterion, it is worth looking at what people were saying in the heat of emotion as a means of gaining insight into their underlying concerns.

The powwow committee people—those on the right side of the room who had no direct links to American Indian family members or home communities and who consequently did not have Indian cards—emphasized their right, as people with some American Indian ancestry, to be included in the membership of the BCIA and to serve on its board of directors and its powwow committee. They argued that the BCIA is for all Indian people, and that they knew their culture, too. These individuals marked their (generic) American Indian identity with pan-Indian symbols such as beaded clothing and jewelry items, bone chokers, Navajo-style silver and turquoise jewelry, and long hair (the latter marker being especially important for men).[7] Their claim was implicitly based on the (objective) fact of their ancestry, their (subjective) desire to identify with that particular aspect of their genetic heritage, and the logic of the official text of the BCIA's bylaws—that membership and committee and board positions are open to "all Indians."

In contrast, the theme that was most prominent and heartfelt among those on the left side of the room—the extended Anishinaabe families, the elder members of which had grown up in rural Indian communities—was that of lived experience. For the most part lacking the specific clothing, jewelry, and hairstyles that have come to signal a Native American identity in popular culture, those on the left emphasized their family histories (and the lack of such histories for the others). This focus on background was conveyed by such quips as "Where were *you* when it wasn't popular to be Indian?" and "You find some old Indian on your family tree and you think you know *everything!*" The point seemed to be that they had been Indian all their lives, that they and their elder family members had, in the succinct phrase of one woman, lived it. The "it" in this phrase must refer in large part to hardships endured in the past. Their parents and other elder relatives had grown up in rural areas, both on and off reservations, and had experienced the poverty, the racism, the punitive boarding schools, and the pressures to conform that characterized American Indian life during the first half of the twentieth century. They had not had the luxury of putting on an Indian identity and then taking if off as suited their mood and circumstances— something they saw the newcomers as doing with ease.

There is a more positive implication as well—that the elder Anishinaabe people had been raised in communities where the values, perspectives, social norms, and habits that constitute the Indian way had been instilled within them, and the subtle features that characterized the Anishinaabe way of life in these rural communities were implanted in the children through constant daily interactions with community members of all ages. Thus, an Indian way of life, whatever that may have meant in a given place and time, was a constant lived reality to the elders who grew up there. Their Indian identity was enacted on a daily basis, in social interaction with other Anishinaabe people, as a constantly reinforced and deeply internalized way of being.

In considering the nature of the Indian identity emphasized by those in the Anishinaabe families, a semiotic approach to identity recognizes the connection between, on the one hand, the past experiences alluded to or implied in the phrase "our elders lived it" and, on the other hand, one's present identity as Indian. The hardship, deprivation, and oppression experienced by those in the rural-raised elder generation (and to some extent, by their urban-raised children as well) were internalized in ways that were not necessarily fully conscious, and through semiotic processes that continue to reverberate and shape the identities of their present-day selves. Similarly, the positive values, social norms, and habits that Anishinaabe people communally constructed in their home communities continue to be reconstituted whenever Anishinaabe people get together. Although the individuals involved are not necessarily conscious (as they need not be, from a semiotic perspective) of these characteristic styles of interaction, they are nonetheless real and serve to build and reinforce a shared sense of Indian identity.

Those in the BCIA who were newer to their Indian identity based their claims on features that can be understood from the perspective of a Cartesian self—the objective fact of their (partial) Native American ancestry and their subjective choice to identify with that ancestry and display the markers publicly associated with it. In contrast, I would suggest that those in the Anishinaabe families based their claims on features that can best be appreciated from the perspective of a semiotic self. The lived experiences—both pleasant and painful—and the continuity of blood ties and social connectedness over time are neither strictly subjective nor entirely objective. Rather, they are a blend of the ideational and the material, they are based on continuity and change over time, and most importantly, they are about community. These Anishinaabeg (or their elders) shared formative experiences on their reservations and in rural enclaves during the early twentieth century, and they identify presently as members of Anishinaabe families that have connections to other urban Anishinaabe families as well as to family members remaining in home communities. From a semiotic perspective on this demonstration of ethnic identity, for those in the Anishinaabe families, identity *is* community.

Chapter 1

Identity and the City

▼ ▼ ▼

The Riverton community needs to heed the
wake-up call to global competition.

—*American Automotive Corporation executive*

In analyzing the complex and subtle question of ethnic identity among American Indian people in Riverton, three types of community seem especially salient: the city of Riverton as a particular kind of urban setting, the official American Indian institutions of Riverton—which constitute the most accessible and visible aspect of the urban American Indian community—and the Great Lakes–area rural Indian communities in which the great majority of those in Riverton's elder Anishinaabe generation grew up. Each community has its own kind of identity, and each has been a significant force in shaping the identities of those who constitute them.

WHY RIVERTON?

As a city whose economy was dominated throughout most of the twentieth century by one large automotive corporation, Riverton exemplifies a one-industry town characterized by the strong tradition of organized labor found in so many midsized cities throughout the Upper Great Lakes region. Along with other similar cities, Riverton became a mecca at midcentury for Great Lakes–area Indian people (and Native Americans from further afield as well) seeking employment not available in or near home communities. At that time, factories producing autos and auto-related parts were booming, and people with few skills and little formal education could find reasonably well-paying and secure jobs. Although it had previously experienced auto-boom prosperity, during the 1980s Riverton came to suffer the devastation visited on numerous Great Lakes–area cities by the drastic downturn in the U.S. automotive industry, rendering the economic future of these cities precarious at best. Riverton is typical of many of those midsized industrial cities in the Upper Great Lakes region that also experienced periods of prosperity followed by decline. Such a political-economic history resulted in a certain kind of urban Indian community, similar in some ways to those of larger cities in the Upper Great Lakes, or to cities in other regions of North America, and yet unique in important ways.

A POLITICAL-ECONOMIC HISTORY OF RIVERTON

Even before the American Automotive Corporation (AAC) decided to locate its fledgling enterprise there in the early 1900s, Riverton had already developed a thriving carriage-manufacturing industry. Then, as AAC built its operations in Riverton, the city's economy became increasingly auto-centered and robust, concurrent with the rise of the automotive industry generally in the Upper Great Lakes region. By midcentury, Riverton's economy was thriving, and the city's quality of life attracted people from all over, people who wanted to live and work in such a prosperous and harmonious community. During this period, migration to the city, which had begun earlier in the century, reached record numbers. Whereas previous influxes of new residents had been based on emigrations primarily from Ireland, Germany, and (slightly later) Eastern Europe, midcentury newcomers to the city came predominantly from the southern United States. These southern migrants were mostly whites from the upper South and the Appalachian Mountains region, but included a fair number of southern blacks as well. Furthermore, increasing numbers of Mexican migrant farm workers began settling in cities throughout the Upper Great Lakes region and taking factory jobs. It was also during this period that the American Indian population in the region (and throughout the U.S.) began to shift rather dramatically from reservations and other rural communities to cities. Riverton was one such destination for Great Lakes–area Anishinaabe people, as well as for American Indians from further afield.

The American Automotive Corporation grew extremely prosperous, and its workers were among the highest paid in the world. This latter circumstance was due to the strong unions recently created by automotive-industry workers throughout the region—unions such as the United Auto Workers, the United Rubber Workers, and the United Steel Workers. Thus, life was good for most people in Riverton, including factory workers, up through the booming war and postwar years, and into the early 1970s. The generations of workers—white, black, Mexican, and American Indian—who had grown up in poverty in rural enclaves of North America were now able not only to buy the cars they helped make, but also to own their own homes, and in some cases even to send their children to college. Then, things began to change.

Between 1978 and 1992, automotive-industry employment in the greater Riverton area dropped from 80,000 to under 50,000—a net loss of over 30,000 jobs. This drastic downsizing was the automotive company's response to an economic slump that hit the U.S. auto industry with devastating consequences for all Big Three automakers (Ford, Chrysler, and General Motors), smaller automakers, and their parts suppliers, in the late 1970s. Due to a number of factors, including rising energy prices, a saturated market for energy-efficient cars, and increased foreign competition, the U.S. automotive industry experienced an economic slide in 1980 unparalleled since the Great Depression. During this time, the Big Three lost $3.5 billion and laid off 250,000 of their U.S. workers indefinitely, while an additional 450,000 workers lost their jobs in supplier industries (Hill and Faegin 1987, 163).

Primary among the strategies that the automakers adopted to reverse this trend and increase their profits was a change in product design that, among other things, used "interchangeable components designed to be manufactured and marketed in many sites around the world" (ibid., 165). This strategy had become cost efficient as transportation and communication became significantly less expensive during the 1970s, but it resulted in job losses for autoworkers in Riverton and other cities around the auto-producing Upper Great Lakes. Once it had become efficient to manufacture components in foreign countries, major auto corporations (including American Automotive) took advantage of the lower wages they could pay in the Third World by opening factories there. After shifting much of their manufacturing operation out of the United States, corporations in the automotive industry eventually succeeded in increasing their profits while at the same time laying off hundreds of thousands of U.S. factory workers.

All cities were hard hit in what was fast becoming the rust belt of the Upper Great Lakes region, but the situation was especially dire in cities such as Riverton, whose economies were dominated by one automotive corporation. In Riverton, the American Automotive Corporation had not only become *a* major employer in the area, it was actually *the* major employer in Birmingham County, with a local annual payroll of more than $2 billion for the county during the 1960s and early 1970s.[1] The loss of jobs with AAC and related businesses resulted in economic depression and the kind of social problems that inevitably accompany such change. By the late 1980s, large sections of the city were abandoned and decaying, and the main street of downtown Riverton had more boarded-up storefronts than viable businesses. Alcohol and drug abuse rates rose dramatically, as did reports of domestic violence. In the early 1990s, the situation in Riverton was looking extremely grim, and prospects for future improvement seemed virtually nil. When I arrived there in the fall of 1993, however, the city did not appear to be nearly as dire as sources had led me to expect.

THE NINETIES: REBIRTH, OR LAST GASP?

The first thing I noticed as I drove around Riverton was that the huge factories that sit like hulking sentries at virtually every major point of entry into the city seemed to be in operation. Smoke billowed from the smokestacks, the parking lots were full, and local newspaper articles told of various plants that were hiring extra workers. It seemed as if American Automotive Corporation had not pulled out of Riverton after all; it seemed that most of the factories were still working, and perhaps even expanding. In addition, the downtown area did not look abandoned, and the campus of Riverton University boasted a huge and impressive-looking new library.

Meeting people in Riverton, I sensed that AAC workers and their union were still a strong and positive presence in the city. The events I attended were sponsored mainly by Native American groups and often had to do with Native American issues and concerns, and therefore had no direct connection to the automotive industry. Nonetheless, there was invariably at each event at least one representative from a union local, showing support, passing out literature, getting signatures on petitions, and so on. And all the people I met—American Indian or not—seemed to have some connection to the auto company: they were either working in one of the corporation's factories, had previously worked there (and were living comfortably on disability leave or retirement benefits), or had family members working there.

Furthermore, the local paper and television news programs carried one story after another of good news for AAC, the union, and the Riverton area in general. Newspaper headlines from 1994 and early 1995 included references to AAC's surge in sales, to "1995 production plans [that] hold promise for area plants," to overtime at the company's factories giving a boost to Birmingham County's economy, to the planned expansion of one particular large plant, and in April of 1995 to the announcement that AAC had set a profit record that year. Furthermore, a historic old plant that had been closed in the late 1980s had recently been remodeled and turned into a glitzy new technology center employing nearly one hundred people. It seemed that the dire predictions made in the late 1980s had been wrong, that the hard times were over, that the U.S. automotive industry in general and the American Automotive Corporation in particular had bounced back to be stronger than ever. There was every indication that the corporation that had seemingly abandoned Riverton had now recommitted to its home community, thus ensuring that the city was well on its way to a full economic recovery. But the longer I stayed in Riverton and the more deeply I looked into the issues, the more I began to doubt the relatively positive image that had been my first impression of the Riverton of the mid-1990s.

First, there was the price the greater Riverton community paid for having AAC extend the lives of a few factories and build a new world headquarters complex there—namely, huge tax breaks. For example, in October of 1994, the Riverton City Council granted AAC a tax abatement on $77.4 million worth of equipment for a truck plant at one of its Riverton facilities, meaning that the auto company would pay only 50 percent of its property tax on that equipment for the next twelve years. Meanwhile, with every new contract it negotiated, the union continued to grant further concessions to the corporation in the form of lower starting wages, longer periods of time until full pay kicked in, and reduced medical insurance coverage.

Furthermore, the new hires that seemed so promising were actually the result of a long battle between the auto company's management and union locals at the affected plants. The corporation was determined to handle increased volume by working current employees overtime and hiring temporary workers, rather than by hiring new full-time workers. The reasoning behind these decisions all came down to benefits: overtime pay is expensive, but not nearly as expensive as having to pay medical, vacation, sick leave, and retirement benefits to new employees. Meanwhile, factory workers who were already permanent employees were experiencing extreme stress from the very long hours spent working on a sped-up assembly line, and this was taking a toll on their physical and mental health. Temporary workers, while grateful for whatever work they could get, would have much preferred to be made permanent and to become eligible for the higher wages and good benefits that went with full-time permanent employment.

By the mid-1990s, most large corporations were limiting their investment in local communities and had begun to think globally. Despite some appearances to the contrary, American Automotive Corporation was no exception. The transnational corporate ethos was succinctly expressed by the new chairman of one of AAC's main divisions in Riverton, who stated early in 1995 that "although [this division of AAC] is headquartered in Riverton, it has customers, competitors, and opportunities around the world—two-thirds of them outside the U.S." He then discussed his belief in "the necessity of being an aggressive global business"—that while the AAC division may be based in the Riverton area, "at the same time, [Riverton] is only one community in the division's global system," and "it is the robustness of the entire system that gives the division the competitive strength necessary to succeed." Thus, he explained, it is important to build plants in the countries where the markets are, adding that "[i]f they don't start making a profit, some Riverton-area AAC plants could be sold or closed—the Riverton community needs to heed the wake-up call to global competition." This AAC executive then expressed bafflement and frustration that his inspirational message of global competition did not seem to be "getting across in this community."[2]

Such a difference in perspective is, of course, entirely predictable when one considers the contrasting positions held by the various parties with regard to the global economy, and this executive (unwittingly, it seems) identified the key factor when he used the term "community." The Riverton community comprises not only factory workers in the automotive industry (current, past, and temporary) but also those who aspire to such jobs. It includes local business owners, service providers, property owners and landlords, and elected officials and employees of the local governments of Riverton, the surrounding suburban cities, and Birmingham County. All of these people would be considerably better off if AAC kept its manufacturing operations in the Riverton area (and would suffer if AAC pulled out). The workers (and potential workers) would obviously benefit from the wages, health insurance, and pensions they would receive if AAC stayed. Beyond that, local business owners and service providers would benefit to the extent that people could afford to purchase their goods and services. Furthermore, landlords would benefit from sufficient individuals and businesses to rent their properties. Finally, governments would benefit both from the corporate taxes levied against AAC and the income taxes of workers earning the high wages AAC paid. The key point is that all this was dependent on AAC remaining in the area.

On the other hand, the corporate executives and owners would continue to benefit no matter where in the world production and sales occurred—to the extent that the corporation profited, these individuals would personally profit. Add to this the corporation's increased profits after taking advantage of lower production costs and cheap (non-unionized) labor in other parts of the United States, such as the rural Southeast, and in Third World countries. It quickly becomes clear that while AAC executives may live in the Riverton area, they are not part of the Riverton community in economic terms. Rather, they are part of the transnational corporate community, and their interests are directly at odds with those of local Riverton community members. In Marxist terms, the various sectors of the Riverton community hold different class positions—the proletariat (current, former, and future factory workers) versus the bourgeoisie (small business owners, professionals, public service workers, local elected officials) versus the landlords versus the capitalists (owners of large, but still local, businesses). All these individuals, however, are disadvantaged under the transnational system. The operative word here is *local:* despite their different positions within the (local) class structure, they are all dependent on the local economy and have no way of profiting from AAC's success in the global economy if AAC leaves the area. The global economy serves as a sort of leveling mechanism that unites all sectors of the local economy and sets their interests against those of the transnational corporation and its owners and executives.[3]

The apparent contradictions, then, between the predictions of doom made in the late 1980s and the signs of prosperity evident in the mid-1990s can be reconciled when one recognizes that it is the corporation (American Automotive) that is prospering. This prosperity helps some community members temporarily by keeping jobs in the area. At the same time, however, the overall transnational corporate strategy is ultimately to withdraw its manufacturing operations from Birmingham County in favor of Mexico and other parts of the world as a means of keeping corporate profits—and the salaries and bonuses of its top executives—high. Thus, while the automotive executive quoted above, and other AAC officials, "heeded," with great enthusiasm, "the wake-up call to global competition," most people in Riverton continued to suffer from anxiety about the future and from a lack of jobs and all the attendant problems that accompany under- and unemployment.

The character, or identity, of Riverton changed drastically between 1945, when it was a prosperous community confidently looking ahead to a bright future, and 1995, when it had become a community in decline, insecure about the future and desperately trying to convince the American Automotive Corporation to keep this or that plant open just a few more years. The identity of the local American Indian community was, of course, strongly influenced by these changes, and to some extent changed its character in ways that parallel the changes in the larger Riverton community. Other factors, however, especially shifts in federal Indian policies, have helped shape the nature of Riverton's urban Indian community somewhat differently throughout the second half of the twentieth century.

AMERICAN INDIANS IN RIVERTON

The area that is now Birmingham County was, of course, originally inhabited solely by American Indians—bands of Chippewa—from about the mid-1700s. At the beginning of the nineteenth century, pioneers poured into the old Northwest Territory (roughly analogous to the Upper Great Lakes states as shown on the map, but minus Iowa), and a series of treaties were made between Indian tribes of the region and the U.S. government. As a result of these events, Indian people were increasingly pressured to leave their traditional homelands and settle on reservations. A number of small reservations were established throughout the Upper Great Lakes region, and in 1934 some of them were successfully incorporated under the Indian Reorganization Act and became federally recognized tribes. A number of others have gained recognition more recently. (See map for locations of most federally recognized tribes/reservations in the region at present.) During the period of the self-determination policy that began in the 1960s, some of these tribes gained significant political and economic power through the success of their gambling casinos and other tribal businesses.

During the mid-nineteenth century, however, and well up into the twentieth century, conditions were poor on virtually all reservations in the Upper Great Lakes region. Much of the land was heavily wooded and unsuitable for farming, and when the value of the lumber was discovered in the late 1800s, unscrupulous schemes by non-Natives resulted in very little of the financial rewards of timbering going to the Indian people. Poverty was a constant problem, there were very few opportunities for Indian people to earn decent wages, and Native land was routinely obtained by non-Natives through tax fraud and other devious means. Furthermore, the advantages promised by the U.S. government for those on the reservation, such as annuity payments, health care, and educational opportunities, failed to materialize. Given the poor conditions on reservations during this time, many Indian families chose to stay on their traditional lands in inconspicuous rural enclaves; many who had already relocated to the reservations left to rejoin family and friends in these small communities. Also, there were some Native peoples in the region—most notably the Miami people of Indiana—who never received reservation lands and have not received land to this day.[4] Thus, throughout the Upper Great Lakes region, many Anishinaabeg continued to live in small rural enclave communities even after reservations had been established.

A number of these communities were located in Birmingham and surrounding counties. Downtown Riverton was an Indian village up until the mid-1800s, when the land was ceded and most of the Native people moved away to other rural Indian communities in the area. So there has always been a Native American presence in Birmingham County. While few American Indians lived in the county during the first few decades of the twentieth century, the Indian population began to increase rapidly starting around 1940. This rapid increase occurred just prior to and during World War II, when Riverton's factories dramatically increased the number of new workers hired for their increasingly productive plants. American Indians—from around the immediate area, throughout the Upper Great Lakes region, and even from other parts of the country—started moving to Birmingham County in large numbers to escape the chronic unemployment of their rural home communities by taking these factory jobs in the city.

Although some came only for a short time to earn quick money before returning to their home communities, many Indian people stayed on in Riverton, married, and raised families there. The result was a steady growth in Birmingham County's American Indian population from the 1940s through the 1970s. In 1980, the total Native American population of the county reached nearly four thousand (out of a total population of about 450,500). As is the case with urban Indians in many cities, Native American migrants to Riverton did not settle into geographically bounded Indian neighborhoods, but rather tended to scatter throughout low-income environs, interspersed with Mexican Americans, African Americans, and other poor minorities (cf. Weibel-Orlando 1991, 23; Lobo 1998). But a genuine sense of community developed early on among those American Indians who kept in touch with other Indian people (in most cases, families from the same home community, or from the same general tribal/cultural group). In the context of relative prosperity and confidence that dominated the Riverton of the 1950s, Anishinaabe people maintained social connections through potluck dinners, bowling leagues, and work parties to help one another with home improvement projects. In the late 1960s and early 1970s, as Riverton's economy began to wane, some of the prominent Anishinaabe families in Riverton formed a number of more formal institutions to address the needs of their community. Primary among these was the Birmingham County Indian Association, which established an Indian Center in downtown Riverton in 1972. Also, a Native American Student Organization was formed at Riverton University, and the Riverton public school system established an Indian Education Program. Most of the staff positions in these organizations and programs were filled, at least initially, with people who had been active in Riverton's American Indian community for a number of years.

In the 1980s, as American Automotive began closing plants and laying off workers, the mood of the city turned from confidence to insecurity. Some younger Indian people moved to other parts of the country (such as the Sunbelt states) to find work, and some of their elders retired to home reservations. At the same time, new migrations slowed virtually to a halt because, just when job opportunities were diminishing in the Riverton area, new jobs were opening up on some of the reservations in the region of the Upper Great Lakes. Indian gaming (casino gambling) and other tribally owned businesses that had begun to proliferate at the beginning of the self-determination era of federal Indian policy in the early 1960s gave rise to a newfound economic success. Consequently, reservation residents were better able to find jobs in their communities, and Indian people who had lost their jobs (or not been able to find jobs) in Birmingham County could sometimes find work by moving to a reservation area.[5] Thus, by the mid-1990s, Riverton's Native American community was somewhat diminished in size from its peak in 1980—the 1990 census shows a Native American population of about 2,900 for Birmingham County (the overall population of the county having dropped to 430,500). Furthermore, there were signs within the community of the despondency that characterized Riverton generally, as AAC continued to go global and hopes of renewed prosperity faded for most local residents. Still, the urban Indian community had survived and was struggling to meet the needs of the city's Native American population as best it could. All the main American Indian organizations, as well as the informal social groups that first developed in the 1950s and 1960s, remained intact and continued to play a meaningful role in the lives of many of Riverton's Indian people.

The political and economic story of Riverton and other midsized, deindustrializing Upper Great Lakes cities revealed, by the mid-1990s, an American Indian community that had stabilized into a distinct pattern. The 80 percent of the population that was of Anishinaabe heritage had become "layered" with regard to people's ages and place of growing up. An older generation of people—in their late fifties, sixties, and seventies at the time of my study—had been the original migrants during the midcentury auto boom. These were the people who had been brought up on reservations and in off-reservation rural Indian communities and then, as young adults, migrated to Riverton for factory jobs. While many had been to Indian boarding schools, the education received there provided them, for the most part, with only the most basic of laboring skills—carpentry, farm work, and machine work for men, and cooking, laundry, and childcare for women. Many people in this generation lacked even these skills. Thus, the opportunity to obtain work that was not dependent on education and yet offered job security, good wages, and benefits was a powerful incentive for Indian people of this generation to relocate to Riverton (and other cities throughout the Upper Great Lakes region). At the time of my study, these people were of retirement age and older, and for the most part were living quite comfortably on the retirement benefits provided by American Automotive.

The children of this generation have had very different lives. As the first in the family to grow up in the city, their connections with the Anishinaabe home communities were sporadic and attenuated during their childhood years. The expense of traveling, the limited amount of vacation days for full-time, year-round factory workers, and the ambivalence felt by many in the parental generation about being Indian and maintaining ties to the home community kept visits back home to a minimum for many families. In some cases, such ties were completely severed. Thus, those in the first urban-raised generation, while having some sense of their Anishinaabe heritage while growing up in Riverton, were able to gain only a partial and often conflicted understanding of this aspect of their identity. On the positive side, though, they had many opportunities their parents had not had as children: they were educated in the regular school systems of Birmingham County, and some were able to go on to college, and even beyond. Furthermore, unlike their parents, who had to work long hours and endure hardships as assembly-line workers in AAC's factories, many people in this first urban-raised generation hold jobs that might be more correctly termed "careers" and are fairly financially secure. They hold positions in social service agencies, schools, local government offices, and businesses—positions that offer personal satisfaction as well as decent pay and benefits.

Of course there are many exceptions to these characterizations of the two generations of Riverton's Anishinaabe population. Some of the original migrants never were able to obtain steady factory work, and if they stayed in the city, it was as members of a marginalized underclass. Conversely, a few in the older generation were able to obtain additional schooling and succeed in white-collar jobs. In the first generation of urban-raised children of those who migrated from reservations, some attained very high levels of achievement, becoming lawyers, doctors, and business executives, while others followed in their parents' footsteps and took the factory jobs that were still available as this generation came of age. Now there is a second generation of urban-raised Anishinaabeg, grandchildren of the original migrants, the eldest of whom were in their twenties at the time of this study, and some of these people are beginning to take their place in the Indian community.

In general, however, the fact that the Riverton area experienced an economic boom at midcentury but has been in economic decline since the mid-1970s has resulted in this layered demographic effect of the American Indian population there. Nearly all Anishinaabe people in Riverton who were retired or nearing retirement age in the mid-1990s had grown up in rural Indian communities before moving to the city, while the great majority of those under fifty-five had grown up in the city. Furthermore, of those under fifty-five, only people above the age of thirty or so were likely to be connected to rural Indian home communities through their parents; those people in their twenties and younger have, at best, only the tenuous connection of grandparents who grew up on a reservation or in an off-reservation rural Indian community. This pattern is in marked contrast to that found in urban areas that have provided more consistent economic opportunities over time. Such cities do not show this layered effect because new migrants are constantly arriving, ensuring that at any given time there will be, within the city's American Indian population, younger people who grew up on reservations as well as older people who were city-raised.[6] Riverton's pattern, on the other hand, is typical of midsized industrial cities in the Upper Great Lakes region, and might well occur in other parts of the country where similar conditions prevail.

As mentioned above, not all Anishinaabe people who migrated to Riverton in the 1940s, 1950s, and 1960s were able to obtain and hold secure factory jobs. Some returned to their home communities, where they could at least be in a familiar setting, surrounded by family and friends. Others stayed on in the Riverton area and raised their families there. These latter families, living in poverty, have been more susceptible to problems of substance abuse, domestic violence, and physical and mental illness than have their more financially secure counterparts. Consequently, their children have not had the same level of opportunity as the children of steadily employed factory workers, and the cycle of poverty has continued, in many cases, into the second and third generations.

Thus, despite the successes of many individuals and families among the Anishinaabe population of Riverton, some of them are living in deteriorating apartments without telephones and are in constant danger of having their utilities shut off. They rely not only on the BCIA's

Indian Center and other social service agencies and government programs, but also on their tribe, if they hold tribal membership, for emergency food and clothing, basic health care services, assistance in having utility services restored, and other such aid. These are the poorest of the poor—those for whom Riverton does not have much to offer—and yet they remain because of family and social ties, and because they may have no place else to go. The economically deprived segment of Riverton's American Indian population is not closely examined in this study, but I would not want my focus on those who are relatively better off to imply that the successful ones represent all—or even the majority—of Indian people in the Riverton area.

In the preceding description, I have specified Anishinaabe people, who make up about 80 percent of Birmingham County's Native American population. But Birmingham County's American Indian population includes people from many different tribal backgrounds including Cherokee, Iroquois, Lakota, Apache, Diné (Navajo), Hopi, and others. While some urban Indian people of these tribal backgrounds do fit the pattern of the two generational layers delineated for Anishinaabe people, the greater distances these other tribal members had to travel from their home communities has obscured the pattern somewhat. Also, those who are relatively new to their American Indian identity—who have only recently become aware of an American Indian ancestor—have no ties to extended Indian families or home communities and therefore do not fit the pattern described for those in the Anishinaabe families.

Chapter 2

Institutions and Identities

▼ ▼ ▼

[The BCIA] was started more as a social group, in order
to be able to say, "Hey! Here's a place where I can
socialize with other Indian people; someplace where
I can let my hair down"—literally!

—*Tom Richards*

In exploring the nature of an urban Indian community, one
might begin with the most accessible and visible aspects of that
community—namely, the city's official American Indian institutions. I use the term "official institutions" to distinguish the formal
organizations, associations, and programs from informal institutions, such as Indian bars (Weibel-Orlando 1991, 120–21; Danziger
1991, 35–36, 47), extended social networks of real and fictive kin
(Danziger: 54–55), and churches with a high proportion of American
Indians among their congregations (ibid., 57–59; Sorkin 1978,
116–19). Through official institutions, individuals are able, at least
in part, to express their American Indian identity, and those who
share such an identity can come together as a community. There are
three major official Indian institutions in the Riverton area—the
Birmingham County Indian Association, the Indian Education Program in the area's public school systems, and the American Indian
Student Organization on Riverton University's campus. The Birmingham County Indian Association has been more central to the social, cultural, political, and economic lives of Native Americans in
Riverton than any of the other official Indian institutions there.
Throughout the United States, such Indian associations and the Indian centers they typically establish have played a major role in
helping Native Americans adjust to urban life.

URBAN INDIAN COMMUNITIES IN THE UNITED STATES

The economic conditions that brought American Indians to Riverton and to other cities in the Upper Great Lakes area at midcentury were not unique to the region. Indian people on reservations across the nation suffered conditions of extreme poverty in the 1940s as a result of disastrous federal policies of the late 1800s and early 1900s. The most important single piece of legislation during the policy period from the 1870s through the 1920s—generally known as the allotment period—was the Dawes Severalty Act of 1887. This act, which was geared toward the assimilation of Indian people into mainstream American society—promoted the division of reservation lands into individual plots for each family in the tribe. The remainder of the land could then be sold to outsiders. Historical evidence suggests that the Dawes Act was originally intended, at least in part, to protect American Indians as they "adjusted" to the life of European American-style farmers. Over time, however, pressure by white settlers wanting Indian land intensified, and "the policy of assimilation shifted to one of exploitation" (McDonnell 1991, 3). Its effect on Upper Great Lakes–area Anishinaabe communities was disastrous: "American citizens took the opportunity to defraud hundreds if not thousands of Indians of their allotments and homesteads" (Cleland 1992, 253). These conditions obtained not only throughout the Upper Great Lakes region, but in most other regions of the United States as well.

The hardship and poverty caused by the Dawes Act were finally recognized by the federal government after being detailed in the 1928 Meriam Report, and the result was a change in policy. Congress passed the Indian Reorganization Act in 1934 to encourage American Indians on reservations to form the kinds of (Western-style) tribal governments that could then be recognized and supported by the federal government. Although this policy was a positive step for Native communities in that it promoted tribalism, as opposed to individualism, it did not do much to address the deep-seated economic and social problems that plagued many reservation communities.[1]

Native people who had not relocated to reservations also suffered poverty in their rural communities due to dwindling natural resources, limited opportunities for wage-work, and very low wages in return for what work they did find. Then, as manufacturing of all kinds began to increase dramatically in urban areas during the war years, the economic pull of job opportunities in cities began to equal the economic push of poverty on reservations as forces contributing to reservation-to-city migrations. Compelling as these economic conditions were, however, they were not the only factor influencing the decision of American Indians to move to cities: new federal Indian policies were at work, as well, and they applied further pressure to American Indian people.

Having turned away from the goal of assimilation in the late 1920s, and having promoted tribalism throughout the 1930s, the federal government then reversed its position and once again embraced assimilation. The resulting termination phase of federal Indian policy that lasted from the early 1940s through the 1950s took its name from the most extreme action implemented during this period—the actual termination of, or withdrawal of federal trust responsibilities from, Indian tribes. The claim was that trust responsibility (the federal government's obligation to fulfill the promises it made in exchange for Indian land) entailed keeping American Indians in a wardship status that was not only demeaning but deterred the assimilation of Indian people into mainstream American society. Thus, the policymakers argued that termination of trust responsibilities would free American Indians to participate fully as U.S. citizens. Toward this goal, over one hundred tribes were slated for termination—and quite a few actually terminated—with devastating consequences. Having achieved a marginal degree of economic security by managing their tribal resources communally, the terminated tribes were plunged into poverty when their tribal properties and assets had to be distributed to individual tribal members and consequently became subject to state and federal taxes. Eventually, most terminated tribes were reinstated and the policy was abandoned, but considerable damage was done while the policy was in force.

The job relocation program, advanced during the same time period, provided the policy pull to complement the policy push of termination. The Bureau of Indian Affairs set up offices in dozens of large cities around the country and, in concert with representatives on reservations, encouraged Native Americans to relocate to cities. In some cases, moving expenses were covered; in other cases, promises of job training or even of actual job placement were made. By 1972, the program had relocated more than one hundred thousand American Indians from reservations to urban areas (cf. Sorkin 1978, 25). Anishinaabe political activist Winona LaDuke has linked the relocation policy of the 1950s to the devastating removal policy of the 1830s[2] as follows: "Removals continued under the so-called Relocation Act . . . under which . . . native people across the country were offered one-way bus tickets to major urban areas" (LaDuke 1999, 121). Although many "managed to find their way back to the reservation" when "promises [of employment and economic opportunity] failed to materialize" (Native American Task Force 1990, 30), tens of thousands of those relocated by the BIA nationwide did remain. These job relocation program participants were later joined by American Indians who came to cities on their own to escape the poverty of home communities and for the greater employment opportunities they hoped the city would offer.

Only two cities in the Upper Great Lakes region were designated for the job relocation program—Chicago and Cleveland—but economic factors brought Native Americans to many other cities in the region as well, including Riverton. And while only one Upper Great Lakes tribe—the Menominee of Wisconsin—actually was terminated, others were slated for possible termination, and the policy produced a general climate of anxiety throughout the region. Such uncertainty about the future of reservation life no doubt factored in the decision of many Upper Great Lakes–area Indian people to migrate to Riverton and other cities in the region at midcentury. By 1990, over two-thirds of America's million-plus Native American population were living in cities (Fogelson 1998, 50), and that proportion continues to increase.

The adjustment was often quite difficult for Indian people during the mid-twentieth century, coming from reservations and other rural Indian communities to cities where many aspects of daily life were unfamiliar, alienating, and confusing. In his ethnohistorical account of Detroit's American Indian community, Danziger offers the following vignette about two Ojibwa men, Clarence and John, to illustrate the problems in adjustment encountered by American Indians new to the city in the early 1940s. He explains that having found an apartment by the end of their first day in Detroit,

> the hungry newcomers bought a few pork chops and potatoes and tried cooking supper on the apartment's newfangled stove. While Clarence fried the meat on the top burner, John cautiously inserted the potatoes and turned on the oven. Several times he tried to light it, then came a loud explosion. It singed the hair on Clarence's face. Pork chops and potatoes flew through the air like grapeshot. Thus began the challenge of urban life. (Danziger 1991, 29–30)

As a means of providing assistance with such basic aspects of daily life as learning how to use unfamiliar appliances, as well as more serious matters such as finding employment and housing, Indian centers arose and flourished in nearly every American city that had more than a few hundred Native people among its population. These centers were established by informal groups of Native Americans, who joined together in urban areas as the Indian population grew.

The most urgent need in the early years of urban Indian centers was to help newcomers find jobs, housing, and transportation, as well as to learn the ropes of urban life. The urban Indian associations that created these Indian centers and kept them going had very limited budgets in their early years. Later, they benefited from the funding made available through the Great Society initiatives of the mid-1960s and through programs for Native Americans that were developed by the Nixon administration during the 1970s. These increased funding opportunities allowed many urban Indian centers to begin offering social services such as substance abuse counseling and economic assistance to the needy, as well as sponsoring political and cultural events. Starting in the mid-1980s, however, urban Indian communities suffered from the budget cuts of the Reagonomics era and its aftermath. Still, many Indian associations, such as the Birmingham County Indian Association, have managed to survive into the 1990s and to keep their Indian centers open, though often at a level greatly reduced from the previous period.

THE BIRMINGHAM COUNTY INDIAN ASSOCIATION

The BCIA has been in existence since the 1950s, when it was formed as an informal social network of rural Anishinaabe people new to the city. The BCIA's history falls generally into three main phases, with each one characterized both by a shift of the participants and a change in the primary mission of the organization. The three phases correspond roughly to the following time periods: (1) the 1950s and 1960s; (2) the 1970s through the mid-1980s; and (3) the late 1980s through the 1990s.

Phase I. 1950s and 1960s: The Social Club

As Tom Richards, a long-time member of the BCIA, indicated in the quote at the beginning of this chapter, the original impetus for the Birmingham County Indian Association was social. Anishinaabe people in Riverton kept in close touch with one another from the start. Not only did individuals and families maintain ties with relatives and friends in home communities, but they also made a point of getting together—mostly in one another's homes—with other urban Indian families from the same home community, or at least from the same tribal/cultural background (e.g., Chippewa or Menominee). Through such an association, facilities could be rented and information disseminated to allow larger groups of Indian people to gather. In interviews, people who had been active in the BCIA during its early years emphasized the camaraderie that having an Indian association afforded them. Joe Niles, who had grown up on a reservation in Wisconsin and has long been active at the BCIA, used the term "social club" to describe the way the Association used to be. He said it was more grassroots during its early years, when the primary purpose was for American Indians who had grown up on reservations and moved to Riverton to be able to "find somebody they had something in common with."

Many interviewees reminisced about the informal potluck dinners and spaghetti suppers the BCIA used to hold, as well as the Indian bowling league started in the 1960s—under the auspices of the BCIA—which continued to thrive throughout the 1970s. Also, a number of people talked about how, back in the old days, the BCIA provided a number of informal services. There was a network through which people could get tips on job openings, loans of vehicles, and help with home repairs by work parties, in which a large group would show up to paint someone's house, fix the roof, or build a retaining wall. All the families were in more or less the same circumstances, sometimes doing all right, sometimes needing assistance. At nearly every social gathering, one family or another was in financial crisis, and the hat would be passed and donations collected for the needy ones. The next time, that family might well be on the giving end, contributing what it could toward helping another family that had fallen on hard times. In other words, social services were provided, but informally.

Phase II. 1970s through Mid-1980s: The Social Service Organization

With incorporation in 1971, and the founding of the Indian Center in 1972, the character of the BCIA began to change. While most of the old-timers recognized the inevitability, and even the desirability, of these changes, they also clearly regretted the loss of the Association as it had been in the beginning, during the 1950s and 1960s. Those who were involved with the BCIA at the time of incorporation agreed that it was the funding that changed everything. Whereas the Association had been strictly social and voluntary, incorporation brought a substantial government grant. At that point, according to Tom Richards, the BCIA became much more like "a white institution" in which record keeping and doing one's job were more important than socializing. While the newly opened Indian Center did serve a social function—in that people could come in and just hang around, have a cup of coffee, and visit with others—the primary function became the provision of social services. (Interestingly, this time period coincided with the beginning of the downturn in Riverton's economy—thus, social services were likely more in demand than previously.)

Another long-time member of the Association, Jack Peters, described the changes that occurred throughout the 1970s, when the emphasis moved from socializing to social services, as follows:

> The older people just felt that the Center wasn't doing what they wanted anymore—that it didn't meet their needs. In the beginning, the need for them was a place to socialize, a social gathering place. To be with their own, to just sit around and have some fun talking. And they weren't so much into having a service agency. When the funding came in, the real grassroots people decided that's not what they wanted. And they left [the BCIA].

Joe Niles made a similar point about what he called the change from grassroots activities to poverty programs. He commented that with the change came a split in which the more highly educated (and sometimes only marginally Indian, according to Joe) professionals held the staff positions (often the board positions, too) and delivered the services, while the really down-and-out received the services. This left no place for the majority of the original community—mostly factory workers who were earning decent wages and benefits and therefore did not require assistance, but who had little formal education, had grown up in rural Indian communities, and still needed the social support of "being with their own."

On the other hand, most interviewees agreed that the services were important, and some spoke with pride of the Indian Center's heyday from the mid-1970s through the mid-1980s, during which an ever widening range of programs was available. Even after the political winds shifted in the 1980s, and funding for Native American organizations became scarce, the BCIA continued to operate its programs and deliver its services. Ron Mitchell, a Menominee Indian who grew up on a reservation in Wisconsin and became involved in Riverton's Indian Center in the mid-1980s, recalled the time they had "had it all": a daycare center; job referral services; drug and alcohol counseling; a liaison to Child Protective Services; health services such as testings, screenings, and routine checkups by a registered nurse (with a doctor on call); and an emergency assistance program that helped indigent clients pay utility bills or buy food. He said there were "a lot of people helped by [the Indian Center]" in those days. In addition to official programs and services, the Indian Center also delivered food baskets to poor families at Thanksgiving and Christmas and held an annual Christmas party, which was not only a social event, but also an opportunity to give out mittens, hats, toys, and candy to the children who attended.

While the focal point during this period was the provision of services to low-income people, the BCIA continued to sponsor events that were primarily social in nature. The annual Harvest Dinner, held on the first Saturday in November, was loosely based on the ghost supper tradition of Great Lakes–area Ottawa (and some Chippewa) communities, in which families gathered to remember those who had died in years past and to "nourish" their deceased loved ones by bringing dishes enjoyed by those loved ones to share with others. The Harvest Dinner carried on the social spirit of the potlucks and spaghetti suppers of the 1950s and 1960s, but on a larger scale and with formal qualities such as speeches by the director and board members, awards given out, and so on.

Also, the BCIA sponsored a social club for teenagers during the late 1970s and early 1980s. It met weekly at the Indian Center for classes and outings. The BCIA promoted traditional culture, as well. Occasionally, it held classes to teach Indian Center members such craft skills as quillwork, beading, and basket making. Ojibwa language classes were held at the Indian Center. Finally, in 1982, the BCIA began producing an annual powwow in a large park outside the city of Riverton. The powwow featured traditional dancing and drumming, ceremonial events, and traders selling Native American craftwork and other items.

Phase III. Late 1980s through 1990s:
The Cultural Center and Political Organization

In the late 1980s, federal funding dried up and the services, programs, and staff of the Indian Center had to be drastically cut. The Center moved to a smaller, less expensive site in a low-income neighborhood several blocks away from its previous downtown location. The annual powwow continued, but only because it had become self-supporting; in fact, extra profit from the powwow became one of the few sources of income the Indian Association had left. At its nadir in the mid-1990s, the BCIA had to let its last staff member go, to conserve the rapidly dwindling funds for rent and utilities.

This change of fortune is consistent with general trends for urban Indian centers starting as far back as the early 1980s, when changes in the federal political climate resulted in drastic cuts in funding for poverty programs. A high percentage of Indian program money was funneled to reservations, as part of the new self-determination policy era, rather than to urban organizations. The timing coincided locally with the pullout of American Automotive and the devastating effects their withdrawal had on Birmingham County's economy.

According to local interviewees, these factors, in combination with irresponsible management and poor planning by certain key staff and board members during the mid-1980s, resulted in a rapid decline of the BCIA's fortunes.

Bleak as the situation had become, the BCIA's downward spiral was reversed in 1994 by a few dedicated board members who managed to secure an emergency grant from the local United Way in the summer of that year. The board of directors used the grant money to hire a qualified director and support staff. As a result, the Indian Center began to take its place once more as an important institution for American Indians in Riverton.

The character of the Association changed, however. The 1950s and 1960s had been a time of informal social gatherings and equally informal mutual aid, while the 1970s and 1980s had formalized both the social gatherings and the financial assistance, turning the focus more toward provision of social services for the needy, and adding cultural learning activities. In the 1990s, although these earlier functions were retained, social services had to be reduced due to limited funding for such programs, and cultural events came to the fore as the primary focus of the Association. Also, political issues concerned the Association more than in the past, and the Indian Center became involved in promoting Native American causes and leading political protests on Indian issues.

One of the main reasons for these changes was the turnover of personnel and membership. As already mentioned, many of the founding Anishinaabe families of the BCIA became disenchanted during the 1970s. They felt there was no place for them in the new structure, which emphasized delivery of social services to the needy. Meanwhile, more highly educated people of American Indian heritage, with little connection to their parents' home communities, joined the BCIA as staff, board members, participants, and volunteers.

This trend became even more pronounced toward the end of the 1980s and into the 1990s. Societal changes in general encouraged local people who had very little knowledge of their American Indian ancestry to claim a Native American identity and become involved in the BCIA and other official institutions. These newcomers were often perceived as "white" (or in some cases, "black") by members of the more established Anishinaabe families at the Indian Center. The newcomers—sometimes dismissed as "wannabes" by the old-timers—were more interested in cultural events that would help them discover their heritage and in political causes to which their education had attuned them, than in offering assistance to the needy or in gathering together simply for social purposes. In the confrontation described in the introduction, these were the members who had only recently become involved in Riverton's official institutions, and in attempting to assert their right to do so, found they did not have the crucial Indian cards to hold up. The overtly political orientation of the newcomers served to further alienate the older Anishinaabeg who were not interested in protests for the purpose of establishing Native American rights.

The other factor that led to the BCIA's new emphasis on cultural events and political issues during the 1980s and 1990s was a change in the social and political climate of the dominant society. With Native Americans having acquired "ethnic chic" in some circles, not only were those with American Indian ancestry encouraged to identify as Indian but also organizations and institutions of the larger society were eager to have "authentic" American Indian performances of some kind at their events. Additionally, as the American public became aware of political issues affecting American Indians, the Indian Center, as Birmingham County's most prominent Native American institution, was called frequently by newspapers and other media, as well as by community and political organizations, for statements on political issues. When political action was called for, the BCIA was the obvious choice for organizing protests, rallies, and other such events.

The staff, board members, and volunteers of the BCIA struggled to meet the expectations put on them in their role as *the* Native American organization in Riverton. For example, when a group of media professionals wanted a "Native American performance" of some sort as the entertainment at their annual banquet and called upon the BCIA to provide a "program," the request was raised at a board meeting, and those present felt obligated to try to accommodate the group. However, very few people at the meeting had the proper regalia and training to put on such a performance, and those who did were very new at it. Finally, one woman, who had a small amount of Cherokee ancestry and was just beginning to learn traditional Native American dances, reluctantly said she would finish her regalia quickly and do the performance with her son, who was also beginning to learn some dances. Another woman, from the southwestern United States and of mostly Mexican heritage, but with one Yaqui grandparent, agreed to do the speaking part—to talk about Native American traditional culture and customs as an introduction to the drumming and dancing performance. There was concern about what she ought to wear—some worried that if she "dressed traditional" she would take attention away from the dancers, so she said she would just wear a sweater and a long skirt, with some Indian jewelry. Then others were worried that might not be enough, but she laughingly assured them, "Don't worry—I'll look Indian!" These kinds of discussions were typical at BCIA meetings as the Association's board members attempted to respond, with limited resources, to the constant requests from local and regional organizations for "real Indians" to come to their events and do authentic performances.

The requests for political involvement were less problematic. There were enough people on the staff and board of the BCIA able to formulate positions on various political issues and get people to participate in political events, and there were a number of important political issues, both local and national, around which BCIA members rallied. These issues included equal opportunities for Native Americans in higher education; efforts to secure the release of Native American political activist Leonard Peltier from federal prison; and inclusion of Native Americans and other underrepresented minorities in AAC's hiring policies.

Even during the difficult economic times of the 1990s, the Indian Center continued to help poor people by offering assistance with emergency food and clothing. These supplies were made available not just to American Indians, but to anyone who needed them, including African Americans who lived in the low-income neighborhood around the Indian Center. One of the BCIA's greatest contributions to the surrounding neighborhood was its federally funded summer lunch program. Each weekday throughout July and August of 1994 and 1995, the Indian Center provided nutritious lunches and recreational activities to neighborhood children, most of whom would otherwise have had no lunch and been without any supervised activities.

Throughout the 1990s, the Birmingham County Indian Association's Indian Center remained an important resource and focal point for the Birmingham County community—Native and non-Native alike. Although the emphasis turned to cultural and political events, the previous provision of social services was retained to the extent that limited funding allowed. The staff and board of the Association continued to try to attract more funding for such programs and services, and looked into the possibility of reopening a satellite office to better serve the outlying counties of the rural region to the east. Even the original purpose of the Association—the opportunity for urban Indian people to enjoy camaraderie with their own—did not vanish entirely. The Harvest Dinner continued to appeal to the original families, as did the Christmas party and the annual powwow, and there were a few older people who still enjoyed stopping by the Indian Center just to have a cup of coffee and visit. For all the changes that occurred, the Birmingham County Indian Association maintained its place as the key official institution by and for American Indians in the Riverton area.

While the BCIA has certainly been the most prominent Native American organization in Birmingham County since its founding in the 1960s, it has not been the only one. Among other official institutions in the area during the second half of the twentieth century, the two most important were the Indian Education Program, implemented in several of Birmingham County's school districts, and the American Indian Student Organization at Riverton University's campus.

INDIAN EDUCATION PROGRAMS

Birmingham County has several Indian Education Programs in place. Riverton's has been the largest, with approximately six hundred students enrolled each year during the mid-1990s; the other programs, in smaller school districts, ranged in size from about fifty to about two hundred students during this period. The history of this federally funded program is long and complex, but the most direct catalyst for its creation was a 1969 study commissioned and funded by the federal government. The impetus for the study was, in part, the increasingly intense criticism being voiced at the time by American Indian political activists. They denounced the deplorable level of education that Indian children had been receiving—in church-run mission schools, in federally run government schools, and, more recently, in public school systems of cities and towns—and the abuses these children had suffered for decades in such schools. The Special Subcommittee on Indian Education that conducted the study stated in their report that they were "shocked by what [they] discovered" (quoted in Josephy 1985 [1971], 156). They concluded by making a number of broad and far-reaching recommendations for "changes— all of which are geared to making Indian education programs into models of excellence, not of bureaucratic calcification" (ibid., 160).

The Indian Education Act, passed by Congress in 1972 in response to the study, made funds available to local school districts to provide whatever special counseling and remedial programs their American Indian students might require to achieve academic success. A central focus of the Special Subcommittee's report had been to "increase . . . Indian participation and control of their own educational programs" (ibid.). This strong recommendation was based on a finding that shocked the subcommittee—the extent to which schools serving American Indians (whether church-run, federal, or public state schools) excluded parents and other American Indian community members from having any input into the educational process. In response, the Indian Education Act specified that Indian Education Programs must be run by a committee of parents. That is, while staff members take care of day-to-day operations, all decisions as to the content of the programs, how funds are to be spent, and what kinds of services will be provided are made by a committee composed of a subset of parents with children in the program. The Parents' Committee is not an informal parents' group, then, but rather constitutes the actual governing body of the program.

Furthermore, student participation in the program is strictly up to students and their parents. It is not a matter of Indian (however that identity might be determined) students being automatically enrolled in the program and receiving services. Rather, each fall a form is sent home with every student in the district, for parents who wish to enroll their children in the Indian Education Program to fill out and return. While most school districts have a place on the form to list one's tribal affiliation and blood quantum, the Indian Education Act does not require such information—it simply states that all "Indian" children are eligible for the program, without specifying what is meant by Indian. This leaves a great deal of latitude for school districts as to how they choose to define Indian, and what, if any, documentation they will require as proof of eligibility. Consequently, there has been a certain amount of variation as to how restrictive or open these programs are.

The general trend in Birmingham County has been for eligibility standards to go from more exclusive to more inclusive. That is, when the funding first became available in the early 1970s, and Indian Education Programs were being established in Birmingham County, most districts required that students have an official tribal membership, or could document that they were at least one-quarter Native American. Over time, though, these districts eased their criteria to the point that, by the mid-1990s, some of the districts had virtually no eligibility criteria other than the parents' self-definition. Such lax standards meant that many (perhaps most) of the students enrolled in Indian Education Programs in Birmingham County, as well as their parents, had very little, if any, connection with a particular tribe, reservation, or other home community.

Knowledge of this situation first surfaced in interviews with staff members of several of the Indian Education Programs in Birmingham County. Many of the interviewees expressed frustration over the number of parents in the program who were not able to list a specific tribal affiliation on the application (rather, they simply put "Indian"), or who showed a very low blood quantum, such as one-eighth or even one-sixteenth. Staff member Carol Johnson, herself only one-quarter Native American (Apache), made a connection between her program's ever increasing enrollment and a growing awareness among the general public of the success of tribally owned and operated casinos in the Great Lakes region, and the per capita payments made by some tribes to their members:

> You know what really gets me? One of my pet peeves? [It] is every year, the number of people that will turn up and want to enroll their kids in the program simply because they think they can then join a tribe and get casino profits. But they don't care *one thing* about Indian education, Indian issues, Indian people, Indian culture. . . . They just say 'Gimme, gimme, gimme!'

At another point in the interview, though, Carol expressed sympathy about the difficulties that can arise in documenting an American Indian ancestry. She talked about the shame and hardship many Indian people had experienced during the first three-quarters of the twentieth century that caused them to hide their identity even from their own children, as best they could. She pointed out that in some cases it is not the student's (or parents') fault that they have little connection to or knowledge of whatever American Indian ancestry they might have. These children have already been victimized in the past, she reasoned, and should not be further victimized by being denied access to the Indian Education Program.

Another consequence of these same general historical circumstances was identified by Sarah Roberts. Sarah was on the staff of a rural school district's Indian Education Program—a district that is predominantly white (i.e., there are very few African Americans or Hispanics in the district)—and had traced her Native ancestry to one Cherokee grandparent. Her program was mainly made up of students who were phenotypically white (in Sarah's words, who don't "look Indian") and who had little, if any, connection to an American Indian community or extended family. Yet Sarah was aware of many other students in her district who were phenotypically Native American (who did look Indian) and were from families generally known and acknowledged to be the Indian families of the area, yet did not belong to the Indian Education Program. The reason is that their parents will not enroll them. She explained:

> [My district] is too near the town where the local leader of the Klu Klux Klan used to live [in the 1930s and 1940s], and there were lots of problems [for Indian people] with that. A lot of people who are now parents, when they went to school they didn't want anything that would single them out. And now they don't want to enroll their kids in Indian Education for fear of singling *them* out.

Sarah was doing her best to work with the students she had and to try to convince some of the other ("more Indian") parents to enroll their children, but she remained frustrated about the situation.

Even among parents who did have their children enrolled in Indian Education, there were dramatic differences in degree of participation, based on similar factors. A Chippewa woman who served as president of an Indian Education Parents' Committee for many years, Marion Weber, explained to me that it was the "mainstream," as opposed to the "traditional," parents who were more likely to serve on the committee. In elaborating on what she meant by this distinction, Marion said that among parents who had their children enrolled in the program, those who had been "raised Indian" were much less likely to get involved in the Parents' Committee than those who had been "raised white." Her assessment was that Indian Education is basically a white program, both in terms of its structure and its personnel, in which Indian-raised people feel uncomfortable and alienated.

In the fall of 1994, Carol Johnson invited me to attend a Parents' Committee meeting in her district—the first of the school year. What I learned there dramatically illustrated what the Indian Education Program personnel face: both the difficulty in attracting "Indian-raised" (in Marion's phrase) parents to participate, as well as the eagerness to come forward and to get involved found in parents who grew up with little or no influence of Native culture. At the meeting I attended, a total of ten parents showed up—two couples, seven mothers, and one father. Three of the parents were phenotypically African American and the other seven were phenotypically European American. (I mention phenotype because to look "white" or "black" means that one has a choice whether to identify as American Indian. Given the power of "social race" in American society as a criterion for treatment of others, people who look Indian are constantly confronted with that identity in a way that those of other phenotypes are not, thus making phenotype an important aspect of American Indian identity.)

From the introductions that people gave during the meeting, and the subsequent discussion, I learned the following. Only one person at the meeting had known her American Indian ancestor personally. While some had known all their lives that they were partly of Native American heritage, several had only found out recently— through family documents or even just from a photograph of an Indian-looking grandparent or great-grandparent—that they were part American Indian.

Parents gave a number of different reasons for wanting to enroll, or keep, their children in the program. One couple, both of whom described themselves as "part Indian," referred to the teasing and abuse they had suffered as children growing up in Riverton, because their American Indian ancestry had been known and reviled. (On the other hand, their own parents had not identified as Indian, and their families had not had connections to Indian extended families on home communities.) These parents were concerned to enroll their own children in the Indian Education Program so they could, in the mother's words, "know they're not 'drunken Indians' or vicious savages like the Indians you see in the movies and on TV." Another woman, who also had suffered shame in her childhood as a result of her (partial) American Indian ancestry, expressed similar sentiments, emphasizing that she wanted her children to learn "pride in their culture."

One man explained that it was his wife (who had not been able to attend the meeting), not he, who had the American Indian ancestry (one Cherokee grandmother). He said this would be his children's third year in Indian Education, and that they were benefiting greatly from the remedial help they received through the program. The other parents, when asked about their interest in the program, all stated variations on a common theme: since they had become aware that there was a Native American ancestor in their past, they wanted their children to "learn about their heritage."

The one person who had known her American Indian relative personally was a phenotypically African American woman, Beth Harper, who explained that she was from Mississippi where, during her childhood, she and her family had lived near a community of "Black Indians." Her father had told her he was half Cherokee, but had not done much to impart the language or customs to Beth and her siblings. They had mastered counting to ten "in Indian," and had learned about some other aspects of American Indian culture, from the Black Indians[3] who had come to visit. Beth was hoping that by enrolling her children in the Indian Education Program, they would have the opportunity to learn more about their American Indian heritage than she had. This prompted another woman, also phenotypically African American and also from Mississippi, to recount that she, too, remembered Black Indians from her childhood, but had not realized until recently that she, herself, shared that mixed heritage. This woman, like Beth Harper, was eager for her children to gain the kind of knowledge she had been denied.

The predominance of parents wanting their children to learn about their heritage, then, accounts for the emphasis on the cultural activities, events, and outings that so strongly characterize Indian Education in Birmingham County. The Indian Education Act of 1972 says nothing of such cultural activities—it specifies only counseling and remedial tutoring as services approved for Indian Education funding (and learning materials that are culturally sensitive, which is a different issue). Yet the leeway given to Parents' Committees in shaping the content of programs in individual districts has allowed for Birmingham County's Indian Education Programs to promote traditional culture as their main focus. Students take field trips to powwows, nature centers, and museums with American Indian displays. They learn how to make moccasins, baskets, dance regalia, and jewelry. In addition, some programs incorporate history lessons into the program, designed to fill in the gaps left by conventional accounts of American Indian life.

According to Carlos Gonzalez, a staff member of one of Birmingham County's larger Indian Education Programs from 1984 to 1993, the cultural emphasis of the program was not useful to many of its current students. Carlos, himself Mexican American, has been closely connected with a network of Anishinaabe families in the Riverton area through his wife, Bobbie, an Ojibwa woman whose family is from a reservation in Wisconsin. A number of people in Carlos and Bobbie's social network had been involved with Indian Education in the 1970s, when the programs were getting started, and Carlos had learned how things used to be from these friends. He explained:

> In the past, when the program first started, if the outreach worker called someone and they told him they were Indian, then he would go to their house and make a visit. And he would want documentation from them, to show him where the bloodlines are from, and give him some background.

Without this kind of documentation, Carlos said, the child could not be accepted into the program.

Carlos told me that the children of those Anishinaabe parents who were involved in the Indian programs in the early years, and who now have school-aged children of their own, often do not enroll their children in the Indian Education Program. Or, if those children are enrolled, it is usually for whatever remedial academic help they might need and not for cultural activities. He explained that children from these families,

> . . . don't need [the cultural programs in Indian Education], because they've got it from home. Their parents know what they want to teach their children. And when they go to visit [older relatives] on the reserves, they get all the education they need. They don't need it from the program office.

He then expressed concurrence with this position, explaining that he and Bobbie teach their own children about their combined Mexican American/Native American heritage through similar informal means within the family structure and on trips to Carlos's relatives in Mexico and Bobbie's family on the home reservation in Wisconsin. Thus, Carlos makes a point very similar to Marion's about those who were raised Indian staying away from Indian Education Programs as soon as they see them as having become white.

These changes parallel those described in the history of the BCIA—an influx of new Indians that results in a withdrawal from the institution by the established Anishinaabe families of the community. A similar trend characterizes the development of the most important institution in the county serving college students—the American Indian Student Organization at Riverton University.

RIVERTON UNIVERSITY'S
AMERICAN INDIAN STUDENT ORGANIZATION

The American Indian (originally Native American) Student Organization at Riverton University began in the late 1960s—a time when renewed consciousness of "Indian pride" and "Red Power" was occurring all across North America. Inspired by the social upheavals of the 1960s, and in particular by the Civil Rights movement among African Americans, American Indians—many of them urban raised— became more visible and vocal during the sixties and early seventies. Major political events that Native American activists engaged in during this period, both inside and outside the system, include the American Indian Capital Conference on Poverty (1964); the Indian Statement on Policy and Legislation (1967); the occupation of Alcatraz Island in San Francisco (1969); the founding of the American Indian Movement, or AIM (1971); and the occupation of Wounded Knee, South Dakota (1973).[4] The general climate of activism, combined with increased American Indian attendance at colleges and universities, led to the formation of American Indian student groups on campuses around the country.

The Native American Student Organization that formed at Riverton University in the late sixties remained active through the midseventies. The group was comprised almost entirely of American Indians who had grown up in Indian communities around the Great Lakes area and had moved to Riverton for one of two reasons: (1) they had come with a spouse or other family member who had gotten a factory job in the area; or (2) having served in Vietnam, they were able to go to college on the G.I. bill. The resulting student organization served a strong social need for these newly urban Indian people, and reflected a political attitude consistent with the spirit of the times.

By the mid-1970s, most of the people who had been keeping the Native American Student Organization going had graduated or left the university, and when no one came forward to take up leadership positions in the group, it ceased to exist as a separate entity. American Indian students found a home with students of another ethnic group—the Hispanic organization—and this arrangement worked well for a number of years. The American Indian students of the seventies, like those before them, became somewhat radicalized by the general social climate of the time and the protests that were being mounted by American Indian activists. Many of those active in the student organization during this time have gone on to effect social change in various ways. Some have mounted successful lawsuits against institutions of the dominant society, and others have led social protests. Still others have worked quietly within the system, as members of tribal councils or as part of county- or state-level governments, to improve the lives of Indian people within their communities and beyond.

During the 1980s, as considerably less activism was apparent in American society, Riverton University abandoned its policy of recruiting students from reservations. Most of the area's American Indian students (and for that matter, most students, regardless of race or ethnicity) tended to be commuters from around Birmingham County, and were often the sons and daughters of those Indian people who had migrated from reservations at midcentury for factory jobs. Many were older students with family responsibilities and had little time to devote to extra-curricular activities. I spoke with one such student, Jeff Parker, who had grown up on an Ojibwa reserve in Ontario and was active with the BCIA and in Riverton's Indian community generally. He reported that, during his time at Riverton, the Native American students had split off from the Hispanic organization and were under their own leadership again. However, Jeff said he had become frustrated in his efforts to get the group involved in important issues, projects, and events on campus. He said there simply were not enough people willing to put in the necessary time, and he had finally just given up. Other American Indian people who had attended Riverton in the 1980s reported similar frustrations and disappointments.

The American Indian Student Organization (AISO), as it is now called, revived somewhat during the mid-1990s from the lethargy and disorganization it had exhibited during the previous decade. It remained small in size—the total number of American Indian students enrolled at Riverton University hovered around sixty at that time, and the number of active participants in the student organization rarely exceeded ten or so in a given academic year. Yet the AISO also became much more visible on campus starting in the early nineties. The composition of the group reflected the same social and cultural changes as that of the BCIA's membership and the participants in the Indian Education Programs. Thus, most members of the AISO during the nineties were people who had only recently learned of an American Indian heritage, or those who had always known they were Indian, but had no connection to a Native American community or extended family. Consequently, the peer support aspect that dominated during the sixties and seventies was replaced by an emphasis on traditional culture. Cultural events sponsored by the AISO during this time include an American Indian art show; performances of traditional Ojibwa folktales (in English); and a lecture by a visiting Aztec medicine man (in Spanish, with English translation). Finally, and most important, in 1993 the AISO began producing its own annual powwow at the university, adhering as closely as possible to the conventions, protocol, and traditions of the BCIA's annual powwow.

Political issues also assumed a renewed focus for the group, but the issues differed from those of earlier times. Whereas in the 1960s and 1970s, political action tended to take the form of individuals developing an awareness of issues they then carried into their post-college lives as leaders and educators, during the mid-nineties the group sponsored events on Native American issues at the pan-Indian level. Examples of such political activities during the mid-nineties include talks by John Trudell[5] (November, 1994) and Vernon Bellecourt[6] (November, 1995) and a showing of the film "Incident at Oglala"[7] with a follow-up speech by the president of a nearby city's Leonard Peltier Defense Committee.

▼ ▼ ▼

All three of Birmingham County's major official American Indian institutions share a common history of identity transformations. Each of the three was founded by people who had grown up in nonurban Indian communities and had moved to the city as young adults. Then, having gone through a transitional phase, each institution ended up with the majority of its leaders, staff, and members being people who had only a tenuous connection, if any, to such a community. This is not meant to imply that these people did not find a genuine sense of community through these institutions. They were sincere in their support of Native American political and social causes and felt a genuine interest in learning more about a cultural heritage that was part of their family ancestry. Their involvement in

Native American organizations was obviously meaningful to them. In terms of the approaches to ethnic identity reviewed in the introduction, those who made up the majority of active participants in Riverton's official American Indian institutions during the 1990s had strong subjective Indian identities. The city's institutions played a key role in helping them develop and strengthen such identities. However, for those who had not known their American Indian ancestors, the disconnection from Indian families and home communities cut them off from a material grounding in a certain kind of American Indian experience. What was most real to those new to their Indian identity were the very markers that most reservation-raised Anishinaabe people had abandoned when they moved to the city.

At the time of my early research, many of these older, rural-raised Anishinaabe people who had founded the city's official Indian institutions still lived in the Riverton area; yet they, for the most part, shunned events sponsored by these institutions. They tended to be put off by the strident politics of the newer participants, and even more so by the overt representations and demonstrations of traditional culture favored by those new to their Indian identity. These older Anishinaabe people tended to avoid direct confrontation, and for the most part they sat quietly by while those in the younger generations confronted the newer Indian people of the powwow committee. Yet they did take part in the protest by holding up their Indian cards, and they referred privately to the events sponsored by the official institutions as white and to those who promoted and participated in such events as "wannabes." Meanwhile, those who were most enthusiastic in efforts to express their American Indian identity looked upon the older Anishinaabeg (who eschew such expressions) as being assimilated.

This seeming assimilation begins to appear as rather superficial when viewed from the perspective of a semiotic approach to identity. Examining the experiences, perspectives, and values of these rural-raised Anishinaabe people and considering the choices they have made in light of their background, new insights into the nature of their Indian identity are possible. The next chapter focuses on the hardships faced by these older Anishnaabe people as they grew up in rural Indian communities during the first half of the twentieth century.

Chapter 3

"Assimilated Indians"

▼ ▼ ▼

That powwow they had over there last weekend
was a crazy bunch of nonsense!
I don't see how anyone can dance to that music—
it's just a lot of racket!

—*Charles Lamont*

The previous chapter ended by noting a paradox: those people who seem to have the deepest roots in traditional Indian communities and reservations are also those who have most actively distanced themselves from symbols of traditional culture; they are therefore often perceived as having assimilated into the mainstream culture by those newer to a Native American identity who embrace such symbols. The choices of the rural-raised generation, however, cannot be reduced to such a simple process as assimilation. This chapter will explore what lies behind the seeming assimilation of Riverton's original Anishinaabe migrants.

MEETING CHARLES LAMONT

In June of 1993, I traveled to a Chippewa reservation located near Lake Superior specifically to locate and interview tribal members who had previously lived and worked in the Riverton area, but had since returned to their home reservation to work or to retire. On the reservation was the Elder Center, a retirement facility that offered both residential care and daytime activities for nonresident elderly people in the community. Working as a volunteer there, I was given the job of driver for Charles Lamont, a full-blooded Chippewa Indian then in his mid-eighties. Through my relationship with Charles, I began to learn what life had really been like for many Indian people earlier in the twentieth century.

Charles was originally from a Chippewa community on a large island about forty miles from the reservation where he was living at the Elder Center. The island is about one mile offshore, and although no bridge connects it to the mainland, a ferry service has offered transport to and from the island since the early 1900s. Charles grew up on the island and, after attending the federal Indian boarding school at Mount Pleasant, Michigan (the location of the Isabella Chippewa Reservation—see map), spent the better part of his adult life working in Riverton and other industrial cities around the same general area. In his later years, he returned home to the island, but then moved into the Elder Center on the reservation when he was no longer able to live independently. Thus, Charles's overall life pattern prior to his retirement—growing up in a rural Indian community, then moving to an urban area to live and work—was much like that of the older generation of Anishinaabe families in Riverton. However, the type of work Charles had done had made his life circumstances somewhat different. Rather than working in one of the relatively lucrative and secure factory jobs that had offered many other Great Lakes American Indians financial stability, Charles had struggled to make a living as a carpenter, working mostly construction jobs, moving around to find work wherever he could.

Charles and I hit it off right away. Though his manner was often gruff and cantankerous, and his conversation liberally peppered with expletives, I quickly learned he was a caring and good-hearted man. He was simply depressed from all the losses he had recently suffered, bitter about having been abandoned (as he saw it) by his family, and desperately in need of companionship. Having lost his ability to drive, Charles felt almost incarcerated at the Elder Center, under the watchful eyes of the staff and with the other residents always wanting to "get in [his] business." That summer Charles and I put many miles on my car as we drove around a four-county area that encompassed both the reservation and the island so Charles could conduct his business and visit friends and relatives. We would stop at the convenience store across the street from the Elder Center, fill the tank with gas (Charles always insisted on paying), stock up on Diet Pepsi and snack foods, and then hit the open road. As we crossed over the boundary leaving the reservation, Charles would invariably exclaim, "Okay, darlin'! Let 'er fly!" and we would be off on another adventure. Those road trips taught me a great deal about Charles and his past. Over the course of the summer and during subsequent visits, Charles gradually told me the story of his life.

The first thing one noticed about Charles was how non-Indian—one might even say, how assimilated—he seemed to be. He was disparaging of the various traditional activities and events the Elder Center staff encouraged the residents to participate in and refused to have anything to do with them. He was scrupulous in keeping his hair cut short and expressed disgust at long hair on men; when asked if he had ever worn his hair long, indignation was evident in his reply: "No! I've always been clean as a whistle!" He wore none of the markers of Indian identity associated with Native American men in both reservation and urban contexts: such items as ribbon shirts, turquoise watchbands, and bone chokers. Finally, he shunned all forms of Native spirituality in favor of Catholicism, to which he had been introduced as a child.

In contrast to his indifference—even hostility—toward his American Indian heritage, Charles actively promoted his identity as a worker and a union man. He was eager to talk about all the different jobs he had had as a carpenter. He had worked first in a small city near his home community—to be called "Morristown"—then in various cities (including Riverton) around the Great Lakes region, and finally back home on the island during his retirement. When we drove around the island, he would point out with pride the buildings he had worked on. And when he showed me the crosses he had made for the Indian cemetery,[1] it was his carpentry he wanted me to admire, not the fact that he had made a contribution to the Indian community. One of Charles's most prized possessions was a card showing fifty years of membership in the Carpenters Union. Also, in telling how his house had burned to the ground several years before, he expressed greatest regret at the loss of two kinds of items. First were the mementos from his marriage (his wife of fifty-seven years had died just a year before the fire); second were the pins he had earned for service to his union, of which, he assured me repeatedly, he had had many.

This lifetime of achievement as a hard worker and loyal union member was responsible, as Charles saw it, for the fact that he was now able to live out his retirement in relative comfort and pay his own way at the Elder Center. Thanks to his social security and union pension benefits, he was able to meet his basic needs and even keep a little bit tucked away for emergencies. In comparison to the retirement packages that American Automotive employees receive, Charles's retirement income was quite meager. His comparison, however, was based on those who had no retirement benefits to speak of—who were indigent and had to be taken on as charity cases. Charles explicitly contrasted his circumstances to those Elder Center residents who were in the latter category, whom he invariably referred to as "damn Indians," and who had their expenses partially or entirely sub-sidized by the tribal government. The way Charles saw it, he now had to help support those who had been too lazy, wasteful, or shortsighted to have provided adequately for their old age. He said it was as if he were being punished for working hard all his life and having some-thing to show for it. Charles resented those he perceived as being "freeloaders," he attributed their present circumstances to certain character flaws (laziness, inability to plan ahead, and in some cases, excessive drinking in younger years), and in turn attributed those traits to their being Indian. Meanwhile, he explicitly and repeatedly differentiated himself from them, emphasizing his own identity as a hard-working, responsible, intelligent, skilled union man, who had supported his family and made contributions to society through his work, and thus could now pay his own way in his retirement years.

The importance of this distinction for Charles, and other aspects of his outlook on life, can be better understood in light of his back-ground. Furthermore, while unique in its particulars and extreme in the severity of the hardships and deprivations it describes, Charles Lamont's life story illustrates, in its broad contours, circumstances and experiences shared by many Anishinaabeg of his generation throughout the Upper Great Lakes region. Loss of land, dwindling subsistence resources, and lack of wage work (or extremely low wages) led to dire poverty for many Native families in rural enclaves and small towns, as well as on reservations. These were the condi-tions that prompted them to migrate, as Charles had done, to urban areas. The majority of the older Anishinaabe people in Riverton—those who appeared to be assimilated—had experienced many of the same general kinds of circumstances and events that had shaped Charles's outlook and identity. Thus, Charles's story is included not as a typical example of Anishinaabe life in the early twentieth cen-tury, but as an in-depth illustration of the kinds of conditions that often prevailed in early twentieth-century Anishinaabe communities.

CHARLES'S STORY

Charles Lamont was born in 1910—a time when, according to Charles, the island was still predominantly Indian (although it had some white communities, as well). There was only one main (un-paved) road, and none of the homes had electricity, running water, or central heating.[2] There were a few basic facilities on the island, such as a general store, a post office, several small churches of various de-nominations, and a blacksmith shop, but all other goods and services could only be obtained by traveling to the mainland. This meant taking the ferry, or walking across the ice—a distance of about one mile—during the several months each year that the lake was frozen.

Charles described a bleak childhood fraught with hardship, deprivation, and loss. He had two brothers, one several years older and the other two years younger, but the older brother had died in a drowning accident when Charles was still quite young. The family— Charles, his younger brother, and their mother and father—lived in a one-room wooden shack along a path by the lake, with other Indian families living in similar dwellings along the shoreline and in other small settlements scattered around the island. Their only source of heat during the long, harsh winters was a wood-burning stove, and Charles recalled long periods during the winter months when the snow was so deep their mail could not be delivered, and they needed snowshoes to walk even short distances.

Although there was no opportunity for Charles and his brother to attend school on the island, they did receive some instruction, mostly in the form of traditional Ojibwa stories, from their paternal grandmother who lived nearby. Charles recalled being afraid to walk home at night after hearing tales of *Mishebeshu,* a malevolent *manitou* (spiritual being) that lived in the lake and ruled the underworld. His grandmother spoke no English, and Charles himself knew very little English during this period in his life, since most of his family members "talked Indian" most of the time.

Even the Catholic church services on the island, which Charles attended with his mother and brother, were in the Ojibwa language. (Charles explained that his grandmother was also Catholic, but she could not join them for church because she had difficulty walking and the distance to church and back was too far for her to manage.) Aside from church services, the only other communal events Charles recalled from his childhood were large gatherings on the Fourth of July. He told me there was singing and dancing at those gatherings, but it was very different from present-day powwows which, according to Charles, are "*nothing* like [what] the *old-time* Indians did!"

When Charles was ten years old, his life was drastically altered by the death of his mother. A short time later, his father remarried ("Christ! He couldn't hardly wait 'til her body got into the ground!"), and Charles reported that his stepmother would have nothing to do with him and his brother except to beat them. As for his father: "He was just a goddamn lump. He didn't want nothin' to do with us kids after our mother died." After a year or so of enduring these conditions, Charles and his brother went to live with their grandmother. During this time, Charles had to work in the summers for his uncle— his father's brother—on a fishing boat. Charles hated having to work for this uncle, who "was just no damn good. All he was good for was drink." The arrangement though—living with the grandmother and working for the uncle in the summers—lasted only a couple of years, because Charles's grandmother was too poor to continue supporting both boys during the months Charles was not working. So, at the age of twelve, Charles went to live and work at a lumber camp on another part of the island.

Although lumbering did not take place during the summer and fall months, a few of the lumbermen would stay on doing "other things" (the only description Charles could give) during the off-season. Charles explained that he had to live there year round, working for the lumberjacks, because he "didn't have no home." One of his jobs during the off-season was to remove "deadheads" (floating stumps) from the bay near the lumber camp. This was a task he dreaded because it was difficult and dirty work and the water was sometimes extremely cold, especially in the late fall. Throughout most of the year, however, Charles's main job was to cook for the lumberjacks.

> C: I worked awful hard—worked like a goddamn *slave* for everybody! . . . I was cooking for six, seven lumberjacks. And I was just a kid. I was up at four or five o'clock in the morning and I'd cook the meal. Then I'd get stuff ready to cook the next meal.
>
> D: Did you have anybody to tell you how to do it?
>
> C: No! I had to learn for myself. I took and put some chicken in, and I'd boil the goddamn thing until it was done! And if I doubted it was done, I tried it! If it was done, I'd eat my share of it.
>
> D: How much did you get paid for that?
>
> C: A dollar a day.

All told, the lumber-camp job lasted about two years. Then came the next big change in Charles's life: at the age of fourteen, he was sent to Indian school at Mount Pleasant, Michigan.

It was in the summer of 1924 that a representative from the federally run Mount Pleasant Indian School came to the island. Charles described how it happened:

> C: [The Indian representative] came around, and wanted to see all the Indian kids he could find, and fill the damn place up.
>
> D: Did you want to go, or not want to go?
>
> C: Well, sure we wanted to go. We wanted to get an education, my brother and I. [Then, after we were signed up] we just waited. There were a whole bunch of us. We all met in [Morristown], we got on a train—we had two trainloads.

D: You must have been kind of scared, to go away from home like that.

C: Well, there was nothin' you could do about it. Nothin' you could do.

Despite his fatalism about going to Mount Pleasant, though, Charles revealed that after the representative had been there, he had gone to visit his grandmother to seek her advice as to whether he ought to go. She had sat him down and had a long talk with him, "in Indian," telling him that he should go to the boarding school, and he should work hard and make something of himself. He wasn't going there to play, she emphasized, but to learn, and he would have to study English and "give up [his] Indian ways." This advice obviously had made a deep impression on Charles—there was intense emotion in his voice as he talked about it, even seventy years later. Sadly, Charles's grandmother was never able to see what he had made of himself at school—by the time he returned home to the island in 1934, she had died.

Charles described his years at the Mount Pleasant Indian School with a mixture of pride and anger—pride in his achievements, anger at the way he and the other students were treated. They had to work hard—each student had a full shift at some type of labor, farm work or custodial work such as cleaning the buildings, stoking the furnace, and repairing the equipment, in addition to a full shift in the classroom. In the summer, when school was not in session, students like Charles, who had no home to go to or no means of getting there, stayed and worked for local farmers at no pay. Charles recalled, with some degree of bitterness, how he had worked long hours in the summers, plowing fields with a team of horses, and had received nothing in return but his room and board. By working during the entire growing season, whether or not school was in session, the students became such productive farmers that they were able not only to meet their own needs, but to supply other Indian schools as well. Thinking that at least this would have provided for good meals at the school, in terms of both the quantity and quality of the food, I asked Charles how the food was. "Lousy!" he replied. "They didn't give us butter or *nothin'!*"

On the positive side, Charles reported that during his years at Mount Pleasant, he had become fluent in English, made good grades, learned how to manage money, and most importantly, mastered carpentry—the trade that had allowed him to earn a decent living throughout most of his life. He also mentioned, with obvious pride, the responsibilities he had been given during his last couple of years at the school. He became especially animated when he talked about being a "major" in charge of the new students (all the government-run Indian boarding schools, and most church-run Indian schools as well, were operated in paramilitary style). He described his role, and how he handled it, as follows:

> C: I didn't take advantage of [the new kids], I just talked to 'em. I called 'em outside and I told the whole damn bunch of 'em what the hell was goin' on, and what the reason was, see? And by God, they understood. They understood.
>
> D: Did you see kids coming in who didn't speak any English?
>
> C: Yes, ma'am, I did. Yes, ma'am. Lots of 'em. And I just pulled the whole damn bunch of 'em, when they come in on a bus, from way up north—they'd put 'em on a bus—and when they dumped 'em off, out in front of the building, I started talkin' to 'em. I told who I was, and I talked Indian, see?[3] And I told 'em what the hell the story was, and how we're going to try to work on 'em, to see how long it's gonna take us.

This leadership role was important to Charles. He said he had been singled out because he was smart, hard working and responsible—traits he felt had served him well all his life (and those his grandmother had exhorted him to develop at school).

In 1930, Charles graduated from the Mount Pleasant Indian school—at the age of twenty—but there was no work. School officials finally found a job for him as an orderly in a tuberculosis sanitarium in Iowa, where he worked for two years before returning home to the island in 1934. There, he married a white woman who was also a native of the island—Charles had known her during his childhood—and they started a family. But there was no work on the island in the 1930s (D: "It must have been hard to find work on the island during the Depression"; C: "Wasn't hard, it was just you *couldn't* find it. There *wasn't* any!"). So, in addition to doing subsistence hunting and fishing, Charles made regular trips to Morristown in search of wage work. He described how he would walk across the frozen lake in the winter and pay the mail truck driver to give him a ride to Morristown. There was also a group of white men living on the island who regularly drove to Morristown looking for work, and who had room for an extra rider, but they would not let Charles join them, though he offered to pay them—the reason, Charles reported, was simply that he was Indian.

Finally, after a year or two of barely scraping by on subsistence hunting and fishing and whatever odd jobs he could find, Charles did land a regular job in Morristown, working as a form builder—thus utilizing his carpentry skills—on a large construction job. The work was hard, but the pay was decent and it was steady, so Charles moved his wife and two daughters to Morristown and worked on a series of related construction jobs for about five years. When the work ended,

Charles and his family moved south to the Riverton area, and he worked construction jobs all around the region. At this point he joined the Carpenters Union, which improved his pay, and with the Depression ending and the war years beginning, there was plenty of work. One of his longer-term jobs was as foreman on a construction crew for several new factories and additions to existing factories in the Riverton area. Charles said proudly: "They could see I was smart, and they made me boss." After several years in that position, he and his family settled in a small city about one hundred miles from Riverton, and Charles traveled when he needed to work in other areas. Having spent most of his adult life working as a carpenter on construction jobs far away from his original home, Charles retired with his wife back to the island in 1975. There he started his own saw-sharpening and cabinet-making business, and also occasionally worked on the construction of vacation cottages and other buildings on the island. During this time, Charles was able to build a house—"a nice, big house, not a little shanty!"—for himself and his wife. Finally, in the late 1980s, Charles retired completely. After his wife's death in 1991, and the fire that destroyed his home in January of 1992, Charles lived in apartments, moving from town to town, all in the general vicinity of the island and the Chippewa reservation. He even lived for a brief time in tribal housing in a large town, where he said he was constantly disturbed, harassed, and even robbed, by the "drinkers and dopers" he had for neighbors. Finally he ended up at the Elder Center on the reservation.

▼ ▼ ▼

Charles was often prompted to tell his story because of a location we passed by in our travels ("That bay is where I used to have to pull out deadheads"; "There's the road I took—it was just a dirt path at the time—to go to my grandmother's to tell her my mother was sick"). Charles said little to indicate that he connected his own experience with his being American Indian, but I, of course, did think in such terms. The poverty of the Indian people on the island was similar to that experienced by most Native communities at the time, as were the social problems Charles alludes to—the excessive drinking, domestic violence, and child neglect that so often accompany deprivation and hardship.

CONDITIONS IN ANISHINAABE COMMUNITIES: 1880-1950

The federal policy known as allotment and based on the goal of assimilation was initiated around 1880 and remained in effect through the first three decades of the twentieth century, with devastating consequences for Native communities. The practice of breaking up communally held land into individual parcels not only resulted in the immediate loss of land (since unused—meaning unfarmed—land could then be sold to non-Natives), it also virtually ensured the future loss of much of the remaining land, since there was no provision for expansion as families grew. If a head of household received an eighty-acre plot (the standard size) in 1890, and if that person had four or five children, by 1920 all those children and their families would have to share the same plot. One more generation, and it would be impossible for the land to accommodate any but a small fraction of the descendants of the original allottee.

Added to this problem was the poor quality of the land. One of the government's earliest strategies (during the 1880s) for achieving the assimilation of American Indians into the mainstream of American society was to turn every Indian male head of household into a European American–style farmer. While any number of objections might be raised with respect to this strategy, the strongest would have to be this: the land to which Upper Great Lakes–area Indian people had been relegated during the treaty period was often the poorest in the region, because it was usually the land that non-Native settlers did not want. The areas reserved for American Indians were typically wooded, with poor-quality soil, and often located in northern areas with very short growing seasons.

Despite these limitations, many families did make the necessary adjustments, clearing part of the land, building log cabins, and planting crops and orchards that they maintained and harvested. However, the very success of these families made the land more valuable to non-Natives, with the result that non-Natives found ways to lay claim to such Indian properties. There are countless examples, during the late 1800s and early 1900s, of variations on a common story. Anishinaabe families would leave their homes during the off-season to go on hunting, trapping, or fishing expeditions or to sell craft items at another location, and return home to find that their property had been declared "abandoned" by the local (white) officials and sold to non-Native buyers. Since Anishinaabe people had little, if any, access to the court system (Cleland 1992, 253), they had no recourse. Similarly, local officials routinely raised taxes on Native-owned land, increasing the amount to the point where the owners could not pay. The property was then seized for nonpayment of taxes and auctioned off to non-Native bidders (cf. Cleland 1992, 253–56; McClurken 1996, 93).

Finally, there were cases where non-Natives simply took land from Indian people, without even bothering to go through the motions of making it look as if due process had been followed. One example of this occurred at the Odawa community of Little Traverse Bay in the northwest corner of Lower Michigan. As non-Natives came to outnumber Odawas in what was quickly becoming prime beachfront real estate, "few Indians could protect their property from the non-Indians who settled in and simply began clearing forest land" (McClurken 1996, 93). Consequently, "within one short decade, between 1872 and 1882, the Odawa found themselves living in small enclaves on the outskirts of the towns they themselves had built" (ibid., 91).

Sometimes more violent means were used, as was the case with the Burt Lake Band of Odawa (in the same general region as the Little Traverse Odawa, but further inland). Having secured their land in the mid-1800s, the Burt Lake Odawa had built a community of homes and small farms, and even had their own Catholic church. Then, in 1900,

> [land speculators] used loopholes in Michigan land acquisition laws to take legal possession of the land. [One of the speculators] claimed the land on which the town of Burt Lake was built. Under the protection of the local sheriff, he moved from house to house, dousing each with kerosene and then setting fire. Only the Catholic church remained standing. (McClurken 1991, 80)

The Odawa landowners could do nothing but leave, seeking refuge with relatives elsewhere.

These methods—declaring properties abandoned, raising taxes until the owners could not pay them, and simply taking land by force— were responsible for many thousands of Anishinaabe people throughout the Upper Great Lakes region having lost their allotments by the early twentieth century. Some had never been allotted land to begin with, and others had land that they could not farm very effectively due to poor soil conditions and a short growing season, or because it was overburdened by too many descendants of the original allottee having to share the plot. Thus, the transition to European American-style farming, self-sufficiency, and ultimate assimilation into mainstream society that the original policymakers had envisioned did not come to pass.

There was, however, another value to the allotments in the Great Lakes region that had not been foreseen when the policy first went into effect. As previously mentioned, much of the land was wooded, and while the trees presented an obstacle to farming, they came to have great commercial value as white settlers poured in, towns sprang up, and lumber was needed for building houses, businesses, and other facilities. This set off a lumbering boom in the late 1800s that lasted until the 1930s, by which time virtually all the old-growth forests had been cleared from the Great Lakes region. Some Anishinaabe families and communities benefited in the short term from cutting and selling the lumber on their land, but they usually did not get full price for it; in any case, it was soon gone and they were left with land void of trees, but still unsuitable for farming (cf. Danziger 1979, 100–101). More often, however, the Native landowners did not even benefit in the short term from the sale of their timber, because they were subjected to the same kinds of tactics that had relieved those with good farmland of their property. A fairly typical example comes from the White Earth Chippewa Reservation in Minnesota. As described by White Earth tribal member, environmental activist, and author Winona LaDuke:

> In 1889, Minnesota ranked second in the county in logging, with the northwestern portion of the state leading the state's production. In 1889–90, 11 million board-feet of timber were taken from the White Earth reservation. In the next year, 15 million board-feet were cut, followed by another 18 million in the 1891–92 season. [In this context,] mechanisms were set in place to pry [timber-rich] land from children at boarding school, blind women living in overcrowded housing, soldiers at war, veterans, and those who could not read or write English. [The result was that] by 1904, 99.5% of the remaining reservation lands were allotted, and ten years later, just 14% of the original White Earth land was still in Indian hands. (LaDuke 1999, 118)

Similar conditions obtained on reservations throughout the Upper Great Lakes region.

As a result of their loss of land, Anishinaabe people missed whatever opportunity they might have had to farm and to profit from the sale of lumber, and they also saw the ability to survive by their traditional subsistence practices rapidly diminishing. Game animals that Native people had relied on for centuries were disappearing along with the forests and other natural habitats, and new laws greatly restricted hunting, fishing, and other subsistence practices. These laws applied to all residents, but they had a disproportionate impact on Indian people, who depended on such practices not for sport, but for survival. Treaties with the U.S. government that had guaranteed Native peoples hunting, fishing, and gathering rights in their traditional territories were ignored during this period. The conditions described below occurred at Bay Mills Indian Community in Michigan's Upper Peninsula. The account exemplifies the numerous factors that intersected to constrain Indian people from being able to meet even their most basic needs:

The people of Bay Mills . . . were starving during the winter of 1930 and petitioned the government for help. . . . The Bay Mills situation was desperate. Because the people had been advised that they had to abide by state game laws, they could not fish without a ten-dollar license, which none could afford. Neither was there work in the woods: the pine timber had been stripped from the sandy plains south of the reservation. To make matters worse, the State and National Forest had purchased this area and now prohibited burning. Because fire is necessary to rejuvenate the blueberry crop, Indians were now denied this one source of cash income. . . . In 1908, Bay Mills people had picked 2,000 crates of berries on the plains at two dollars per crate. Now, . . . this cash income denied, Chippewa County was forced to pay aid to keep the Bay Mills people from starving to death. (Cleland 1992: 268)

While the particulars varied, these same general kinds of conditions were duplicated in Anishinaabe communities throughout the Great Lakes region, on both sides of the border,[4] during the first several decades of the twentieth century.

Desperate as conditions were for reservation communities such as Bay Mills, many off-reservation settlements fared even worse because they were not recognized as legitimate Indian communities and therefore did not have recourse to even the minimal and unpredictable government aid provided to the reservations. In this context, wage work became increasingly important to Anishinaabe people after the turn of the twentieth century.

In the Great Lakes area, one of the earliest wage-work opportunities for Indian people was the lumber boom of the late nineteenth and early twentieth centuries—the same lumber boom that stripped them of so much of their land and traditional subsistence. Work in lumber camps offered Native people in northern and rural areas the advantage of being able to stay near their homes and still earn money, such as Charles Lamont experienced. Similar stories could be drawn from virtually every Anishinaabe community in the Great Lakes area (cf. McClurken 1996, 94; Danziger 1979, 112; Cleland 1992, 256). Another common type of wage labor was farm work: American Indians would either work for non-Native farmers near their own communities, or would travel further afield on a migrant circuit. In addition to these forms of wage labor, rural Indian people sometimes commuted to factory jobs and other more urban types of work available in nearby towns and cities.

Of all the strategies Anishinaabe people devised to meet their basic subsistence needs, none was able to stand alone as the means of supporting a family. Therefore, the most common practice in Native communities was to combine any and all types of work in their ongoing efforts to get by. This was the case on reservations in the United States and on reserves in Canada, as well as in the many smaller enclaves, often called "Indian towns," that dotted the rural landscape of the Upper Great Lakes region until well into the twentieth century. One such community was located about thirty miles to the northwest of Riverton, near a town to be called "Whitfield." Bob Miller, a factory worker in his late fifties at the time of the interview, grew up in Whitfield's Indian town, and describes the various ways people tried to make a living.

In addition to the hunting, fishing, and trapping that were practiced year round (mostly by men and boys), and the gardening and gathering of wild foods such as berries that took place during the warmer months (mostly by women and girls), some of the people of Whitfield's Indian town supplemented their income by making traditional black-ash baskets for sale to whites. Bob tells of one family of thirteen—a couple with eleven children—who needed to sell baskets to survive: "They didn't have a car, and they just got out and walked. . . . They would pack up all their baskets on their backs, and hitchhike, walk, to get up to [a tourist area hundreds of miles away] to sell those baskets" (Jackson, 510). This family, along with others from Whitfield's Indian town and Anishinaabe people from all around the Upper Great Lakes area, also used to walk and hitchhike to farms and orchards in areas such as northwestern Lower Michigan, eastern Wisconsin, and western Minnesota to pick crops at harvest time each year. Whole families would camp out until the harvest was complete and they could receive their meager wages and return home, or move on to a new location where a different crop needed picking.

Closer to home, Bob's father and other men in Indian town were sometimes able to find wage work of various kinds. Speaking specifically about his father, Bob explains:

> B: He had about, I'd say, eight or nine different jobs. Mostly farming and lumbering—he did quite a bit for the [white] farmers. He dug ditches for farmers to put the tile in. He knew how to do it, him and my uncle. They had a lot to do around here, [because] they were just starting to [get ditches put in]. My dad dug some long ditches in them days.
> D: And he did lumbering work, too?
> B: Right. He used to do it by hand. The old hand-saw, you know, him and his brother. He retired from that when they wanted him to use a power saw. He called it "the machine," and he didn't want to go that way—he wanted to do it his own way, with the hand-saw. (Jackson, 493)

These kinds of jobs, as well as factory work, were most often performed by men. Women sometimes took factory jobs, too, or they earned wages working as domestic help in the homes of whites, or by providing basic health care services such as delivery of babies and treatment of routine illnesses and ailments with traditional herbal remedies.

Despite all these different kinds of work, people in Whitfield's Indian town remained very poor. Though Bob emphasized that his father was a good provider, he admitted that there were times, especially during the winter months, when "things got a little skimpy" with regard to food. The family ultimately lost their land when Bob's father had to sell it as the only means of obtaining the $200 necessary to bury his mother (Bob's grandmother) when she died in the mid-1940s. Similar circumstances forced other residents of Whitfield's Indian town to sell their land for far less than it was worth, and by 1950 the entire area had been taken over by non-Native farmers.

While some communities fared relatively better than others, the overall conditions for Upper Great Lakes–area Anishinaabeg during the first half of the twentieth century were generally dismal. One consequence of the grinding poverty and oppression that many families faced, year after year, generation after generation, was that alcoholism (and related problems of domestic violence and child abuse and neglect) became prevalent. Alcohol and its accompanying problems continue to plague Native Americans today. In writing about Great Lakes–area Chippewas, Danzinger calls alcoholism "the undisputed number one health problem on every reservation" (Danziger 1979, 193), and cites statistics from Minnesota showing that Native Americans as a group have the highest proportion of alcohol-related problems in the state. Those statistics are as follows: for "trouble in the family because of drinking," 69 percent for reservation Indians, compared to 18 percent for blacks and 14 percent for the general population; for "trouble with the law because of drinking," 50 percent for reservation Indians, compared to 11 percent for blacks and 10 percent for the general population; for "trouble on the job or missed work because of drinking," 44 percent for reservation Indians, compared to 8 percent for blacks and 3 percent for the general population. Similar statistics can be cited for other Great Lakes states: for example, in Michigan, according to a 1990 report, child neglect due to alcohol abuse by parents was responsible for 93 percent of the cases in which children were removed from Native American homes—a much higher proportion than occurred in the general population (Native American Task Force 1990, 20).

These statistics are from the last quarter of the twentieth century (mid-1970s for Minnesota, and late-1980s for Michigan), but the conditions they quantify are deep-seated and prevailed throughout the twentieth century. Charles Lamont's case has already been detailed. Another example is that of Andrew Williams, a resident of Riverton in his late forties who looked much older because he had spent most of his life drinking heavily. Although he received "per capita" (a share of casino profits) payments from his tribe and veterans' benefits due to disabilities resulting from his service in Vietnam, he was not able to maintain an apartment, and so remained homeless. From time to time, he was picked up by the Riverton police, who referred to him as "the Chief," and was booked on drunk and disorderly charges, though Andrew was virtually never a bother to anyone. He seemed to feel fairly comfortable at the Indian Center, which he often used as an address for receipt of his checks and other important mail.

One day, while Andrew was at the Center (in a somewhat intoxicated condition) having a cup of coffee, he told me a little about his past, growing up on a Potawatomi reservation in Wisconsin. He said he had had a twin brother, Peter, and that when they were seven, Peter had become seriously ill. There had been no one to care for him or take him to the doctor because all the adults had been drinking. The result was that Peter died. Andrew told me this story in a flat, matter-of-fact tone—he did not volunteer any further explanation or context for the event of his brother's death.

Another example of the tragic results of alcohol abuse among Great Lakes–area Anishinaabeg comes from a story told by Rob Evans, a young man interviewed in Riverton. Rob was a member of a Minnesota Chippewa tribe, but he had never lived in that tribal community. Rather, he had spent his early childhood (during the late 1960s) in a foster home in Minneapolis, and later was adopted by a white minister and his wife. Rob recalled that as a very young child, when he was with the foster family, he was taken occasionally to a public building (most likely the Department of Human Services) to visit with a woman, whom he had known simply as Susan. He also recalled that there was always another child visiting there, too—a girl about three years older than Rob. He had never understood why he went to see Susan until one day when he was taken to a funeral, and his foster father lifted him up so he could see into the casket. In it was Susan, and his foster father said, "That's your mother." He then pointed to a little girl, cowering in a corner, whom Rob recognized as the one he had always seen when visiting Susan, and said, "And that's your sister." After that, Rob was adopted and never had any further contact with his sister while growing up, nor learned anything further about his family of origin.

Later, as an adult, Rob had finally been able to gain access to his adoption records. In his file was a report that described a visit by Child Protective Services workers to a filthy apartment in Minneapolis where

Life Before the City

Great Lakes area "Indian Town" community—c. 1890.
(Emerson Greenman Collection)

More substantial dwelling in a Michigan Odawa community—c. 1910.
(Emerson Greenman Collection)

Methodist ministers at a meeting in Lower Michigan—c. 1920.
All those standing are Anishinaabe except the third from the left.
(James H. Potts Collection)

Gathering of Anishinaabe families at a Methodist Sunday School
near Lake Superior—c. 1895.
(Michigan Historical Collections Topical Photo Collection)

Anishinaabe families at a Wisconsin lumber camp—c. 1880.
(Emerson Greenman Collection)

there was no food, no heat, and evidence of much alcohol consumption. No adult was at home, but a baby was found abandoned in a crib, small and sickly, wearing nothing but a tee shirt. Rob said that it had dawned on him, as he read the description, that "that baby was me." Although he was not able to learn anything about what had happened to his sister from reading that report (she was not mentioned, and must have been removed from the home at some other time), Rob did finally manage to locate her. He described her as suffering from fetal alcohol syndrome, which greatly impaired her ability to function, and said she lives in a group home in rural Minnesota. Rob had established as much of a relationship with her as was possible and was visiting her whenever he could.

Such disturbing conditions and events were not often talked about openly—it seemed significant that Andrew was somewhat drunk when he told his story, and Rob was one of only two people I interviewed who preferred not to be tape recorded. But given the prevalence of alcohol abuse and related problems in Native communities throughout the twentieth century, it is inevitable that many people who grew up in such communities were affected, directly or indirectly, by the ravages of alcoholism.

Such a context of impoverishment and hardship allows insight into why Native people sometimes came to see Indian boarding schools, despite all their faults and shortcomings, as the best chance their children might have for a decent future, and why the students themselves often felt they needed to go. Numerous written accounts document the harsh conditions at such schools. For example, Noriega (1992) describes how Indian boarding schools deprived parents and other elder relatives of seeing their children for many years—and sometimes permanently—and Irwin and Roll (1995) emphasize that Native children in such institutions were subjected to treatment that was often physically, emotionally, and sexually abusive. As summarized by BraveHeart and DeBruyn:

> The destructive and shaming messages inherent in the boarding school system, whether . . . [federal] or [church], were that American Indian families are not capable of raising their own children and that American Indians are culturally and racially inferior. Spiritually and emotionally, the children were bereft of culturally integrated behaviors that lead to positive self-esteem, a sense of belonging to family and community, and a solid American Indian identity. (BraveHeart and DeBruyn 1998, 61)

Given such horrendous conditions and outcomes, I expected Indian people who had been to such schools to describe their experiences there with anger and bitterness. This, however, was not the case. Invariably, former students from these schools talked about what they learned there and the opportunities they enjoyed as a result of having attended the school. Even Charles Lamont, who was more outspoken about the negative aspects than most, concluded that he was very glad he had gone to Mount Pleasant Indian School—that it was that school, and that school alone, to which he owed all his successes in life.

On the other hand, the extent to which they seemed to have internalized the values of the dominant culture, which included disparagement of Native people who did not assimilate in this way, was striking—as evident in Charles's account of telling the new students "how we're going to try to work on 'em, to see how long it's gonna take us." His use of "we" and "us" shows that he had come to identify with the authority of the school. He aligned himself with those whose mission was to "work on" the new students in such a way as to rid them of their Native American customs, beliefs, habits, and practices, which could then be replaced with those of the dominant culture. Alice Littlefield, in interviewing former students of the Mount Pleasant Indian School, found similar sentiments expressed by many interviewees. For example, one student said, "One of the most important things [was] you learned to work there; that's why later in life, most of these people weren't lazy, 'cause they learned to work there" (quoted in Littlefield 1996, 18). The implicit contrast, of course, is to more traditional Indian people who, in pursuing subsistence practices rather than wage work, are seen as lazy.

The boarding school, then, is a key element, if not the key element, in the assimilation process for most of the students who attended one. But an argument might also be made that the process had already begun in the home community, before the student ever reached the boarding school. Decades of interference by church and government officials had already resulted in American Indian communities having lost many of their traditional ways to the process of acculturation. Since assimilation and acculturation are essential to understanding twentieth-century Anishinaabe people, it is time to take a closer look at these terms and their meanings.

ASSIMILATION AND ACCULTURATION

The term "assimilation" is usually used to mean the loss, by an individual, of the markers that served to distinguish him or her as a member of one social group, and the acquisition of traits that allow that person to blend in with, and succeed in, a different social group. While in theory this might apply to any instance of culture switching, the term is virtually always used to refer to members of a minority group, or a colonized people, becoming absorbed in the majority, or dominant, society.

The term "acculturation," while very similar in concept, has a slightly different meaning. Probably the most often-quoted definition of acculturation is Linton's, according to whom the term "comprehends those phenomena which result when groups of individuals having different cultures come into continuous first-hand contact, with subsequent changes in the original patterns of either or both groups" (Linton 1940, 463–64). Linton is careful to phrase his definition in such a way as to allow for the acculturation process to go in either direction, so to speak, as well as for mutual change to occur. Nevertheless, this term is almost never used to refer to a dominant group borrowing elements from a minority or colonized group, or even of mutual culture sharing. Rather, it is used nearly exclusively to apply to situations where minority, low-status, and marginalized groups change according to the patterns of the larger, more powerful group.

Thus, the phenomenon described by "acculturation" is very similar to that described by "assimilation," and in fact the two words are often used interchangeably. However, it can be argued that there is a very important difference between these concepts that ought to be maintained. Linton, in defining acculturation, speaks in terms of groups, and this is key to understanding the phenomenon. No matter how much change individuals within an ethnic group might undergo in making adjustments to a dominant society—giving up such distinctive cultural features as ancestral language, religion, styles of dress, and traditional foods, and replacing them with their dominant-culture counterparts—they can still maintain their collective identity as a group. Barth makes essentially the same point by insisting on the importance of the boundary between groups, rather than on the content within a group, when considering matters of ethnic identity. No matter how much of the content becomes attenuated and even lost entirely, the group can still maintain its ethnicity if it continues to function as a group and to redefine the nature of its ethnicity as it continues to adapt and evolve. In contrast, "assimilation" refers to the eradication of cultural differences through absorption into the body of the larger society (from the original physiological meaning of "assimilate," defined by the *American Heritage Dictionary* as "to consume and incorporate into the body"), and therefore is best applied to individuals.

Scholarly studies of the relationship between American Indians and the dominant U.S. society can be generally grouped into two main categories: the acculturation studies of reservation communities conducted by Boasian anthropologists from the 1930s through the

1950s (e.g., Redfield, Linton, and Herskovitz 1936; Linton 1940; Bruner 1957; Herskovitz 1958); and the "urban Indian" studies carried out primarily by sociologists during the 1960s and 1970s, many of which focused on issues of assimilation (e.g., Ablon 1964; Tax 1978). My study is concerned not only with adjustments of individuals to urban life, but also with conditions in the home communities they left behind. In fact, from a semiotic perspective, in which the strict distinction between the individual and the community is blurred, both aspects of this (ultimately false) dichotomy should be considered together. Therefore, I will address issues of both acculturation and assimilation as these processes have affected the Anishinaabe people of the Upper Great Lakes region during the twentieth century.

A strong case can certainly be made that by the early 1900s, most Native communities in the Upper Great Lakes region had become at least somewhat acculturated in that they had replaced many of the overt features of their indigenous culture with European American counterparts. Christian missionaries having arrived in the area as early as the seventeenth century (first Jesuits and later Protestants—mainly Methodists), there was at least one church in virtually every Native community throughout the Upper Great Lakes region by the turn of the twentieth century. Many community members were active Christians. Those who were not Christians were far more likely to be simply non-religious than to be adherents of indigenous spiritual practices such as shaking-tent rituals (establishing direct contact with spiritual beings) or the ceremonies of the Midewiwin society of men and woman who perform healing rituals. The Native language was still widely spoken in Anishinaabe communities in the early years of the twentieth century. By midcentury, however, it was only the older people who were fluent in Ojibwa, and most of them were also fluent in English, which they used in the majority of their daily interactions.

European American-style clothing had been adopted by virtually all Anishinaabe people long before the turn of the twentieth century, and by the year 1900, most men had abandoned the long hair of their forebears for the short hair favored by European American men. (Several interviewees, in showing photos of their relatives from this time period, made a point of commenting on how they were trying to "look white" in their clothing and hairstyle.) With regard to food, some older traditions, such as using maple syrup for seasoning, making corn soup (an indigenous specialty), and eating game animals such as muskrat and raccoon (along with the deer, rabbit, poultry, and fish also enjoyed by European Americans) continued well into the twentieth century. However, these foods were increasingly displaced by store-bought foods and government-issued commodities as subsistence food supplies diminished. Furthermore, as opportunities for wage work increased along with pressures to supplement traditional subsistence practices with cash income, Anishinaabe people were able to afford more manufactured items and therefore relied less on traditionally crafted goods. (The exception was when traditional craft items became sought after by whites, in which case they become products of cottage industries for sale to non-Natives, rather than for the household.) As more people worked away from the community, there were fewer people left to keep traditional communal gatherings and activities going. This further eroded the already greatly reduced ceremonial life in most communities, and by the mid-twentieth century, traditional gatherings and events such as naming ceremonies, ghost suppers, and Midewiwin rituals had become rare occurrences in many areas.

Thus, when individual children left these communities to go to Indian boarding schools, they were already half assimilated. That is, they brought with them a minimal amount of traditional cultural heritage in terms of religion, dress, dietary habits, ceremonies, and language (although language was perhaps the most tenacious feature of indigenous culture and often the last to be abandoned, as seen in the case of Charles Lamont). Therefore, one might argue that the schools' job was more a matter of instilling features of European American culture into the students than of eradicating the last vestiges of Indian culture—though they sought to do both. The schools were effective, and the majority of graduates went on to urban jobs or returned to do wage work in their home communities. In either case, they were likely to live in a way that appeared[5] more European American than Anishinaabe, and to raise their children to speak English and acquire other habits and customs of the dominant culture.

All these adjustments and adaptations that constituted the acculturation of communities and the assimilation of individuals were limited in a very important way. As cultural, behavioral changes, they could go only so far: to the extent that American Indians have been defined in European American ideology as a separate (and inferior) race, they were (and still are, in many instances) prevented from becoming fully accepted into the dominant society.

RACISM

As already noted, it was often the case that the more acculturated Anishinaabe families and communities became and the more improvements they made on their land, the more likely they were to lose their land to non-Natives to whom it had become valuable. Yet

Native people usually had no real recourse in the courts because laws tended to favor non-Native interests, and local officials failed to protect Indian peoples' rights, however "civilized" (by European American standards) their habits and lifestyles may have become. Even as late as the 1940s, Anishinaabe people were subject to racist practices that prevented them from owning property. Tom Richards explained the effect this had on his mother, a full-blooded Chippewa from Whitfield's Indian town who had married a non-Native (white) man from the same area:

> The home that [my parents] bought [in Riverton] in 1940 had a deed restriction against selling it to American Indians. It was, of course, legal at that time. They could have had their home taken away from them in court because she was Indian. So [my mother] apparently had a lot of contact with the law that was very bad. (Jackson, 692)

Tom also relates a story his great-aunt used to tell about how his uncle (his mother's brother) was constantly getting arrested:

> The local police would just come up [to my uncle] and say "Oh, we think you've been poaching," and they would throw him in jail. [Also, one time] he had been doing work for [a white farmer] cutting wood, and [the farmer] said he could have the wood that was on the ground. So [my uncle] hauled the wood away. Then another farmer from next door came along and [accused my uncle of stealing the wood], and they started fighting. So the police threw [my uncle] in jail and *then* he asked the first white farmer [for whom my uncle had worked] what had happened. (Jackson, 691)

These kinds of local abuses of power, whether written into formal documents or informally practiced by local law officials, were commonly directed against Indian people all around the Upper Great Lakes region until at least the middle of the twentieth century.

In addition to these official, legal forms of exclusion, harassment, and intimidation, Anishinaabe people were constantly the targets of racist acts by non-Native individuals in or near their communities, for example, Charles Lamont's being denied a ride by other out-of-work laborers who did not want to share their car with an Indian. There are countless other references in my interview material and fieldnotes to these constant reminders of "racial inferiority." For example: a very bright and successful Menominee man told of how, back in the 1940s, he had been barred from college prep courses in his rural Wisconsin public high school because, he explained, the Indian curriculum was industrial arts only. A middle-aged Chippewa woman who had grown up in a small town in northern Minnesota reported with bitterness that her father had always been called "Chief" by the local whites—"and that was as a degradation, not as an honor." An older Miami woman described how, as a child at a rural school in northeastern Indiana, she had been teased mercilessly by white children who had thrown rocks at her and her sister on their way home from school because they were Indian.

These indignities, large and small, are all examples of abuses encountered by people who had been assigned to the social race "Indian," and were thus assumed to have the traits thought to be inherent in that "race"—laziness, ignorance, low intelligence, savagery, and slovenliness. Furthermore, as in the case of Charles Lamont, these racist attitudes can be internalized by Native people themselves, who then attempt to distance themselves from their Indianness, or at least to live in such a way as to show that they are not *that* kind of Indian. Even for those who left their home communities and traveled to places where they were not known by others, their physical appearance might still cause them to be categorized as Indian and treated accordingly. Again, this happened despite the fact that many such individuals had mastered the art of dressing and behaving in a European American way. Becoming assimilated in outward appearance through clothing and manner, language and religion, was not enough—the bottom line remained that "once an Indian, always an Indian."

One interviewee, a middle-aged Chippewa man named Walter Gardner, related the story of his great-uncle Hank. After graduating from a Catholic Indian boarding school in Minnesota, Hank had gone on to Carlisle Indian School in Pennsylvania to study engineering. Walter described this uncle as very intelligent, always well-groomed and well-dressed, and speaking good English. However, as an American Indian, he had been unable to find work in the profession for which he had been trained and ended up having to support himself as a field hand on a large farm in California. When Walter was ten (in 1955), he traveled with his family from Minnesota to California to meet Uncle Hank. They found him "impeccably dressed in a suit," but living "in a tin shack" (Jackson, 20). Though he had "worked hard all his life, tried to save," in his old age he still "didn't have a car, didn't have [his own] home—he was almost homeless, in a shack that had only cold running water . . . and an outhouse" (Jackson, 21). While the family was visiting, the uncle suffered a heart attack and died. Walter, with understandable bitterness, summed up the situation: "He had graduated from Carlisle Indian School with a degree in engineering, and there he was, dying in an irrigation ditch" (ibid.). In concluding the story of his great-uncle with this stark contrast, Walter was making an intentional commentary on the injustice of racial discrimination.[6]

While not the only force in the lives of Walter's Uncle Hank and the other people discussed above, racial discrimination on the part of the dominant society operated as a powerful constraint on the choices and opportunities of Great Lakes–area Anishinaabeg (and other American Indians) throughout the twentieth century. Racism has certainly left emotional scars on those who have suffered from it and no doubt has deeply affected their sense of ethnic identity. Even more importantly, however, racist policies have became a force in keeping Indian people from improving their economic circumstances. The three factors discussed above—Anishinaabe communities' acculturation, individual Native people's efforts to assimilate, and the racism that made it difficult for those communities and individuals to improve their circumstances—were all prevalent during the first half of the twentieth century.[7] In that period, these factors combined to create a kind of Indianness that seemed more based on economic than on cultural criteria.

POVERTY

When I began research for this book, I expected that people who had a Native American identity in Riverton's urban Indian community would be able to give me information on elder family members from whom they had learned about their culture and who had been relatively traditional (in some sense). I was eager to find out what constituted Indianness, but soon learned that when interviewees described their elder-generation Native American family members, they had very little, if anything, to say about traditional culture. A theme that did come up, however, over and over again, was how poor those relatives had been.

In addition to Walter Gardner's story of his great-uncle, another account comes from an interview with a middle-aged man named Larry Harmon. Larry had grown up in Riverton and told me he had not really "known [he] was Indian" until he was in his early teens, when his mother had finally told him they were Ojibwa. I knew from previous conversations with Larry that as a child he had made numerous trips with his family to an Ojibwa reserve in Ontario to visit some of his mother's older relatives. So I asked how he could not have realized he was Indian—did he not understand that if his relatives were Indian that made him Indian? Larry replied that, in fact, he had not known those relatives were Indian. The only thing he noticed about them was their ruralness and their poverty: "[They lived in] run-down shacks . . . and I'd be ashamed to even say I knew anybody who lived in one of them. Backwoods, more or less. You know—dirt floor, stuff like that." Larry could think of nothing about these relatives that he would describe as Indian in any cultural sense.

Similarly, another middle-aged male interviewee, who also grew up in Riverton, told me about all the different American Indian families his parents took him to visit when he was a child. The one common feature that united these families, he explained, and that distinguished them from all the non-Native families he knew, was their living conditions. They all lived in "one-room shacks, they slept in the same room, no plumbing, no kitchen. . . . [I]t was bad." When I asked if there had been anything else about these Indian friends and relatives that set them apart from non-Native people he knew, he could think of nothing. What characterized the Indians, in his experience, was simply their rural poverty.

Finally, there is a story told me by Rosemary Smith, who was in her mid-thirties and had grown up in Riverton during the 1960s. Rosemary described how, when she was little, her (Chippewa) grandmother used to "pile us kids in the car, and we'd go see her relatives." These relatives lived in a small town about a half-hour's drive to the northeast of Riverton; their houses were "overgrown," dark, and dusty, and "they did not have indoor plumbing . . . they didn't have gas, they were cooking over a natural fireplace" (Jackson, 738). This was all Rosemary remembered about these older relatives—siblings and cousins of her grandmother's—most of whom had died by the time Rosemary was ten or so. She definitely did not think of them as Indian.

Rosemary said she finally made the connection between those relatives being poor, living in a rural area, and being Indian when she worked on a project with the BCIA teen group. She explained that a white church group in a small town in the BCIA's rural service area to the east had hired some of the kids in the Native American teen group to help repair the homes of some Indian people near their town. When Rosemary saw these houses:

> I think that was the first time I realized—"Wait! These are the same houses my relatives lived in! These probably *are* my relatives that this church group is coming to help!" And it was kind of amazing, like, "Wait! My *Uncle Joe* lived in a house like this!" (Jackson, 740)

Rosemary told me that, having made that connection, she felt quite uncomfortable in her role of do-gooder, helping "the poor Indians."

For these interviewees, as well as others who told similar stories, the Indianness of their older relatives seemed to constitute nothing more than a particular style of rural poverty. This position is similar to that taken by Judith Friedlander in her analysis of Mexican Indian identity. Having designated a fieldwork location—the town of Hueyapan—that was unambiguously considered to be Indian by outsiders and residents alike, and having lived there for two years investigating the nature of the Hueyapenos' Indian identity, Friedlander concludes:

> To be Indian in Hueyapan is to have a primarily negative identity. Indianness is more a measure of what the villagers are not or do not have vis-à-vis the [H]ispanic elite than it is of what they are or have. [And despite changes over the years in local culture], the villagers are still Indians by virtue of the fact that they continue to lack what the elite continues to acquire. (Friedlander 1975, 71)

Friedlander makes a compelling case for this perspective—that rather than a cultural or ethnic category, Indianness, at least in this region of Mexico, is merely a matter of class. To be poor, in a certain (rural) way, is to be Indian, and to be Indian is to live in rural poverty.

Ruth Behar makes basically the same point—that in much of Mexico, Indianness is more a matter of class than of race or ethnicity—in describing Esperanza, the Mexican Indian woman whose life story forms the primary text in her ethnography, *Translated Woman*. She writes:

> [Esperanza] neither speaks Nahuatl—as did ancestors beyond the reaches of her memory—nor makes crafts to sell. Her "Indianness" does not merit any special attention from bureaucratic agencies; [she] . . . is part of the vast marginal Mexican population that has been internally colonized to think of itself as desended from Indians and yet can claim no pride or virtue in that heritage. (Behar 1993, 10)

To some extent, this perspective might certainly be applied to Upper Great Lakes-area Anishinaabeg in the twentieth century.

There is no doubt that conditions of rural poverty characterized the great majority of Native communities, both on and off reservations. Add to this poverty the extent to which those communities had given up their traditional beliefs, practices, and customs in their efforts to acculturate, and it becomes difficult to determine where to locate the ethnic identity of Anishinaabe people, if not in their rural poverty. A particularly succinct first-person statement on the relationship between being Indian and being poor is made by Ron Paquin, a Chippewa Indian who grew up under conditions of extreme deprivation in Michigan's Upper Peninsula during the 1940s. In his autobiography, Paquin tells about being sent to a Catholic Indian school at the age of seven, and how this caused him to reflect on his own identity: "I knew I was Indian and I didn't know it, if you can figure that. Being Indian wasn't important, anyhow, because I felt so bad about being poor and raggedy" (Paquin 1992, 7). One last story, told by a Chippewa woman named Sharon Nelson, provides a final illustration of the way in which being Indian often seemed to mean nothing other than being poor during the first half of the twentieth century.

Sharon, a Chippewa beadworker in her fifties who had grown up poor in a rural area and attended public school in a nearby (white) town, told of an experience she had recently had at a Rendezvous. She explained to me that a Rendezvous is an event put on by white people, which supposedly replicates eighteenth-century Native American gatherings in every detail. They insist that everything within the grounds—crafts, dance regalia, drums, structures, and clothing and jewelry worn by participants—be absolutely authentic to the historical period and tribal culture being replicated. Sharon had been invited by the organizers of a particular Rendezvous to participate by selling her beadwork there; while she was quite skeptical of the whole concept, she finally agreed, but came to regret that decision.

As it turned out, the organizers—two non-Native women—were in awe of Sharon and drove her to distraction by following her around all weekend, asking her repeatedly, "What's it like to be a real Indian? What's it really like to be Indian?" Sharon was taken aback by these questions and had no idea how to respond, until finally, near the end of the weekend, she lost all patience and blurted out: "You want to know what it's like to be Indian?! I'll tell you what it's like! Being Indian is having to rely on government commodities for food. It's being the one kid in your class called forward to have your head inspected when an outbreak of lice is reported in your school. It's getting thrown off the bus on your face in the dirt. *That's* what it's like to be *Indian!*"

This story, which not only illustrates poverty but also discrimination (whether based on race or class hardly seems to matter), is most likely one to which many rural-raised Anishinaabeg in the Upper Great Lakes region can relate. But the industrial boom that—nationwide—brought tens of thousands of Native people to cities for factory jobs, beginning in the 1940s, has had a tremendous impact on the Anishinaabe people of the Great Lakes region, greatly attenuating the equation of Indianness with rural poverty.[8] These jobs offered the best chance most Anishinaabe people had of escaping the crushing poverty and entrenched racism of their home communities. And many were able to get hired, despite the limitations of their backgrounds, because factory jobs were plentiful and required little, if any, training or experience. There was one thing, however, that was necessary for success in factory work—the ability to behave like a good proletarian (working-class person). Proletarianization must be considered alongside assimilation, acculturation, racism, and poverty as processes that helped shape, and in some cases obscure or perhaps even obliterate, the cultural identity of Anishinaabe people during the twentieth century.

PROLETARIANIZATION

In writing about the American Indian boarding school system as it was developed between 1880 and 1930, Alice Littlefield argues, quite persuasively, that "'proletarianization' better characterizes the efforts of the federal Indian schools than assimilation; to the extent that assimilation was accomplished, it consisted very largely of incorporating some Native Americans into the lower strata of the working class" (Littlefield 1993, 43). Littlefield points out that specific individuals certainly influenced federal Indian policy with their views on the nature of the "Indian problem" and how to resolve it. She takes a broad political-economic perspective, however, in emphasizing that it was the "changing labor needs dictated by the larger economy" that were most often "decisive in decisions to expand or retrench particular programs" (ibid., 44). Specifically, the crucial factor was the shift from family-run farms to larger, corporate-type farms.

Up until the 1880s, Anishinaabe reservation communities had generally been quite successful in maintaining themselves through exploitation of their own communally held resources and the small-scale production of goods within household economies. The government's allotment policy changed all that. Furthermore, prior to the 1880s, local day schools provided to reservation communities had allowed children to remain with their families and continue to participate in the household economy and social/ceremonial life of their communities, while learning the basic skills needed to function adequately in interaction with the non-Native society. These circumstances were drastically altered as boarding schools sprang up, and day schools were closed on the premise that they were no longer needed. As described above, these schools deprived families of their children and subjected children to deprivation and abuse. Another aspect of these schools was the regimentation that served to "proletarianize" the students in their charge.

Charles Lamont's story has revealed the conditions at the Mount Pleasant Indian School during the late 1920s. The emphasis on manual labor, the restriction of academic learning to the most basic skills, the military-like discipline, the spartan living conditions—all of these features served the purpose of instilling proletarian habits, skills, values, and expectations into the students. These same conditions characterized all the Indian boarding schools of this era, whether church- or government-run. The following description illustrates how, during the many years Native children spent at Indian boarding schools, every aspect of their lives was controlled down to the last Foucauldian detail.

Basil Johnston, an Ojibwa author originally from Cape Croker, Ontario, has written about his years at a Jesuit-run Indian boarding school during the 1940s in his memoir, *Indian School Days* (1988). The Garnier Residential School for boys was located in Spanish, Ontario, and was referred to informally as "Spanish" by the students. Although Canadian rather than American, and run by the church rather than the government, the routine at the Garnier school was comparable to that at Mount Pleasant and other U.S. government-run Indian boarding schools. The United States and Canada had very similar systems, and the churches used the same basic techniques as the government(s) to assimilate and proletarianize the students. The following excerpts are from the chapter "A Day in the Life of Spanish":

> 6:15 A.M. Clang! Clang! Clang! I was nearly clanged out of my wits and out of bed at the same time. Never had anything—not wind, not thunder—awakened me with quite the same shock and fright. . . . Clank! Clank! Clank! went the washbasins as they were flipped right-side up on the bottom of a long shallow sink that resembled a cattle-feeding trough. . . . 6:45 A.M. Clang! Clang! Clang! Boys shuffled into line as slowly as they dared without having their names inscribed in the prefects' little black books. It would have been easier to line up immediately without waiting for the bell, but that would have been surrender. . . . 7:25 A.M. Clang! Clang! Clang! For once the prefect did not have to yell to bring about peace and order. . . . Silently we filed into the refectory which, from the state of the furnishings and settings, was a more appropriate term than "dining room." There were sixteen long tables of an uncertain green flanked by benches of the same green. On each table were eight place settings consisting of a tin pie plate, a tablespoon and a chipped granite cup. In the middle were two plates of porridge which, owing to its indifferent preparation, was referred to as "mush" by the boys. . . .

And so forth, throughout the day. Each boy was assigned a number that was used exclusively instead of his name. There were chores, drills, classes, study times, work details, always signaled by the clanging bell. Finally, "9:25 P.M. The lights were switched on and off in a radical departure from the bell clanging as a signal for all the boys to return to their bedsides. 'Kneel down and say your prayers.' We prayed, imploring God to allow us release from Spanish the very next day" (Johnston 1988, excerpts from pp. 28–47). This arbitrary regimentation and discipline did not serve any purpose other than to train the students for the menial wage-labor jobs that were considered the only type of work Indians were capable of. Meanwhile, the allotment policy had decimated home communities to the point that manual labor for others—whether on large farms, in forests, or in mines— had become one of the few ways Native people had of surviving.

Littlefield emphasizes that it was rural labor, in particular, that U.S. government policy prepared American Indians for during the period from 1880 to 1930, and that "the federal school system had been successful in helping to incorporate thousands of indigenous youth into the rural wage labor force" (ibid., 58)—with Walter Gardner's great-uncle Hank serving as a poignant illustration. But then, by 1930, the U.S. economy had become sufficiently industrialized so that "an expanding rural proletariat was no longer needed." Littlefield concludes that "in view of these developments, it is not surprising that federal Indian policy during the New Deal era shifted toward the revival of tribal economies, polities, and cultures that the BIA had earlier tried to destroy" (ibid.). That is, the government's policy shift (Littlefield contends) was not motivated from a humanitarian impulse based on what might be best for American Indian people and communities. Rather, it was economically motivated—the Indians were no longer needed as cheap labor for (European American/white) farmers and owners of mines and timber stands, and therefore it was best to get them back onto the reservations where they would not be competing with other Americans for jobs.

Littlefield's analysis can be fruitfully extended to include subsequent policy shifts. In the 1950s, with urban industrialization having reached its peak, the government abandoned those New Deal policies designed to strengthen tribes. It now set out to terminate those very tribes, while at the same time relocating individual American Indians to cities, where job training programs took over the task of proletarianization to prepare their clients for factory work. Then, as the industrial era began to wane in the late 1960s, federal Indian policy once again turned to supporting tribal communities.

"MARRYING OUT"

Before leaving the rural-raised Anishinaabeg to focus on their urban-raised children, there is one more aspect of their assimilation that deserves mention—the high rates at which they married non-Natives (whites). As I got to know people in the Anishinaabe families, it seemed that virtually everyone in the rural-raised elder generation that I met or heard about had a non-Native spouse. Similarly, almost all those I came to know of in the first generation of urban-raised Anishinaabeg had only one parent who had grown up in a rural Indian community—the other parent was non-Native. This is consistent with statistics on the demographics of urban Indian populations across the U.S., which show significantly higher rates of interracial marriages (mostly to whites) compared with American Indians living on reservations—a situation that makes perfect sense when considering the numbers of American Indians in any given city, compared with non-Indian people. The consequence for American Indians, who comprise a very small proportion of the urban population in most U.S. cities, is that "the overwhelming percentage of potential marriage partners will be non-Indian" (Gonzales 1998, 216).

Among the now-elderly cohort in Riverton's Anishinaabe community, this tendency to "marry out" may have been a result of the kinds of pressures toward assimilation described above. Or, it may have been a cause leading to further assimilation on the part of these rural-raised urban Indian people. Most likely, it was both. The relevant point is simply that the great majority of rural-raised Anishinaabe people in Riverton did, for whatever reason, have non-Native spouses who participated to varying degrees in the life of the urban Indian community.[9]

▼ ▼ ▼

In this chapter, I have sought to convey the kinds of conditions that shaped the early life experiences of the generation of urban Anishinaabeg (especially those in Riverton) who were in their late fifties, sixties, and seventies during my stay in Riverton. These people are seen as assimilated by younger people who are enthusiastic about expressing their Native American identity, and who show little understanding of why it might be that older people are reluctant to engage in such expressions. Certainly the term "assimilation" has some relevance here in designating one process that older, rural-raised Anishinaabeg have been through, but there are also important ways in which these people have retained a strong sense of their American Indian identity. Even to the extent that these older people have attempted to assimilate, however, their choices cannot be fully understood or appreciated without knowledge of the other factors—the acculturation of their communities, racial discrimination, and chronic conditions of rural poverty—that they experienced in their younger years. Finally, it is important to recognize that much of what appears as assimilation might be better characterized as proletarianization—a very selective favoring of the traits necessary to accommodate to the demands of wage work.

The rural-raised generation is the cohort for whom salvation came in the form of urban migration and factory jobs, and who consequently made the adjustments necessary to function and succeed in that setting and role. They may not have been "good" *Indians* with respect to the more overt features of traditional culture, but they were certainly good *proletarians*. This distinction is no doubt lost on the "new Indians"—those who have only recently discovered some Native American ancestry and who are often referred to as "wannabes" by those with strong connections to Anishinaabe home communities. The distinction is recognized at some level, however, by the urban-raised children of the Anishinaabe people who grew up in rural communities. These grown children must struggle to understand the conflicting signals about being Indian that they received from their Anishinaabe parents and other elder relatives as they were growing up in the city. This first generation of urban-raised Anishinaabeg have had to come to terms with the choices their parents made—choices they see as having (partially) deprived them of their American Indian heritage, but that at the same time provided them with opportunities far beyond those their parents had.

Chapter 4

"Paper Indians"

▼ ▼ ▼

We [urban-raised American Indians] are what we call
"paper Indians," meaning we have pieces of paper that
state who we are. [But] we had no ties with our heritage;
we had no ties with our culture; we had no ties with the
reservation. How can you have a tie to something you
know nothing about?

—*Michelle Duncan*

By the mid-1990s, the active participants in Riverton's official American Indian institutions were, for the most part, people who had grown up in Riverton and were currently in their thirties, forties, and early fifties. However, this generalization blurs a distinction that needs to be made between those urban-raised people who grew up in families with parents and other elder relatives who had not come from an Indian home community,[1] and those who grew up in families with parents who had been raised in Indian communities.

The present chapter will explore the experiences of the younger urban-raised generation of Anishinaabe people, again focusing primarily on childhood and adolescence, but will be based almost entirely on the subjects' own descriptions of their early life experience. My aim is not only to illuminate the ethnic identity issues that are of such importance to the urban-raised generation of the Anishinaabe families, but also to glimpse the original migrant generation from yet another perspective, as seen through the eyes of their adult children.

"PIECES OF PAPER"

In the confrontation described in the introduction, the ultimate statement of Anishinaabe families demonstrating their American

Indian identity, and silencing those they call "wannabes," was the dramatic act of holding up their Indian cards. These "pieces of paper," which Michelle Duncan (an urban-raised member of an Anishinaabe family) refers to above, are the official cards documenting membership in a recognized American Indian tribe. The positive message at the meeting was that those who held such cards had a connection to a tribal community—something the "wannabes" did not have and could not obtain. Furthermore, it was through this connection that the lived experience of the elder generation was invoked by their now middle-aged children, along with the fact that the "wannabes" had no such experience. This was most dramatically summed up in the angry accusation, "You find some old Indian on your family tree and you think you know everything," followed by the condemnation implicit in that succinct phrase, "*Our* elders *lived* it!" The clear implication of the previous statements is: "You do not know everything—in fact, you don't know anything—because your elders did not live it. Your elders—your parents' generation—are for all intents and purposes 'white.' In contrast, our elders are Indian, and they've got the childhood experiences to prove it."

Thus, an Indian card seems to serve as an indexical marker for the tribal community in which one grew up, invoking certain experiences, and ultimately an authentic Indian identity. It should be noted that it was the younger members of the Anishinaabe families—the first urban-raised generation—who were actively engaged in confronting the "wannabes" and who first started holding up their Indian cards—with their elders then following suit. Yet, it needs to be emphasized that it was their *elders'* experience that they invoked. It was their elders, not they themselves, who had "lived it," and it was their elders' home reservations that were represented by the Indian cards.

Michelle Duncan, referring to those pieces of paper, brings out another side of the Indian card symbolism. That is, for those who grew up in the city with few direct ties to their parents' home communities, an Indian card may be virtually the only connection they have to that community, and hence to the Indianness it engenders. For the urban-raised Anishinaabe people, then, the Indian card might represent the negation of an Indian identity as much as a demonstration of that identity, because such a piece of paper is clearly a poor substitute for "our heritage," "our culture," "the reservation." This negation is subtly, yet hauntingly, conveyed by the term "paper Indians," which not only refers to the possession of that all-important piece of paper. In addition, it evokes an image of an identity that is paper-thin—a sort of cardboard cutout or caricature of the flesh-and-blood American Indian people who have experienced their heritage and their culture in the context of daily life in an Indian home community.

This paper-thin connection to an American Indian heritage will be explored in this chapter. As I observed and interviewed people raised in Riverton by parents who had grown up in a rural Indian community and then migrated to Riverton to find work, I was struck by the uncomfortable tension they exhibited with regard to their American Indian identity. On the one hand, they were proud of their Native American heritage and expressed their Indian identity openly. Through their involvement in Birmingham County's official Indian institutions, these city-raised Anishinaabeg helped organize and participate in traditional powwows and other ceremonial events, provided social services and economic assistance to low-income American Indians, engaged in political activism in support of Native American causes, and assisted with programs designed to educate the public about American Indian traditional culture. In short, these first-generation urban-raised Indian people tended to be verbal and vocal about their Native American heritage: they *talked* about being Indian—in public settings, among themselves, and with their children. However, in the discourse of life-historical interviews, their descriptions of childhood experience had a very different tone. In that context, many of these urban-raised Anishinaabe people talked about an elusive American Indian heritage that hovered around the margins of their childhood, not quite present, yet never completely absent. Furthermore, it was in descriptions of the past that their complex and difficult feelings came to the fore, as they expressed the pain, confusion, and shame that seems to have constituted the most salient aspect of their American Indian heritage. One such interviewee was Michelle Duncan.

"BUT . . . I DON'T *KNOW* WHO I AM!"

Michelle Duncan, in her forties at the time of the interview, had moved to the Riverton area with her family when she was five and her father got a job at one of AAC's factories. Michelle's mother was non-Native (white), and her father was a full-blooded Odawa, but that American Indian heritage was not readily apparent to Michelle during her childhood. Her father did keep in touch with his extended family who still lived in their home Odawa community in northwestern Lower Michigan. However, while he identified these people as American Indian, he would not admit that they were family. Michelle recalls her father saying, "We're going to see some Indians." He would then take the family to his home community and visit people that Michelle eventually learned were her father's first cousins—but that relationship was never explicitly acknowledged.

Similarly, Michelle shared childhood memories of her family going to visit other families around the Riverton area, and of hearing her father and some of the other adults "talk in a funny language." She later found out that language had been her father's native Odawa (a dialect of Ojibwa), but this was never explained to her at the time.

There were other ways in which Michelle's father had hinted at his—and therefore Michelle's—American Indian ancestry without actually telling her the family background. For example, Michelle told of her father's response when she was in elementary school and was upset because an older boy from the junior high school next door had said to her, "You're nothing but a dirty little squaw, and the only thing you're good for is to throw down on your back." Michelle went home crying, and told her father, who responded by saying, "You're going to run across that. . . . All you can do is just hold your head up high, be proud of who you are." In the interview, Michelle described a response to her father's words that gave voice to what she could not directly articulate at the time of their conversation: "But wait a minute, Dad. I don't *know* who I am! What *am* I? Am I white, or *am* I that dirty little squaw?" Michelle continued to be confused about this question for many years.

In considering Michelle's description of her childhood experience, it is important to acknowledge that it is not the experience itself that is being discussed, but rather Michelle's narrative account—her reconstruction of that experience. Furthermore, a primary component in Michelle's narrative, and in other examples to follow, is what was said (and not said) about being Indian. The junior high boy said something hurtful to Michelle about being Indian; she went home and told her father about it; he, then, gave a cryptic answer that left her confused; and she said something in response, if only to herself. In analyzing the memories, perceptions, opinions and attitudes expressed by Michelle and other Anishinaabeg of her generation, I will be relying on what they said about things that were said in the past: that is, I will be concerned with discourse at two levels. Thus, before pursuing further analysis, I wish to make explicit the theoretical perspective on which I will be drawing.

▼ ▼ ▼

"What we cannot speak about, we must pass over in silence."

—*Wittgenstein*

The notion that culture, social life, and ethnic identity are constituted primarily through discourse has been gaining prominence in anthropology and related disciplines for the past thirty years.[2] There is a closely related phenomenon that, while nearly always implicit in social analyses that focus on discourse, has not received nearly as much explicit attention as has speech. I refer to *silence*.

Silence, too, can work as an active force in constituting and/or transforming cultural and ethnic identities; far from being a "neutral" and "passive" background, silence can, under certain circumstances, act to shape individual identities and group social life in profound and enduring ways. One scholar who does explicitly raise the issue of silence is linguist Alton Becker who, in proposing six kinds of contextual relations that act as "constraints" on particular instances of languages use, includes "silential relations, relations of a text to the unsaid and the unsayable" (Becker 1984, 136). Unfortunately, he does not elaborate on this particular "contextual constraint." Feminist sociolinguist Susan Gal also appreciates the potential for (women's) silence to constrain discourse. In showing how "links between linguistic practices, power, and gender are themselves culturally constructed" (1991, 76), Gal emphasizes that "silence, like any linguistic form, gains different meanings and has different material effects within specific institutional and cultural contexts" (ibid.). Finally, ethnographic treatments of silence, though rare, do exist. For example, Richard Bauman (1983) explores the role of silence in a Quaker community; Mary Black-Rogers (1988) discusses the importance of "no-talk," or silence, as a strategy for showing respect among Ojibwa people; and in what is perhaps the best known ethnographic treatment of silence, Keith Basso (1990) analyzes the uses and meanings of silence in Western Apache culture.[3]

In considering the childhood experiences of the first urban-raised generation of Anishinaabe people in Riverton, I will continue to employ a semiotic perspective, focusing on silence as it emerges in their narratives as told to me. However, it is not the silence of the interviewees themselves that emerges from the interviews—rather, it is their recollections of their *parents'* silence on certain topics and in certain situations and contexts.[4]

"SHHHH! DON'T EVER SPEAK OF THAT!"

From as far back as he can remember, Jake Benson knew there was something wrong on his father's side of the family—that "somebody had done something they were real ashamed of." Jake had grown up in Riverton, and although two of his father's brothers also lived in that same city with their families, and Jake occasionally saw these relatives, he had never gotten to know them. Furthermore, Jake recalls that on a trip to western Lower Michigan—he was about ten—the family was driving through his father's hometown when they saw a large group of people out on the front porch of a house they were passing. He knew it was his father's family—he recognized some of his aunts and uncles—and could see that they were having a family reunion. But Jake's father just drove on by, saying he wanted nothing to do with that "Benson trash."

This is how Jake described the way he grew up—knowing there was something unspeakable about his father's side of the family and haunted by questions of what it might be. Finally, in 1991, at age forty-five, Jake learned the answer: the Bensons were Ottawa Indians. Thus, explicit confirmation of his American Indian heritage came late to Jake. However, certain experiences and interactions with his father earlier in his life, especially during his childhood, had left Jake feeling very much like Ron Paquin: he "knew [he] was Indian, and [he] didn't know." Some further background on Jake and his family will help make sense of this seeming contradiction.

Jake recounted that his father had come to Riverton around 1940, just after having graduated from high school in the western Lower Michigan town where he had grown up, to take a job at an auto factory in the area. Then, much later, when he was in his mid-thirties, he married a younger woman (who was non-Native/white), and they started a family. Jake was the second of three children and the only boy. He reported memories from a very early age of his father commenting on his coloring in relation to that of one of his sisters, who was considerably lighter. One comment that had made a strong impression on Jake was his father saying, "Jake's so dark, he always looks dirty." Furthermore, according to Jake, his father had openly favored the sister who was light-haired and fair-skinned. Jake had not known what to make of this, and had only become further confused when he started school.

It was a Catholic school, and the other students were either Mexican or white. Jake recalled thinking he should belong to one group or the other: his coloring was too dark for him to fit in with the white kids, so he tended to socialize more with the Mexicans, but he knew he was not Mexican either. Like Michelle, Jake had experienced confusion as a child about who he was in terms of racial/ethnic identity. But, whereas Michelle had been able to get at least some kind of response, however cryptic, from her father, Jake had been able to get nothing from his except reinforcement that he was "too dark" and somehow "dirty."

Jake also recalled that his father had warned him once, when the two of them were alone, about "Indians": "He told me that if I ever got in a fight with one, to bite him, kick him, scratch him—never let him up. Do anything I could to hurt and humiliate him—make sure he'd never come back and try me again. . . . And there was an absolute hatred in his voice for them." So Jake had known that there was some shameful secret about his father's side of the family, that he and his father both had dark coloring and there was something wrong with dark coloring, and that his father feared and hated Indians. Certainly there were hints at the connections among these factors, but Jake's father had maintained a resolute silence as to what those connections might be. Jake could only guess and wonder.

Tom Richards also reported mixed messages about his Indian heritage, although for Tom the fact of that heritage was more overt. As explained previously, Tom's mother had grown up in Whitfield's Indian town and maintained close ties with relatives from her home community whom she would take Tom and his siblings to visit. Similarly, relatives from his mother's extended family sometimes stayed with Tom and his family in Riverton. He described these contacts as follows:

> We would go socializing with my mom's relatives almost every single weekend. [The relatives] didn't have telephones, yet they all managed to meet about the same time on Saturday afternoon in Whitfield. . . . There were a lot of social activities, dinners. . . . I remember when everyone got together at our house to help put up a stone and cement retaining-wall terrace in front of the house. All my [maternal] relatives showed up. (Jackson, 688)

Overall, Tom described considerably more contact with his American Indian relatives than did Michelle—whose father's family had lived much further away—and certainly far more than Jake, who had hardly ever visited with his father's brother's families, even though they lived in Riverton.

This contact had given Tom some sense of his Chippewa heritage. For example, in discussing his maternal grandfather's extended visits to their home in Riverton, Tom said:

> As far as the Indian heritage itself, [my grandfather] talked an awful lot about his dad making ax-handles and making baskets. Some of my earliest memories are [of] Indian baskets all over the house—my mom's laundry basket was a large, probably two-bushel basket that was all handmade of black ash. (Jackson, 689)

However, it is important to keep in mind that this was Tom talking as a middle-aged adult about his childhood memories. At the time, these were not Indian baskets that were all over the house—they were just baskets. And while Tom eventually learned that making ax-handles was a skill typically practiced by the Chippewa people of the area up into the early twentieth century, he had not realized when his grandfather was telling him about the ax-handles that he was learning about his Indian heritage. Tom reported that at the time he was a child, his mother and other relatives did not talk much about "Indians" at all, especially with regard to their own family. Furthermore, in addition to the silence that surrounded the family's American Indian heritage, Tom also was witness, more than once, to his mother's outright denial of being Indian. He recalled occasions in his childhood when the subject of his Native American ancestry came up with outsiders (for example, school officials), and he heard his mother insist that his appearance was due to the fact that his (non-Native) father, not she, was Indian.

Thus, even Tom, with his close ties to an extended Chippewa family that lived nearby, described a childhood filled with silences about certain aspects of his Indian ancestry and outright denials by his mother of her own ancestry. A similar story was told by Greg Wilson, a man in his early thirties, who was just beginning to get involved in Riverton's American Indian institutions at the time of our interview.

Unlike Jake, Michelle, and Tom, Greg's American Indian heritage came from both parents. His mother and father were both from a Chippewa reservation in Michigan's Upper Peninsula, though his mother had spent most of her youth at the Catholic Indian boarding school at Harbor Springs. After his mother had graduated from school and returned home to the reservation, she married Greg's father, who had just returned from military service, and the couple moved to Riverton because they had heard that "the shops were hiring." ("Shop" is an informal term that factory workers often use for the factories where they work.) This was in the early 1960s—the last time there were large numbers of openings that brought American Indians and other migrants to Riverton for factory jobs. Greg's father was hired at an American Automotive plant, where he worked full-time on the assembly line. Greg's mother attended college at Riverton University and was active in the Native American Student Organization; she later got a job with a social agency serving a predominantly American Indian clientele.

Greg's parents maintained close ties with their home reservation, traveling north for a lengthy visit at least once a year, so Greg had grown up knowing his Chippewa relatives. Furthermore, since both of Greg's parents were Chippewa, he had been more unambiguously aware during his childhood of being Indian himself than most of the other people profiled here. He described these connections as follows:

> D: [Asking about Greg's school experience in Riverton] So you didn't have a group of Indigenous[5] kids [to hang around with]?
> G: Not in school. [As part of the Indian Education Program] I'd sometimes be able to be with Indigenous children . . . interacting socially with them . . . going on different field trips. But still . . . it wasn't [the kind of] day-to-day thing [that] . . . a lot of other children get, . . . on reservations and those sorts of things. They have a constant kind of contact. But I guess I can't really deprive myself of all that [i.e., present myself as all that deprived] because . . . I've spent a lot of my summers at [the reservation]. And our family's huge. My mom has, like, five sisters and two brothers. And my dad has two sisters. . . . Just about everybody up there's related to us . . . that we know. So I got to hang out with a lot of my cousins during the summers, and we were all in a . . . group.

Despite the fact that Greg at first presented himself as deprived because his contact with other "Indigenous children" was not a "day-to-day thing," a "constant kind of contact," he did then describe a degree and kind of connection with his parents' home community that is considerable compared with what Michelle described, not to mention Jake, who had virtually no such connections. Even Tom, with his regular weekend visits to his mother's Chippewa relatives, did not have the opportunity for the kind of immersion in reservation life, "hanging out" with a whole group of [American Indian] cousins, that Greg described. Despite these close ties, however, and despite the fact that Greg's parents had not denied being Indian the way some of the other parents did, Greg still described some of the same kinds of ambiguities and silences reported by the others.

For example, Greg told me he had known from conversations he had overheard between his parents that when they had moved to Riverton, during the time both before and after Greg was born, there had been concerted efforts on the part of whites in his neighborhood to get the family to leave: "The neighborhood [my sister and I] grew up in, there was a lot of prejudice. And from what I understand . . . the first couple of years my parents lived in that house . . . [people] would be out in the front of the house telling my family to leave— that they weren't welcome in the neighborhood." Greg, curious about these disturbing events, had tried to find out more, yet he could never really get his parents to discuss them with him. He referred to his father being a "strong man" and "persevering," but at the same time being unwilling to talk about this difficult time. It was only shortly before the interview that Greg's mother had finally told him about the things that happened during that period. Similarly, when Greg was beat up on his way home from school for being Indian (as often happened), and when he was called "nigger" because of his dark skin, and "girl" because of his long hair, he had tried to discuss these incidents with his father (the parent most often there when Greg arrived home from school). Greg "didn't understand why things were happening the way they were." He "knew [he] was an Indigenous person," that he was "different," but he had no understanding of why that difference provoked so much hostility on the part of some of his schoolmates. Yet he could get no explanation from his father, who refused to discuss such matters.

Greg reported being frustrated in his efforts to glean information from his elder family members during his growing-up years. His father had remained totally silent on such matters, and his mother "knew a lot more than what she told." Greg had been especially bothered, and remained so even at the time of the interview, by his paternal grandfather's unwillingness to share his knowledge of traditional culture and family history:

> My grandfather on my dad's side was kind of remorseful about how . . . he thought things had turned out. There was money set away for [our tribe], and he's waiting for that money to be paid . . . , because [tribes in our region have] not been paid for yet.[6] And he was very, very mad about that whole situation. He felt, and still thinks, that he should get that money. And he still thinks that until he gets that money, he's not going to tell anybody what he knows. And I know he knows a lot. Our ancestry comes from strong people—comes from some chiefs. But he won't say. Until he gets his money from [the government] . . . , he's not Indian! [Laughs] And you know, he's seventy-seven now so he's getting up there. And I don't know if that's ever going to happen. I wish he'd share it, but I've tried many times to ask him, and he just moves on to a different topic.

These silences on the part of Greg's parents and grandfather were not about the fact of being Indian. (Greg, of course, took his grandfather's "I'm not Indian!" in the ironic sense in which it was intended.) Yet they had nevertheless left him, during his childhood and adolescence, with many unanswered questions about the prejudice he experienced (the negative side of being Indian) and about his traditional cultural heritage and family history (the positive side of his Native American identity).

These silences on the part of the elder Anishinaabe relatives were interpreted by their adult children as having a number of different causes or motivations. However, the theme that emerged more than any other was shame—shame at being Indian. A story told by another woman, Doris Morgan, also focuses on shame as a powerful force in perpetuating silence, not only her Indian father's own silence, but that of a member of his elder generation, as well.

Doris, a volunteer at Riverton's Indian Center, was in her mid-forties at the time of the interview. She told of having just discovered that her father, who had worked all his life in one of AAC's Riverton-area factories, was a full-blooded Potawatomi; yet she could not recall a single time he had ever spoken of, or even hinted at, this heritage. Doris has very dark coloring—brown skin, dark eyes, and black hair—like her father (her mother was white), and had always wondered why this was. Like Jake, Doris explained that as a child, she had known she was not Mexican; she had also known she was not African American, although she, like Greg, had sometimes been called "nigger" by her classmates in school. But this topic had never been discussed in the family. So upon discovering her Potawatomi heritage while looking through some old documents from her father's side of the family after his death, Doris had wanted to learn more. Consequently, she took the opportunity, during a visit to her father's aunt, to ask, "Is it true we're Indian?" Although the two of them were alone in the house, Doris's great-aunt looked around hurriedly as if to make sure no one could overhear. Then she whispered fiercely: "*Shhhh!* Don't *ever* speak of that!" She added, as if to explain the importance of maintaining this silence, "Indians are *dirty!*"

This act of silencing—the great-aunt's reaction to a (seemingly) benign question—is shocking in its strength and intensity. Her "*Shhhh!*" has a brute force that no doubt stemmed from the brutality of countless earlier experiences that served, time and time again, to shock her into the deep conviction that being Indian must never be spoken of—that Indians are dirty. The partial answers, omissions, ambiguities, and outright denials described in the other narratives may be less dramatic than the great-aunt's fierce insistence on complete silence. Yet they, too, appear as brute forces, pushing against the childhood awareness of young people just beginning to wonder who they are, abruptly precluding questions that could not even be fully formulated, let alone given voice.

FILLING THE "HOLE IN OUR HEART"

As adults, these urban-raised Anishinaabe people not only had learned how to formulate those questions—they had also become tenacious in seeking their answers within the knowledge and practices of the cultural heritage they had come to feel was their birthright. They sought, as Michelle Duncan explained it, to fill the "hole in [their] heart":

> The majority of us [city-raised Indian people] walk around with this hole in our heart. We know we're different, that there's a piece of our life that is missing. And once we can [find out] what's missing, and fill that hole ourselves, then we see a whole person emerge. We start asking questions, and we become these enormous sponges, and we just want to absorb, absorb, absorb. And it fills that hole.

This absorption process was evident to one degree or another in the current life choices of virtually all the first-generation urban-raised Anishinaabeg I spoke with or interviewed, including those profiled here.[7]

All five of these interviewees presented themselves at the time of the interview as having a strong sense of Native American identity and a commitment to Riverton's various urban Indian organizations. Michelle had served for a number of years on the board of the Birmingham County Indian Association; Tom, who had gone to college and later earned an MBA, was using his business knowledge to assist Native American groups and individuals in the Riverton area who wanted to start their own businesses; Jake had become active on the committee that organizes and produces the BCIA's annual summer powwow; Greg was an officer in Riverton University's American Indian Student Organization; and Doris volunteered her time at the Indian Center, helping develop programs and activities for American Indian children. All five attended at least some of the various Native American functions and events that occurred in the Riverton area throughout the year. Finally, all five had become involved in attempts to recover in their personal lives something of the heritage they felt was lost to them.

Michelle, in addition to having collected documentation on her father's family (birth certificates, school records, marriage licenses, etc.), had begun seeking out older Indian people around the area over the past several years, learning all she could about traditional spiritual beliefs and practices. Jake had become an amateur genealogist, tracing his father's side of the family several generations back, and learning a great deal in the process about large-scale movements of Native people around the Great Lakes area back into the early nineteenth century. Doris had been involved in helping document the ancestry of members of her father's family's Potawatomi tribe, which had recently received federal recognition. Greg had joined a traditional drum group and obtained regalia for powwow dancing. Finally, Tom had become a family oral historian of sorts, seeking out older relatives on his mother's side of the family and conducting tape-recorded interviews with them about Chippewa culture and language, so he could document their knowledge before they died and took their memories with them. These efforts to reclaim a positive Native American identity played a significant role in the lives of Jake, Doris, Michelle, Greg, and Tom; yet each reported a negative consequence as well—that such overt interest in and public displays of American Indian heritage had caused problems with the parents who had struggled so hard not to be known as Indians. (The one exception was Doris, since her father had already died by the time she began to get involved in Riverton's American Indian community.)

Jake, of course, had the most difficulty in this regard. His genealogical work, as well as his involvement in Native American activities such as powwow dancing in full regalia, had resulted in total estrangement between him and his father. At the time of Jake's father's death in 1993, he and Jake had not spoken in five years. Still, Jake had done what he could to make peace with the father with whom he had experienced such difficulties. And he chose as his vehicle the heritage his father had renounced so violently: "I went back [to western Michigan, where my father had been buried] and scattered his ashes in the woods. And I used smudge, and did the Indian ceremony over him, because he wasn't buried Catholic. So I figured that was the least I could do, even though I don't fully understand the traditional ways." Jake emphasized that he now felt "resolved" about his relationship with his father.

Michelle's story starts out sounding very much like Jake's, but finds a happier resolution. She reported that, when she started to get involved with the Indian Association, her father had "thrown an absolute fit. He did not talk to me for almost a year. Because I was acknowledging the fact that I was Native American." But, she went to say, "He's accepted it now. He's accepted it, once he realized that it was okay—it was okay to be Indian." Similarly, Tom's mother, who had come to no longer deny her Chippewa heritage, had started to accompany Tom occasionally when he attended powwows and other American Indian events around the area, and to show interest in the work he was doing advising American Indian entrepreneurs.

Greg's case is slightly different, since he is the only one being profiled here whose parents were both Native American, and since he is about ten to fifteen years younger than the other interviewees. When Greg became involved in American Indian activities and traditional practices, his mother was quite accepting right from the start. After all, she herself had been active in the American Indian Student Organization at Riverton University when she and Greg's father had first moved to Riverton in the mid-1960s. Also, Greg's mother's work at the social service agency had kept her aware of political issues, and Greg recalled that even when he was quite young, his mother had been active in efforts directed toward improving the conditions of American Indian people in the Riverton area and elsewhere. Finally, she had herself reclaimed her traditional culture in that she learned how to do beadwork in the Chippewa style when Greg was in his teens (something she had not learned as a child, since she had been away at boarding school), and she became quite accomplished and renowned for this talent. Thus, Greg's mother was already predisposed to be supportive of Greg as he began to get involved with the AISO and to pursue traditional drumming and dancing.

With Greg's father, however, it had been a different story. Greg described his father's reaction to his recent involvement in traditional Native American practices, and how he (Greg) felt about that reaction, as follows:

> [My father] used to be involved [in some traditional ceremonies, during his youth on the reservation], but I think he's put [those things] away for the time being. And I get upset—like, two years ago, when I returned to the Circle, and began dancing and singing, [my father] didn't want anything to do with it. [And it bothered me] 'cause [some of] those songs are for him. There are specific songs—he's a veteran of the armed services. And I was kind of upset, because he didn't dance those dances.

However, Greg then went on to explain that he knew

> a lot of Anishinaabe men—old people, *real* Chippewa people that have knowledge, and they don't go to powwows. They stay home. Because they have reached a connection with that other world, and they know when negative and positive energies are working, and they know how and why they work. Now, I'm not saying the powwow is a bad thing. It's a good thing for our people, to express themselves and have an identity of themselves. But another thing that the powwow can do, that was brought over with Anglo people, is to promote prejudice, resentfulness, and jealousy. And that's why some of the old Anishinaabe people stay away.

In this way, it seems, Greg had made peace with his father's choice. Greg was pursuing one traditional path with his drumming, singing, and dancing, and his father was choosing another traditional path by not participating. The important thing, Greg seems to be saying, is that both father and son were following Anishinaabe tradition, each in his own way.

All of those profiled in this chapter, and many other first-generation urban-raised Anishinaabeg as well, were struggling to fill the "hole in [their] heart"—to make sense out of the American Indian heritage that lurked in the shadows of their childhood experience, and to bring that heritage out into the light of day. For this generation, Riverton's official American Indian institutions provided a much needed community that made information on traditional Native practices and beliefs available, encouraged political activism on behalf of Native American causes, and provided opportunities for socializing with others of American Indian ancestry. Most importantly, these institutions created an atmosphere in which it was not only okay to be Indian, but in which American Indian heritage was respected, valued, even celebrated. Furthermore, while many in the rural-raised parent generation had come to have only a marginal connection, if any, to the official institutions, most of these elder Anishinaabeg were gradually coming to terms with the choices their grown children were making; they were starting to recognize that a new climate in the dominant culture rendered these choices harmless in a way that similar choices could not have been in the past.

Even the urban-raised generation, growing up in Riverton in the 1950s, 1960s, and early 1970s, had to endure social ostracism, racist slurs, and at times even physical attacks. The childhood experiences of the elder, rural-raised generation were more fraught with such difficulties, further intensified by the extreme poverty that plagued most Indian communities throughout the first half of the twentieth century. In their search to understand their own childhood experiences, many first-generation urban-raised Anishinaabeg had begun reinterpreting their parents' contradictory statements, denials, and silences with a new understanding and sympathy.

This often took the form of recognizing their parents as workers in the dominant society. While regretting and perhaps resenting their parents' (seeming) assimilation, they had come to respect their proletarianization (though they did not refer to it as such), and to sympathize with the hardships inherent in that transformation and with the coping strategies their parents had had to develop to survive. The urban-raised Anishinaabe people came to appreciate—in both senses of the word—the obstacles their rural-raised parents had to overcome and the sacrifices they had to make in order to achieve success in an alien environment, thereby giving their children advantages and opportunities that they, the parents, had never had.

THE EFFORT TO BECOME "A NORMAL WHITE PERSON"

Both Jake and Michelle portrayed their fathers as having suffered prejudice in the factories where they worked. Their fathers had spoken very little about the problems they faced on the job, but a brief comment here or there had given a glimpse into the abuse they endured. For example, Jake reported that his father was called "Indian Joe" in the shop (his name was not Joe), because he "looked like a pure blood." He expressed a general belief that his father had felt ridiculed and humiliated at work. Also, it is clear from the way Jake talked about his father's drinking that he saw it as tied to the shame experienced, in the shop and elsewhere, about his Native American heritage—the primary source of the demons Jake mentions below. After discussing his father's shortcomings as a parent, Jake went on to say, "[But] I understand that in a lot of ways, he was a good dad. And he had his demons. . . . He didn't want to be identified [as Indian]. . . . He would never admit to being Indian." Jake had gained this sympathetic perspective only in his adult years, as he struggled with the demons from his own past (including alcoholism, from which he was recovering at the time of the interview) and with his identity.

Michelle talked about these same kinds of issues with regard to her father, but she made a more explicit connection between her father's anger, his drinking, and his situation at work:

> My father was an alcoholic. A very sad man. Even though he tried not to be. And I understand now that it was because he was denying who he was. He was denying who his children were, and there was a lot of anger that he suppressed over the years. And to get rid of that anger, he drank. And my father got in many fights [with coworkers], because they would call him "Chief," or they would make derogatory comments. . . . And he has a lot of scars from his battles.

This denial of who he was and who his children were was primarily caused, according to Michelle, by her father's experience at an Indian boarding school, where he was beaten for speaking his Native language—"that was the beginning of his humiliation, of his punishment for being who he was." Therefore, "he said that his children would not suffer that discrimination—to the point that he even listed us as 'white' on our birth certificates."

Michelle saw her father's drinking as the result of shame and anger deeply rooted in childhood experience and exacerbated by abuse suffered on the job. Yet, despite the extreme hardship Michelle saw her father as having endured, she also saw a positive side to his work experience. After having depicted her father's life in the shop, Michelle continued, "And it's sad because, well . . . [but] it's *not* sad! I'm really, really proud of my father, because the more discrimination that he suffered, the harder he tried. And when he retired, he was one of the top two electricians for his entire . . . *division!*"

This theme—that despite the racial prejudice suffered in the shop, or perhaps in some way because of it, the role of worker came to be of central importance as a means of achieving admiration—was echoed by Jake, as well. He explained how he saw this kind of dynamic operating in his own father's life:

> His whole life revolved around the job. I guess he wanted to be a 'normal white person' somehow—that was very important to him. And he had to show that he was smarter than everybody else. And better at his job. . . . My mother and him worked at the same factory, and they'd talk about the shop all night long. They'd sit and drink and I'd just hear about the shop, the shop, the shop.

So the factory, and the role of worker, took a central position in the lives of the fathers of Jake and Michelle, as constructed in their narratives. Unlike the American Indian heritage that was only hinted at, the worker identity that Jake's and Michelle's fathers had struggled so hard to develop was quite openly presented within the family.

Like Michelle and Jake, Greg showed pride in his father's achievements as a worker and provider, particularly in how well he had managed his finances for a secure retirement. Greg, too, tied in his father's success as a factory worker with the hardship he had suffered. Greg explained:

> He's gonna make sure he . . . retire[s] with full benefits. He was raised in a kind of a semidysfunctional home, and he had to learn the hard way what a job meant, and what money meant. And how valuable it was. And he came down here [to Riverton] with a focus on what he wanted to do, and what he needed to do. And when he retires, I think he's going to . . . feel very self-gratified by what he has done.

Thus, in discussing their fathers' strong identities as workers and their successes on the job, Greg emphasized childhood hardship, Michelle cited both discrimination in the job setting and the abusive boarding school experience, and Jake implied similar troubles, both on the job and during childhood, that his father had endured. In discussing his mother's work situation, however, Greg could be more unambivalently positive. He clearly indicated that her success as a social services worker—having made it in a professional position—had been a source of pride for him while he was growing up.

Tom's situation was somewhat different, since in his case it had been only his mother who was American Indian. While in many cases Native women worked outside the home, whether at professional or (more often) working-class jobs, Tom's mother had been able to stay home and care for her five children, since Tom's (non-Native) father had a factory job that provided enough income for the family to live on. Therefore, Tom did not have any stories about his mother trying to fit into the world of work outside the home. However, he did talk about how hard she worked, during the years when Tom and his siblings were growing up, to acquire the habits and skills of a homemaker so valued by the dominant society. After describing his mother's efforts to maintain a clean and well-ordered home, along with her shunning of Indian ways even within the home, Tom offered the following sympathetic explanation for his mother's choices:

> It was hard for my mother, because she was the youngest, but she was the only one who finished high school. And they had by that time moved into Whitfield [which was nearly all white], and so I think she tried then to be a different person, unfortunately. Which happens a lot. She tried to leave it all behind her, and pretend it never happened. (Jackson, 691)

The "it" in the previous sentence refers to her family's life in the Indian town community where Tom's mother had spent her early childhood years, and all the hardships and prejudices her family had faced there.

Tom had gained insight into his mother's conflicted identity when he did some oral historical research, as an adult, into his mother's family background. He had found out from a non-Native older woman who had lived in Whitfield all her life that his maternal grandmother, who had provided midwifery and healing services for both Natives and non-Natives during the 1920s and 1930s, had used indigenous spiritual practices as well as medicinal remedies. However, when Tom had tried to discuss this with his mother, already in her seventies at the time, he found that

> [she] has a real problem because she wants to identify as being a Christian, and so she still has problems talking about [her mother's Native spir-

itual beliefs and practices]. So it has been very difficult for her. And none
of the other family members have spoken about [her]. . . . None of my
mother's brothers and sisters ever mentioned their mom. (Jackson, 690)

He reported that he had been at least partially successful more recently in getting his mother to discuss the spiritual aspects of her
mother's healing practices and other matters of traditional spirituality, but it had not been easy—he had really had to "drag it out of
her." During his childhood, she had been resolute in her determina-
tion to be a Christian and a European American–style homemaker
and mother, and to have nothing to do with the sorts of practices her
own mother had engaged in. Despite his interest in his grandmother's traditional ways, however, Tom conceded that his childhood growing up in Riverton was no doubt eased by having had a
mother who was more or less like those of his (non-Native) friends.

Thus, Michelle, Jake, Greg, and Tom each recognized, looking
back, the benefits they had reaped as a result of their parents' efforts
to be like "normal white people" and in so doing to give their children, insofar as was possible, the chance to live the lives of "normal
white people." These urban-raised Anishinaabeg had enjoyed a level
of financial security while growing up that had been entirely unavail-
able to their rural-raised parents during their childhood years. This financial stability had led to opportunities in adult life for the next
generation, as well. Jake chose to follow in his parents' footsteps and
had worked for twenty-five years at the same factory where they had
worked (and about which they had talked incessantly while he was
growing up—"Sometimes I think they loved the shop more than
they loved me"). Michelle had gone to college and secured a professional career as a substance abuse counselor. Tom was a successful
businessman while Greg, the youngest of the group, had just recently
returned to college at the time of our interview.

All four of these urban-raised Anishinaabeg (and Doris) were well
aware that their lives were considerably better in material terms than
their rural-raised Indian parents' lives had been, in large part due to
the hard work and sacrifices of those parents. That is, first-generation
urban Anishinaabe people like Jake, Michelle, Doris, and Greg saw
the worker identity their fathers developed—or, in Tom's case, his
mother, who chose to provide a good home for her children as a
homemaker—as a key factor in allowing them to enjoy the benefits
they had. But they saw their parents' worker identity as having come
at the price of their Indian identity. Becoming "like a normal white
person" (in the shop and in the home)—the means of succeeding
and providing a good life for their children—had also meant

"putting away" their Anishinaabe practices. However, despite the considerable constraints on the Indian identity of their parents, each of the urban-raised Indian people being profiled here also included in his or her narrative something else. Each recalled at least some shred of a positive identity about being Native American that had been conveyed by their Indian parent when they were growing up.

One such incident has already been quoted—Michelle's father's having told her to "hold [her] head up high" and "be proud" of who she was. On another occasion during her childhood, after having seen Indian people on television portrayed as "blood-thirsty savages," she recalled asking her father straight out, "Are we Indian?" His response, Michelle reported, was to say, "Yes, we are. But not like they show on TV." Michelle added that "he just let it go at that"— that the topic had not been open for discussion. Yet Michelle at least was able to get confirmation that they were Indian, and reassurance that being Indian did not mean they were like the Indians portrayed so negatively on television.

Tom reported that despite his mother's reluctance to talk about the spiritual (and therefore non-Christian) aspects of her mother's healing practices, she had been very proud of her mother's ability to effect cures for physical ailments and illnesses, using traditional Chippewa herbal remedies. There had been "many times [during my childhood] when my mother talked about her mom, because of her mom going around healing people" (Jackson, 690). Tom explained that the fact that his grandmother had healed by traditional Indian means was very important, because many of her patients had been non-Native people who either could not get a conventional doctor to come to the Whitfield area, or who had tried a conventional (non-Native) medical treatment that had failed. He reported that his mother had been quick to point out, with pride, that her mother had had a very high success rate with these patients, by using the Indian ways.

Similarly, Greg's mother had always been open about some aspects of her American Indian identity. While she had never been forthcoming with information about traditional ways, her involvement with American Indian organizations and causes, mentioned above, had always given Greg the opportunity to see her exhibiting a positive Indian identity in a different sense. In contrast, Greg's father had mostly been "busy at the shop," and, as mentioned above, had "put away" his traditional practices by the time Greg was born. Still, as Greg looked back on his childhood from an adult perspective, he described his father as all along having been "a good Anishinaabe man" who, as an Anishinaabeg, knew that the first part of his life was supposed to be for his children to be the most important thing in his life—to provide for them, and to make sure they started on their way. A lot of elders of our [reservation] community have come before my father and have told him that it is time for him to take his place within the community. And he has told these men that he is not a chief, and all he needs to do right now is make sure that his family is safe and that he finishes his job.

Thus, whereas the other first-generation urban-raised Anishinaabeg saw their parents' proletarianization mainly as part of an assimilation that worked at cross-purposes to valuing and expressing an American Indian identity—to being Indian in some sense—Greg interpreted his father's dedication to his job and to providing for his family as the primary means through which he expressed his American Indian identity, and lived as a "good Anishinaabe man."

Finally, even Jake reported that his father had some positive things to say about Indians. Jake described how his father would express admiration for things Indian (but not where his own family was concerned). "He would talk about the way an Indian would do something in the woods, or . . . about hunting game. Things like that. Or he would talk about the way they lived . . . in the old days." Furthermore, Jake reported that his father had talked about how some day "our society as a whole" would collapse, and then "the people up north will be strong again." Jake explained that this was an old Ottawa belief that the Indian people would someday have to teach the white man how to live. Though Jake's father had "never acknowledged that it was an Indian belief," he still had expressed, in veiled form (substituting "the people up north" for "Indians"), his admiration for the traditional ways of his Ottawa ancestors.

During the interviews, I did not directly elicit examples of times during childhood when parents had shown pride in their American Indian heritage, exhorted their children to have pride, or simply expressed positive attitudes about Indian people and culture in general. Rather, these statements seemed to arise unbidden as a sort of counterpoint to the predominant themes that inevitably emerged— themes of confusion that interviewees had felt about their identity, their parents' unwillingness to discuss such issues, and the hardships parents had endured both at the time of the interviewees' childhood and in the past of the parents' own childhood. Clearly, as part of their need to fill the "hole in [their] heart," these first-generation urban-raised Anishinaabe people needed to find some hint of positive identity in their childhood experience, however oblique or fleeting. This allowed them a sense of continuity between a past characterized most strongly by its lack of a positive Indian identity, and a present in which such an identity had come to have central importance.

In seeking to recapture a heritage that their parents chose to put aside, these grown children of (seemingly) assimilated American Indians are, of course, not so different from the grown children of assimilated parents of other ethnic groups in the United States who strive to reverse the effects of the melting pot and reclaim their ethnicity. This phenomenon has been most closely studied in the case of various "hyphenated Americans" of European origin, or "white ethnics." The first huge waves of European immigrants came to this country in the late 1800s and early 1900s, and the first analyses of the adjustments made by succeeding generations go back to the 1930s. One of the foremost scholars on European immigrants of this era was Marcus Lee Hansen, who, in a seminal essay, described the movement away from, then back toward, ethnic heritage, which typifies the generations. This movement was most succinctly summed up in a phrase that has subsequently been echoed, elaborated on, and challenged by sociologists studying immigrant groups in the United States: "what the son wishes to forget the grandson wishes to remember" (Hansen 1952 [1937], 143). The typical pattern for such ethnic groups, as documented and discussed in numerous sociological studies, is that the original immigrant generation, who came to the U.S. as adults, retained their Old World ways, especially within the family, much to the chagrin of their U.S.-born children; these first-generation U.S.-born children grew up to be hyper-Americans, attempting to eradicate all traces of their ethnic past; the next generation, born in the United States to assimilated parents with all the advantages of being mainstream (white) Americans, eventually came to regret that their parents had deprived them of the cultural heritage of their grandparents and sought out ways to reconnect with that heritage.

What is different about the American Indian generational pattern is that the first two generations in the European American ethnic model are collapsed into one generation of urban American Indians.[8] That is, those Anishinaabeg who originally migrated to cities were like the European immigrants who left the old country (analogous to the reservation). At the same time, however, they were like the first generation of U.S.-born ethnics in that they worked hard to assimilate to their new sociocultural environment. Thus, their children—the "paper Indians" of this chapter—who were the first generation born in the city, might best be equated with the second generation of U.S.-born European ethnics in that both groups seek to reclaim the heritage denied them by their assimilated parents. Certainly there is some merit in such an analogy, but there are important differences as well.

First, there is the matter of social race. Many of those in the original migrant generation of Anishnaabeg (and to some extent, their children as well) were "racially marked" by their appearance and did not have the option of fully assimilating, no matter what behaviors they adopted. This stands in contrast to white ethnics, who, with the proper behavioral adjustments, could successfully blend in to the mainstream of American (white) society.[9]

Perhaps an even more important factor, however, is seen in the case of second-generation ethnic European Americans raised by parents who had grown up in the United States with no direct contact (in most cases) with the old country. These parents had, for the most part, enthusiastically embraced the ways of their American peers (as opposed to those of their European-raised elders), leading to the adoption of a fairly unambiguous American identity in their adult lives. In contrast, the urban-raised Anishinaabeg grew up with parents who were at the same time from "the old country" and attempting to assimilate. Thus, the first-generation urban-raised Indian people describe an ambiguity, an ambivalence, a poignant tension in their parents' ethnic identity—what appears to them now as a fragmented identity, as they recall how their parents struggled to maintain some connection to extended family and home community, while at the same time attempting to "leave it all behind [them] and pretend it never happened."

The "pretending it never happened" and similar efforts described by the grown children of the original Anishnaabe migrants are portrayed in the narratives as having a forced quality to them—not the casual forgetting of things that are unimportant or the natural forgetting of things that simply recede in time. Those phrases might better describe the "forgetting" that Hansen and others have attributed to the first-generation of U.S.-born European ethnics—the original immigrants' "sons." The forgetting on the part of the generation of American Indians who migrated from rural communities to cities, as perceived and portrayed by their adult children, seems at times more like the kind of forgetting that Freud discussed as repression. That is, it seems to be the motivated forgetting that results from "shutting off" something too painful or traumatic to remember (Freud 1914, 148). Consequently, the "paper Indians" have need to recover those memories they see their parents as having "shut off," and that heritage they felt was "put away." This need is qualitatively different from that of most second-generation white ethnics (as well as those of partial American Indian ancestry who lack ties to Indian elders or an Indian community). Where the latter have the option of being "normal white people," many of the former do not; where the latter choose to "remember," the former need to fill the "hole in [their] heart."

"HOW CAN YOU HAVE A TIE TO SOMETHING YOU KNOW NOTHING ABOUT?"

In the narratives of the first-generation urban-raised Anishinaabeg, it is the fragmented identity of the parents that gives force to their silences, because it gives content to those silences. I use the term "fragmented identity" to describe the parents' ethnicity as conveyed by their grown children, rather than "dual identity" or "bicultural identity," because the image conveyed is not simply one of wearing two hats or shifting styles, as these latter terms imply. True, there is some degree to which those in the rural-raised generation do make such conscious shifts. However, the narratives of their grown children suggest a level of conflict, ambivalence, and inner turmoil ("demons") in their parents that implies a lack of integration and resolution with regard to these issues, as well. That is, these are aspects of identity that manifest themselves intrasubjectively through semiotic processes that occur within the individual, both above and below the level of conscious awareness, rather than simply through a single (or dual) conscious subjectivity.

Implicit in each omission, each cryptic response, each denial, is the harsh, brutal experience that makes discussion of certain issues so difficult. As portrayed in the narratives, those traumatic experiences were present in the parents' silences, and it was this presence that bore into the hearts of their children. E. Valentine Daniel, in writing about the experiences of torture endured by Tamils during outbreaks of ethnic violence, concludes: "What persists in this and many other interviews such as this is the drone of silence—a silence that does not settle for the anthropologist whether it is a silence of a not-being-able-to-speak or of an ought-not-to-speak" (Daniel 1996, 150). Similarly, in an interview study of how Jewish Holocaust survivors retell their traumatic memories, psychologist Henry Greenspan discusses the struggle for words—a struggle that often ends in failure:

> If the silence between the words strikes us in survivors' written memoirs, where only space on a page marks its presence, it strikes harder when we can hear that silence as an abrupt halt, a gasp for breath, the agonized deliberation that may surround the choice of a single word. In embodied speech, the silence between the words becomes a fully palpable, sometimes consuming, presence. (Greenspan 1992, 147)

Daniel and Greenspan are confronting directly the silences of their interviewees, while I am encountering a discourse by my interviewees about the silences of their elders. Still, it is reasonable to speculate that those silences, as recounted by interviewees, have a force similar to the silences described by Daniel and Greenspan. That is, urban-raised Anishinaabe people have no way of knowing, as they recall their childhood experience, whether a given silence on the part of a parent was a "not-being-able-to-speak" or an "ought-not-to-speak." Given this ambiguity—along with the fact that both kinds of silence arise in the context, or from a background, of trauma—their parents' silences are transformed from absences into powerful presences, "fully palpable, and sometimes consuming." Thus, the absences that those in the urban-raised generation perceive as having made a "hole in [their] heart" were also presences. Far from being unconditionally empty or silent, these absences, as dynamic semiotic signs, are filled with a cacophony of competing messages—a mix of pride and shame, acceptance and rejection, whispering of something lost but not saying what it was. So now, in their adult lives, the first urban-raised generation of Anishinaabe people of Riverton speak of their efforts to determine what it is they lack and to reclaim it. They seek to replace that powerful silence of their childhood with the powerful voice of a strong, positive American Indian identity.

This, then, is my answer to Michelle Duncan's rhetorical question in the quote at the beginning of the chapter: "How can you have a tie to something you know nothing about?" I would say that she and others with her background in fact do know a great deal about their Anishinaabe parents' background and heritage. That is, they are not connected to an Indian heritage only by "pieces of paper." Part of their connection comes through the "presences in the absences" discussed above—such palpable silences and emptynesses carry "trace" meanings like that of Derrida's linguistic sign, "a monument . . . stonelike . . . a text without a voice" (Derrida 1982, 24). In deciphering this "voiceless text," the urban-raised generation do form ties with their heritage, their culture, and the home communities of their Anishinaabe parents.

In pondering their recollections from childhood, they uncover clues to the hardships their parents have suffered, they catch glimpses of how their parents were treated by non-Natives in Riverton, they receive hints that their parents had pride, however conflicted, in their American Indian heritage. These clues, glimpses, and hints act semiotically as signs, permeating the lives of the next generation in a way that ties them, albeit ambiguously and ambivalently, to their parents' American Indian heritage. They constitute a powerful ongoing discourse within these urban Indian families of what being Indian is about in the present, while at the same time these messages spring from deeper roots, extending back through chains of semiosis to the parents' own present and past experiences. These chains served to tie the children—however partially, ambiguously, and at times unconsciously—to the often difficult and sometimes brutal experiences in the city, in the shop, and in the rural Indian home communities that had forged certain aspects of their parents' ethnic identity. Moreover, these ties have also been reinforced from another direction.

Each time the family visited the home community, got together with other Indian families in Riverton,[10] or had Native friends or family come to visit at their home, the urban-raised children were witness to a certain kind and level of Anishnaabe culture or identity. For, while the parents and other Anishinaabe relatives may have seemed assimilated in terms of the more overt features of culture content—food, clothing, hair style, language[11]—they constantly demonstrated, in the patterns of their daily interactions, a certain kind of Indian identity. These patterns of characteristically Anishinaabe habit, style, and practice in the elder generation, formed during their childhood years in their home communities, were not readily perceived as Indian by their children. Yet at some level, the interactional and behavioral patterns no doubt registered on those in the younger generation, giving them a direct connection to an American Indian heritage that, though subtle and seldom fully recognized, was nonetheless "fully palpable." As a semiotic process occurring neither within the individual participants (subjective) nor in an easily definable exterior form (objective), the Indianness of the participants was emergent within the mutual engagement of participants in social interaction with one another.

For the most part, those who formed the core of these Indian gatherings were members of extended Anishinaabe families. These families, in turn, formed links through space between urban and rural settings, and through time as younger family members interacted with their elders, whose memories reached back to, and whose habits found their roots in, much earlier times. The next chapter will consider the role of families in the contemporary Indian community in Riverton as well as in the rural home communities of the early twentieth century, and will emphasize more positive aspects of Anishinaabe community life.

Chapter 5

Family Ties

▼ ▼ ▼

There are lots of big families that you just don't see
around [the Indian Center]. They've got quite a few
members, and we don't see them around here.

—*Joe Niles*

In describing the history of Riverton's official American Indian
institutions, I have explained that as the climate, mission, and personnel of these institutions changed over the years, the original
founding members—the generation of Anishinaabe people who first
migrated to Riverton—tended to become alienated and fall away. In
Jack Peter's words: "When the funding came in, the real grassroots
people decided that's not what they wanted—and they left." It was at
least a year before I began to recognize that the real grassroots people
had left, and it was another six months or so before I started to understand where they had gone. Many of them still lived in Riverton,
and yet few of them participated in the events and programs of the
official institutions.

Through interviews with Joe Niles and others among the few
grassroots people who stayed involved with the Birmingham County
Indian Association over the years, I was finally able to gain some insight into another whole layer of Riverton's American Indian community. I came to see that beneath the surface of the highly visible
and readily accessible official institutions lay a patchwork of extended Anishinaabe families that had picked up where the BCIA and
other official organizations had left off in the early 1970s. That is,
when the BCIA and Riverton University's AISO stopped functioning
as social clubs (or when their social function was eclipsed by other
priorities), the original Anishinaabe migrants to Riverton simply

shifted venues, continuing their social activities outside the purview of the official institutions. And, since the closest associates of these rural-raised urban Indians tended to be their own relatives, the core of their informal social groups was nearly always extended family (or groups of interrelated families) from the same home community.

This chapter will consider the role of families in the Anishinaabe communities from a very different perspective. It will return to the home communities of the early twentieth century, as well as to the contemporary urban Anishinaabe community, to consider the positive aspects of family life—the importance of kinship ties, the strength of family bonds, and the complexity of the networks that bind Anishinaabe communities together. Anishinaabe communities had already become quite acculturated by the early twentieth century, but there were continuities with the earlier culture, and these continuities provided the basis for an Indianness that, while quite different from the open and explicit expressions of traditional culture favored by the younger, urban-raised generation, nonetheless constituted a strong and positive American Indian identity.

The primary locus for these continuities is, I would suggest, the relationships that were maintained within and among extended families in the Anishinaabe communities throughout all the cultural, political, and economic changes they have undergone. Among those who grew up in rural Anishinaabe communities during the first half of the twentieth century, such family connections continue to hold a place of central importance, even in Riverton and other urban settings. This chapter will explore the nature of these kinship networks and their significance to Anishinaabe identity, for some of the deepest values, beliefs, habits, and practices of traditional Anishinaabe culture were engendered and perpetuated within families. A description of the traditional Anishinaabe belief system shows how certain models of the kinship system and certain aspects of the worldview mutually reinforce one another, and how both underlie rules of social interaction. The Anishinaabe worldview and social practices define a particular and subtle form of Indianness among Anishinaabe people, a form of Indianness identifiable in their interactions, not only with one another, but with non-Anishinaabe people as well, and even, in certain ways, with the non-human environment.

EARLY TWENTIETH-CENTURY ANISHINAABE KINSHIP RELATIONS

In the earlier description of hardships faced by Anishinaabe people in their home communities during the first half of the twentieth century, I focused on the Whitfield-area community known by non-Native outsiders as Indian Town. The people who lived there had a Native-language name for this town. For privacy reasons it will be called here by a different Native-language place name: *Zhashkooning*. Through interviews with people who had themselves lived in this community, or who had elder relatives who had lived there, it was possible to learn something of the kinship relations that sustained community members through difficult times.

For example, Tom Richards learned from interactions within his own extended family about the community spirit that characterized family life in the early twentieth-century Zhashkooning community. His great-aunt Grace, who had grown up in Zhashkooning during the 1910s, had told him how relatives "would share—one person had a team [of horses], another one had a boat, another one had woodworking tools. When someone would get married, they would get together and build a cabin" (Jackson, 690). Similarly, Bob Miller, who had lived in Zhashkooning with his family until the age of ten, described family life in the 1940s and the importance to people of getting together:

> They didn't want to stay apart too much. They wanted to come back, see if anybody was sick or something like that. . . . I remember quite a few times when I was a little guy, a lot of . . . [relatives] would come over, or we'd go to their place. 'Cause they stuck that close. [My dad and I], we'd go visiting. I remember, we went all over the place. Then they'd come visit us . . . [and] we'd fix a meal or something for them, what[ever] we had. (Jackson, 481)

In another interview that included Bob's wife, Nancy, the two of them talked about how the Indian families would help each other out. Bob began by saying that his mother used to bake bread for many of the families around the neighborhood. Then Nancy continued: "She used to . . . make fifteen loaves of bread at a time. The Matthews family[1] didn't always have a lot of food . . . I know Bob's ma often made things for them, so their kids had food. If you had it, you helped somebody else" (Jackson, 508). Bob added that his father shared his hunting catch with this family, and with others who were in need: "If they didn't have enough food . . . we'd go over there and visit them and take 'em some food." Then he explained that when they could, the Matthews family would reciprocate: "[Sometimes] when I was selling baskets, they'd give me some to sell." In this way, those who were doing relatively well at one time could help out those who were having trouble, and then at another time, the former recipient could be the provider of assistance.

In addition to visits that individual families made to one another's homes to help out, visit, check on each other, and exchange food, goods, and important news, there were also larger gatherings. These larger gatherings joined networks of extended families, until the whole Zhashkooning community was included, and often visiting kin from other communities, as well. Bob Miller described these gatherings, which took place on a fairly regular basis, as he remembered them from his childhood:

> They always made a habit [of getting together, because they] didn't want to get out of contact with all the [relatives] living around Zhashkooning. So they'd get a big pot and throw [some] corn, and potatoes . . . and everything in there. And they'd have a fire under there. Then all the families would get together . . . way back where the woods was. It was kind of a long walk back there. They let you know by word of mouth, telling you a certain day was when they'd get together. I think they probably went home late at night, 'cause I remember that [my dad] used to carry me on his shoulders. (Jackson, 480)

These gatherings would occur once every month or so during the warmer months of the year, and continued for as long as people remained living in the Zhashkooning area. Even after that location had been abandoned because financial hardship forced many people to sell their land, extended families still kept in close touch by gathering at each other's homes on a regular basis (as in Tom Richards's descriptions of his family's visits to Whitfield-area relatives when he was a child during the late 1940s).

The larger gatherings that Bob Miller recalled from his childhood appear to have been of the general type referred to by many interviewees as "camp meetings." These events were common occurrences throughout the Upper Great Lakes region during the first half of the twentieth century. They drew Anishinaabe people from a wide radius—perhaps as far as fifty or sixty miles away, or even further. These were considerable distances given the limited means of transportation available and the poor road conditions in rural areas. For several days, Native families would camp out together, sharing meals, visiting, and (in the evenings) singing and dancing. These gatherings were generally Christian in form, with church-type services held, Christian prayers given, and so on. This is not surprising in light of the role that Christian churches had played in most Anishinaabe communities since at least as far back as the mid-1800s. The Zhashkooning community was no exception, and Rachel Richards and her Aunt Grace both recalled fondly how the community would gather for Sunday services at the church there. Similarly, many other of my older interviewees mentioned the churches in their home communities as important meeting places.

These basic features—a community closely knit through kinship ties, in which everyone kept in touch with one another, helped each other through difficult times, gathered together for social events, and congregated for religious ceremonials (whether indigenous or Christian)—have been documented by the missionaries, fur traders, and other early sojourners among the Great Lakes Anishinaabeg, as well as Indian agents, archaeologists, and ethnographers. Even Charles Lamont, whose later childhood was so severely compromised by a neglectful father, an abusive stepmother, and an alcoholic uncle, recalled that before his mother died, he and his brother had gone with her to the Catholic church in their island Anishinaabe community. Also, Charles reported attending large Chippewa gatherings on the Fourth of July that featured feasting, singing, and dancing. These kinds of experiences were reported by virtually all those who grew up in an American Indian community, and they must have mitigated the negative impact of the oppressive conditions that also characterized these communities. Therefore, life in Anishinaabe communities included not only the poverty, the oppression, and the social problems, but also the strong and supportive kinship networks that sustained community members. In these communities, family members stuck together, helped each other out, shared resources with one another, and kept up close ties with extended kin that lived in other Indian communities throughout the region.

Another description of how these family bonds of mutual support were maintained comes from Agnes Jones, who grew up in a Chippewa community in Michigan's western Upper Peninsula in the 1920s. Her (non-Native) husband had mentioned that whenever they had gone to visit Agnes's aunt, it "didn't make any difference what time of day it was, she always put some food on the table." Agnes continued: "All Indians were that way. My ma used to take us kids to visit [elderly relatives], and I remember, they always had a gift; they always had . . . a dish or something [to give you]. It wasn't very big, but they always had something." These kinds of comments were made by many of my older interviewees who had grown up in rural (reservation or off-reservation) Anishinaabe communities.

Whether considering the negative or the positive aspects of family and community life, however, one still might question what, specifically, was *Indian* about these communities. The kinds of kinship ties of mutual support and the communal events that have been described as characterizing Zhashkooning and other early twentieth-century Anishinaabe communities have been well documented as typical of the moral economy of indigenous Upper Great Lakes–area societies as well as other aboriginal societies throughout North America. However, they are not unique to traditional Native American societies by any means. They are among the criteria cited by Durkheim as characterizing the mechanical solidarity of small-scale societies in general and have been well documented by generations of anthropologists working around the world in small communities (bands, tribes, and peasant villages), which are almost by definition kin-based.

Furthermore, in the United States these same features have been shown to typify ethnic enclaves in both rural and urban settings. New immigrants typically band together in neighborhoods where the primary social units are extended families, and the same is true of other ethnic or racial minorities that tend to be economically disadvantaged. The assistance people give one another within the extended family networks they maintain can make a dramatic difference in the level of well-being attainable by individuals and families. Among other ethnographers, Carol B. Stack (1974) has demonstrated, with exceptional clarity and insight, how these strategies worked for a poor, urban African American community during the 1960s. However, Stack also points out a maladaptive aspect to the general strategy of generosity and reciprocity. She explains that when someone is fortunate enough to get a windfall (such as a small inheritance, or winnings from gambling) and to save part of it from encroachment by "the system," he or she must, by the social rules of obligation, distribute it to kin who are worse off. Consequently, no one ever really gets ahead.[2] Overall, though, in the African American community studied by Stack, the assistance and comfort provided through extended kinship networks tended to far outweigh the deficits.

In any case, such comparisons raise the question: since close family ties, sharing, reciprocal support, and community gatherings are typical of many kinds of small-scale, marginalized, or poor communities, is there anything uniquely Indian about the Anishinaabe communities? In order to address this question, further information is needed about the role of kinship in the traditional Anishinaabe world, or "culturally-constituted environment" (Hallowell 1955).[3]

"ALL OUR RELATIONS": THE EXPANDED KINSHIP NETWORK OF *ANISHINAABE BIMAADIZIWIN*

Raymond Fogelson, in discussing the importance of the notion of community to Native American identity, comments that in many traditional American Indian societies, kinship serve[s] as a metaphor for social and political relations that [can] . . . be inwardly intensive, such that everyone [is] . . . related to everyone else through direct descent, clan affiliation, or adoption, and [can] . . . be outwardly extensive, such that the idiom of kinship [can] . . . be used as a means to establish and structure relations with strangers and alien societies. (Fogelson 1996, 53)

In traditional Anishinaabe society, kinship functions both "intensively" and "extensively."[4] According to Hallowell, there are no special terms to designate affinal relatives (in-laws); rather, "all persons in the social world of the [Anishinaabeg] are assimilated to classes of kin that in our kinship system fall into the category of blood relations" (Hallowell 1992, 52). Thus, in a very real sense, "*all* [Anishinaabeg] are kin of some sort" (ibid., emphasis in original). Furthermore, one of the most important things about knowing the specific kind of relation someone else is to oneself is that it signifies how one is to behave toward that person. In the traditional Anishinaabe world, when traveling to a distant community, one must be careful to establish which category of kin (however distant) one is dealing with before one can even know what type of greeting is appropriate. To behave inappropriately (i.e., the way one might behave with a different category of kin) is to risk insulting the other party and creating ill will between the two people. Thus, a central feature of social life in traditional Anishinaabe culture is learning the proper behaviors for each kin category, as well as which individuals belong to each category.

This principle of proper kinship behavior that characterizes all social relations within Anishinaabe society is not confined to the domain of human beings. It also extends to include entities that, in the European American tradition, are considered part of the natural world, or the environment. In her recent book, *All Our Relations,* which discusses the struggles of Native communities in the face of environmental devastation wrought by the dominant society, Anishinaabe activist Winona LaDuke explains that

Native American teachings describe the relations all around—animals, fish, trees, and rocks—as our brothers, sisters, uncles, and grandpas. Our relations to each other, our prayers whispered across generations to our relatives, are what bind our culture together. The protections, teachings, and gifts of our relatives have for generations preserved our families. These relations are honored in ceremony, song, story, and life that keep relations close—to buffalo, sturgeon, salmon, turtles, bears, wolves, and panthers. These are our older relatives—the ones who came before and taught us how to live. (LaDuke 1999, 2)

These animals—as well as the spiritual beings who serve as "bosses" over each species—are very much a part of the everyday Anishinaabe world. Similarly, thunder is not considered a natural process, but rather is a class of powerful beings—*Nimkii,* usually glossed as Thunderbeings—who sometimes come to the aid of their human "grandchildren." In the traditional Anishinaabe world, in addition to the central role that kinship plays in human relations—where even those in faraway villages can be incorporated into one's family as clansmen or (potential) inlaws—many elements of the nonhuman world are placed within the kinship system as well.

Furthermore, in the Anishinaabe world, states of being and realms that are considered imaginary, or fictitious, or illusory in the tradition of the European Enlightenment—such as myths, dreams, and visions (and the ghosts, culture heroes, and other beings inhabiting these realms)—are very much a part of the daily lived reality of the Anishinaabeg. In such a world, the community includes many kinds of beings in addition to the living human beings who inhabit the village, and all must be taken into account. Consequently, rules governing appropriate behavior with those in various kinship categories (same generation vs. one-generation-removed, male vs. female, etc.) are applied not only to living humans, but to those who have died, to mythical beings, and to spiritual beings associated with the natural world, as well.

The paramount demand in Anishinaabe social life is the effective and consistent management of all these various relationships, with their many types and orders of beings, in such a way as to always behave appropriately and respectfully in the prescribed manner. To conduct oneself in such a manner is to achieve *Anishinaabe bimaadiziwin,* which can be translated as "to live well in the Indian way." In the spirit of *Anishinaabe bimaadiziwin:* good relations are maintained with "bosses" of plant and animal species by treating their representatives in the corporeal realm with proper respect; mythical beings are considered to be present when stories about them are told, and they are accorded the hospitality shown any (other) visiting kinsman; Thunderbeings are summoned and honored with offerings of tobacco (thrown into the fire) as human members of the grandparent generation are given tobacco; family members who have died are not only remembered, but also assisted on their journey in the spirit world by the living, who "eat for them" at ghost suppers or Feasts of the Dead; and those who are not yet born are formally taken into account when family and community decisions with long-term consequences are made. Underlying all these relations is the uniquely Anishinaabe notion of power.

THE ANISHINAABE NOTION OF POWER

Drawing on Hallowell's ethnographic writings, Mary Black (1977a) argues persuasively that, for the Anishinaabeg, a particular notion of power or, more precisely, "power-control" underlies and permeates key aspects of the traditional belief system. Furthermore, this notion of power integrates the belief system (and the anthropologist's understanding of it), bringing together seemingly unrelated or even contradictory beliefs and practices into a consistent worldview. Her starting point in explicating the power-control concept is the *other-than-human person* category—a term Hallowell gave to all the nonhuman beings that people the Anishinaabe social world and are included in its kinship networks. It is in the hierarchical ranking of "persons" that the power-control notion comes to the fore.

In general, other-than-human persons, though related to humans, have more power than humans; humans must seek "blessings" from their other-than-human elders just as children must seek care, protection, and training from elder human relatives. Furthermore, while the powers of other-than-human persons are inherent, the powers of human persons must be achieved, and the means of that achievement is through relations with their other-than-human kin. The blessings (i.e., powers) humans can receive from their other-than-human "grandfathers" range from simply the "ordinary apparatus for successful living" (145) to more extraordinary powers such as the ability to heal, to do bodily harm to or bewitch others, and even to change one's physical form.

Such powers—whether ordinary or extraordinary—are rarely discussed, for to do so would be disrespectful to the (other-than-human) bestower of the powers. Given this injunction, and given the penchant for other-than-human persons (and even some human persons) to change form at will, there is a certain degree of uncertainty in the Anishinaabe world as to whom one is really dealing with in any particular encounter. Therefore, Anishinaabe people typically exercise caution in all interactions with persons (both human and other-than-human) so as to avoid showing disrespect to, and thereby incurring the wrath of, a person who might be more powerful than they.

The goal for most Anishinaabeg most of the time, Black explains, is simply to maintain one's autonomy—to avoid being controlled by one's environment while at the same time not controlling anyone else. The environment in which one seeks this autonomy includes "other people as well as other natural beings or forces that could affect one's outcomes or render one helpless" (ibid.). Thus, Anishinaabeg avoid interfering with other persons in any way, and resent being interfered with by others, not only in actions, but in words as well—that is, Anishinaabe people do not generally question each other's motives, second-guess one another, or offer unsolicited advice. If someone behaves strangely or makes a decision others see as foolish, the typical Anishinaabe response is, "That's just his (or her) way."

A concept closely related to this particular notion of power-control is that of responsibility. Those with relatively greater power, who are in a position to control others (e.g., anyone in a leadership position), do not take advantage of their rank to order others around, but rather consider themselves responsible for those in their charge, most often immediate family members. For this reason, Black points out, the common English gloss of "boss" or "owner" for the Ojibwa root that refers, roughly, to being "in charge" is really not quite right. She reports that "the favored translation of a sensitive bilingual" relied on the notion of being responsible for others as the definition of the leadership role, adding that, for Anishinaabeg, "the idea of bossing is generally rejected" (ibid.). This has implications, of course, for the category of other-than-human persons discussed above as bosses or owners of the plants and animals. Although this term has become conventional, it should not be taken to mean boss in the European American sense, but rather refers to one who takes responsibility for the well-being of others with less power. Thus, Anishinaabe people have not traditionally had a position anything like "chief" as conceived by Europeans. Rather, experienced people in the community took on leadership roles as needed.

In the Anishinaabe worldview, then, responsibility, together with power, control, respect, and autonomy, form a semiotic web that guides Anishinaabe thought and action at a very deep level and permeates virtually all aspects of life. In addition, a complex set of rules governing behavior toward various kinds of relatives (one's own generation versus those older or younger, those one cannot marry versus those one can potentially marry, etc.) serves to guide and constrain social relations. The conceptual elements of this worldview consist of the internal forces that persisted in Anishinaabe communities even as external forces from the dominant society brought about change.

Before returning to the rural communities to learn about some of the specific ways in which the traditional worldview of *Anishinaabe bimaadiziwiin* prevailed there, it is time to clarify the use of such terms as "indigenous" and "traditional." This is not an "authenticity claim"; there is no question that huge cultural and social changes have occurred since the European invasion began. Rather than denying these changes in my use of the words traditional or indigenous, or implying that aspects of social and cultural life predate the arrival of Europeans, I use these terms simply to refer to beliefs and practices, habits and customs that are "indigenized," whatever their ultimate source might have been. This is basically what Native people mean when they refer to the old ways or Indian ways. The point is not that it was done exactly this way before Columbus landed, but simply that it is the way things are (or used to be) done in Anishinaabe communities by the elder generation, and that this differs from the way things are done in non-Native communities and the dominant society generally. This is also what Nancy Lurie (1971) refers to as "contact-traditional"—a phrase that captures both sides of the issue, recognizing that while of course there have been changes since European contact, there is still something essentially Indian, and therefore traditional, about the practices and beliefs being so termed.

With these qualifications in mind, we can now turn to the rural-raised generation's descriptions of the old ways or the Indian ways they remember from their early years in Upper Great Lakes–area Anishinaabe families and communities.

FAMILY PRACTICES

One of the most important of the indigenous customs still practiced in the Anishinaabe communities of the early twentieth century was the use of Native healing techniques. Tom Richards has described his maternal grandmother's healing practices; in another interview, Tom's mother, Rachel, described how her mother would pick a bunch of "ordinary weeds" and "boil them together," and "people that was dying" would be "up walkin' around." Similarly, Ron Mitchell defined his mother as having been a "medicine woman—a healer." Another example was given by Agnes Jones, who recalled how she used to take her mother to "pick medicine" in the fall: "I'd take her different places . . . and she'd have her little hatchet . . . and she'd get her stuff and put it all in separate bags. We'd come home and she'd take 'em all out to dry out, and then she'd tie 'em all up, and put 'em into brown paper bags and tie and hang 'em up places." Agnes also tells of an uncle who went picking: "He always wanted roots. . . . I remember, I used to have a cough, a cold. And I'd be at his place, and he would get the root just for me to chew." Since Agnes was always the "sickly one" as a child, her mother would "doctor her": "She'd just go outside . . . and whatever she picked, she'd just pick outside, and bring it in, and . . . maybe she'd shake it, dust it off, or something. And then she'd mix it for me. And it was my kidney medicine." A number of interviewees spoke of being treated by their parents and other elder relatives with such remedies.

Sometimes, when directly asked, interviewees would discuss the ritualistic aspects of picking plants to be used for medicinal purposes. Agnes's sister, Marjorie, told of how their mother "had to talk [in Ojibwa] to whatever she was picking, and put her tobacco down, and tell what she was gonna use it for." Similarly, Bob Miller reported that when his father killed an animal by hunting or trapping, he always talked to it, explaining to the animal his reasons for needing it.

Older interviewees described such Indian practices with attitudes ranging from pride, to matter-of-fact acceptance, to embarrassment and shame. Many of these traditional customs and beliefs did coexist comfortably with Christianity and other elements of European American culture in Anishinaabe communities. At the same time, however, there was a growing awareness of how these Indian ways were scorned, ridiculed, and even reviled by the surrounding, non-Native society. For this reason, the children did not always seek such knowledge from their elders, and in some cases even actively distanced themselves from it. For example, Agnes Jones explained that she used to sit in the car while her mother "picked medicine" because she did not want to have anything to do with the old Indian ways. (In the interview, however, she expressed regret that she had not asked more questions of her mother and other elders, and paid better attention when they had tried to explain such things to her.) Similarly, those growing up in the Anishinaabe extended families in which the Indian ways were still being practiced reported that it now seemed possible that their parents and other elders may have even tried to hide knowledge of these practices from their children.

For example, at Bob Miller's second interview, he told me that since our first interview, he had gotten to thinking about some of the things his parents had done when he was little. These were things that his parents "didn't show us kids much of," but that he had come to realize were part of their traditional spirituality. One of the main things he remembered was how the adults, when they got together for meetings, would send "all us kids out to play, and then they'd hold their meeting inside; they didn't want us kids to know what they was [doing in] there . . . 'cause it was a lot of the old [Native practices]" (Jackson, 484). Then Nancy Miller picked up the theme:

> One of [Bob's] sisters went through his mother's things, after she had passed on [in 1975]. . . . She had a lot of purses, and every purse had a tobacco pouch [in it]. And everybody in the family said, "Why did she

always carry this tobacco?" Because we didn't see that part of it. Whenever she, you know, did her—I guess you'd call it her "Indian ways"—she didn't do it around any of us, not even around her [younger] sisters. . . . But I saw her, at a powwow [in the early seventies], and she would go up and talk to elder people, and she would hand them something. And so now, I think what she was doing [was handing them a little pouch of tobacco]. (Jackson, 485)

In addition to these uses of tobacco, and those described above (offerings to plants and animals), other interviewees recalled parents and other elders throwing tobacco into the fire during thunderstorms (as a means of making offerings to the Thunderbeings), without giving any explanation why this was done. These cryptic actions on the part of their elders were sometimes confusing to children, and sometimes caused them shame; but as often, they were simply accepted as the way their parents did things.

Within the same extended kinship networks through which people sustained one another in more material ways, knowledge of indigenous practices was reinforced among the adults and passed down—overtly or tacitly—to the children. These forms of indigenous knowledge, whether fully understood or not, were among the Indian ways that were shared by members of early twentieth-century Anishinaabe families and served to reinforce their ethnic identity. The Anishinaabeg, unlike their non-Native neighbors, and despite the extent to which their communities had acculturated to the dominant society, continued to live in a world where kinship relations organized social life and guided appropriate behavior, not only among humans, but with other-than-human persons as well. This was a world where some beings had important powers—or more accurately, a kind of power/control/responsibility—in relation to other members of the (extended) kinship system.

So far, this chapter has presented the positive manifestations of the use of (spiritual) power by other-than-human persons to help the Anishinaabeg. It has described the respect and reciprocity shown these beings by humans, and the healing and spiritual assistance used by Anishinaabeg to help one another. But spiritual power could take negative forms as well. Malevolent spiritual beings and antisocial spiritual practices are the subject of the following section.

BAD MEDICINE

In addition to the manitous (other-than-human persons/spiritual beings and forces) that are "grandfathers," or "uncles," or "elder

brothers," and therefore are kindly and helpful toward human beings, the traditional Anishinaabe world also includes malevolent
manitous (generally not designated by kinship terms). The most important of these is *Mishebeshu*, a giant snakelike creature that rules
the lower realm of underground and underwater. (It was this creature, as portrayed by his grandmother, that so frightened young
Charles Lamont that he was afraid to walk home at night after hearing her stories.) Other evil manitous include *windigo* (giant cannibal
creatures of the north), and skeletons that engage in various forms of
mischief to the detriment of human beings. When Native people
stray from the path of *Anishinaabe bimaadiziwin*, they become vulner-
able to being harmed by these malevolent manitous.

Similarly, when Anishinaabeg fail to show the proper respect to
other Anishinaabeg, they run the risk of being spiritually attacked by
the slighted person. A distinction is made in the realm of human spiritual practices—generally glossed in English as "medicine"—between
good medicine and bad medicine. The healing practices described
above constitute good medicine, but similar powers can be used to do
harm to others. Malevolent spiritual practices[5]—bad medicine—can
be used to cause harm (victims becoming ill or injured, losing a family member to illness or accident, or even dying) or to manipulate
(people behaving in ways they would not ordinarily choose, such as
becoming attracted to someone while under the influence of a specific
type of bad medicine referred to as "love medicine"). A third major
type of medicine, "protection medicine," mediates between good and
bad medicine in that it does good by protecting the holder/creator
and others from being victimized by bad medicine. The primary
means of effecting such protection is to keep a medicine bundle—a
small pouch containing objects (feathers, stones, shells, animal claws)
carefully chosen for their spiritual powers. Despite the existence of
such means of protection, however, those who practice bad medicine
are nonetheless feared in the traditional Anishinaabe world. Finally,
while all kinds of sorcery, including the use of love medicine to bewitch another, are feared, the most dreaded sorcerers are those, usually called "bearwalkers" in English, who can change their shape and
do bodily harm to their victims.

In all its forms, both mild and severe, bad medicine is a salient aspect of the traditional Anishinaabe social world, despite the fact that
all Anishinaabeg are generally thought of as kinsmen. According to
Hallowell, Anishinaabeg are more likely to suspect those in faraway
communities (distant kin through blood and marriage) of attempting
to harm them through spiritual means, but "sorcery may also em-
anate from individuals of one's own community and even from one's

own [close] relatives" (Hallowell 1955, 147). Bad medicine was a significant presence in early twentieth-century Anishinaabe communities, and part of the experience of those who grew up in these communities. Furthermore, it continues to this day as part of the explanatory system of some Anishinaabe individuals—a few whom even grew up in urban areas.

Among contemporary Anishinaabe people, sorcery is seldom discussed with outsiders. But when such practices are referred to, the specific form is usually bearwalking. As mentioned above, bearwalkers are those who can garner enough power to be able to change shape, and in their altered form to cause harm and misfortune to befall their victims. While any number of forms might be assumed (e.g., a ball of light, an owl), that of the bear is most common, hence, the name. I had learned about bearwalking from reading ethnographic sources, but had assumed such phenomena would not have occurred in the lives of contemporary Indian people—even the older ones—given the changes that had come about through many years of contact with the surrounding non-Native society. Thus I was quite surprised, when interviewing older Anishinaabe people in Riverton, to hear one story after another that alluded, though often obliquely, to this phenomenon, and to other forms of bad medicine.

The first mention of such an incident was at the interview of Ron Mitchell. He had been talking about his father, a lay minister, and his mother, a medicine woman. Having told me that it had not been a conflict for his mother to be both a Methodist and a medicine woman, he added the explanation: "Because she was doing it for the good, not for the bad. You have different kinds of medicine—there's good and bad medicine." He then elaborated as follows:

> If you're strong enough in good medicine, you can overcome the bad medicine. And there's people that can put spells on you and they'll make you do things that you don't normally do. And there's people that can transform—spirits that can change. [D: I've heard about that.] Yeah. That's for real. I've seen it happen. . . . I was nine years old, and it was a guy . . . he changed from a person, human, to a bear. I looked at him, kind of looked away, and looked back, and there he was—a bear! I looked away again and looked back, and he was the same again. Most guys that can do that, most of them are evil. And I know of another guy [Albert] who was harassing this other person [Ben]. And Ben told Albert not to do it anymore, and he put the good medicine on himself [i.e, Ben practiced protection medicine]. And then Albert came over in the form of a bear at night—people have these things happen at night. Albert [transformed], and he came to Ben's house to do him

harm. And Ben took his gun out and shot at the bear. Didn't kill him, but he hit him in the shoulder. . . . And then [the bear] hobbled off. The next day, . . . Albert had a shoulder wound, and he couldn't explain how he got it.

Ron Mitchell is unusual for the forthright manner with which he discussed these incidents. Perhaps it is because we had already established a friendship through working at the Indian Center together and he knew me to be nonjudgmental about such matters. In any case, his candor is not typical.

Bob Miller also was unusually forthcoming with such a story, but he prefaced his account the way Native people often do (when they are willing to discuss such matters with non-Natives at all), by suggesting that I would not believe him. I had just been asking him about the use of tobacco in showing respect to plants, animals, and thunder, which had brought up the topic of the old Indian ways. Without any further prompting from me, Bob told me the following:

> Now here's something you won't believe. I don't know if [anyone else you have interviewed] has mentioned it but somehow my dad had that belief . . . that sometimes a [person] could change into something else. [They could change into] whatever they wanted. He said sometimes spirits can change—he let us kids know that. If we told somebody else [i.e., non-Native], they didn't believe it. Somehow he seen it done. . . . He [and my mother] went to the reservation once. They was walking up through [the woods] there, and somebody changed into an animal. Would you believe that? He seen it happen. And my ma was with him, and they both seen it happen. He said it's hard to explain, but they changed into an animal. And he said "Maybe, somehow or other, maybe that person knows the spirit. Somehow they changed theirself into an animal." I don't know how, but I'm not gonna doubt him. 'Cause a lot of things happened back in them times. Maybe if people believed in it enough, if [they] believed in the spirit or something like that . . . maybe they could change themselves. (Jackson, 478)

From this story, Bob went on to tell about his mother's healing practices as an example of good medicine.

A final example of a bearwalking reference was the most surprising because the woman who made it, Sue-Ellen Butler, was only in her early thirties at the time of the interview and had lived in Riverton all her life. However, her mother was from an Anishinaabe community in southern Ontario and had kept Sue-Ellen and her other children in close touch with the relatives who remained there. Once I was talking with Sue-Ellen about mutual (Indian) acquaintances in her mother's home community, and when I mentioned one man's name, Sue-Ellen became visibly distressed. She then told me that there had been a falling-out between this man—a distant relative—and the rest of the family, and that this man had subsequently become a bearwalker. She explained this all very matter-of-factly—she simply wanted me to know with whom I was dealing.

Most people, however, were not so direct about such matters. This is not surprising since they had come to expect they would be disbelieved, and perhaps ridiculed, by non-Natives when they said such things. But quite a few people made some kind of allusion that indicated bearwalking was a part of the "culturally constituted behavioral environment" of the Anishinaabe communities in which they grew up. For example, the following was told by Yolanda Hartwick, who was in her late sixties at the time of the interview. Though Yolanda had grown up in an urban area near Riverton, her parents were from a Chippewa reservation a couple of hundred miles away, and they had kept very close ties with their home community. Yolanda described a "medicine bag" given to her by her parents when she was about fifteen years old as follows: "It was . . . to keep evil spirits and things [away]. 'Cause you know, Indians would be jealous of you if you were a young maiden . . . and my dad and ma [gave] me this thing to wear around my neck—it's like a little leather thing, and you could tie it in a little pouch to carry" (Jackson, 389). While evil sorcery was not specifically mentioned, it seemed clear that Yolanda's parents wanted to give her the power of protection medicine, in the form of this medicine bundle, to shield her from whatever bad medicine might be directed toward her as a result of jealousy.

Given how reluctant people were to speak of such matters, a conversation Tom Richards taped between his mother, Rachel, her sister Margaret, and their Aunt Grace is an especially valuable resource. Although the older women knew they were being tape-recorded, the atmosphere was very informal, as it was just family; thus, it seems safe to assume that things were said that might well not have been said in the context of a formal interview with a non-Native anthropologist. An excerpt from that conversation[6] sheds light on the question of malevolent spiritual forces at work in the Zhashkooning community during the first few decades of the twentieth century. (Aunt Grace was born in the late 1800s, Rachel's sister Margaret in the 1910s, and Rachel herself in the 1920s. This conversation was recorded in 1970, and the first event discussed had taken place shortly before the recording was made.)

G: [My son] Clarence was telling me about some old Indian that he and Sam Waters [an older Chippewa man, about Aunt Grace's age] met. [This old Indian] was telling Clarence and Sam that he could make bearwalk. And Sam believed him pretty bad, you know. He told Sam: 'Go ahead and dance . . . or I'll make you bearwalk.' [Laughter] Clarence said old Sam's feet was going to life. And Sam was dancing and dancing. He was afraid that old fellow would make him bearwalk!

R: Those old Indians was scared of a lot of people, weren't they?

M: Well, they could change themselves into something. They could change into anything.

R: Grandpa said [that after Grandma died she] used to come and set on the tree by the house [in the form of an owl].

G: He said that if . . . [after people died], they changed themselves into an owl, and then the owl would come there to those people and do something to harm them . . . then they'd die.

R: Um-hmm. That's how they used to do their bearwalk, like that. They'd change themself into the certain thing, and then the first thing you'd hear, that's how those people was killed by that. (Jackson, 578)

Aunt Grace concluded this part of the conversation by saying: "Yeah, I can remember our folks telling us stuff like that. That's how people would do."

Elsewhere in this same tape-recorded conversation, Aunt Grace recalled how her mother and aunt used to go "back into the woods and . . . hunt for love medicine. . . . They used to look for two ferns . . . that was growing like twins—that was love medicine." While Aunt Grace did not reveal on this occasion (if she even knew) to what use this love medicine was put, Ron Mitchell told a story of something that happened on his home reservation during the 1940s that illustrates how love medicine could be used:

There was a minister—he was a traveling evangelist preacher. And he and [his wife] already had seven children. But there was this girl who wanted him for *her* man. So what happened is that she got to him somehow—they don't know how. But she used some medicine on him. And he . . . ended up leaving his wife and marrying that girl. . . . They even had a kid.

Ron then went on to tell how the preacher changed as a result of being bewitched by the girl's love medicine: "He drank after that; it was like a religious guy going into the ways of the world—he just did a 180-degree [turnaround]." Ron concluded this story by commenting that nobody would ever have expected this man to change like that—implying that his having been bewitched by love medicine was the only reasonable explanation.

Anishinaabe communities in the Upper Great Lakes region made many changes to accommodate to the surrounding European American/Canadian society. And yet, as the foregoing examples show, certain basic underlying principles of the traditional Anishinaabe worldview continued to guide their actions. The relationships people maintained with all persons in the kinship networks, both human and other-than-human, the good medicine they practiced within families and the bad medicine they feared from strangers and tried to protect themselves from—all these aspects of their experience were rooted in a semiotic system that persisted even as the material conditions of the culture underwent radical change. The fact remains, however, that the main communal activities in early twentieth-century Anishinaabe communities seem to have been, on the one hand, attending church services and, on the other hand, gathering for outdoor celebrations that were dominated by Christian, as opposed to indigenous, symbols and social forms. Thus, one might be tempted to conclude that, despite some remaining survivals of traditional Anishinaabe beliefs and practices, these communities were for the most part Christianized and Westernized. I would suggest, however, that even some of the most acculturated-seeming institutions and celebrations of these communities were very Indian (and more specifically, very Anishinaabe), though not entirely in the way one might expect.

MAKING IT THEIR OWN

The imposition of Christianity onto Native North American communities is part of the legacy of the internal colonization of Native peoples by the Canadian and United States governments. Missionaries were among the first whites to settle in Native communities, and remained a presence up through at least the early twentieth century, having expanded their influence by establishing the church-run Indian boarding schools discussed above. Their expectations were high—in general, Christian missionaries "wanted Indians to renounce pagan idolatry and to embrace Christ through the public act of baptism"; that is, they "expected total change and they were, as a result, constantly disappointed" (Cleland 1992, 79).[7] These expectations, and the disappointment that resulted when they were not realized, sometimes led to brutal retaliations by missionaries against American Indian people. There was also the issue of material exploitation of Native communities in the name of Christianity. Lakota scholar Vine Deloria, Jr., with characteristic irony, sums up the historical relationship between (white) Christian missionaries and Native Americans:

> One of the major problems of the Indian people is the missionary. It has been said of missionaries that when they arrived they had only the Book and we had the land; now we have the Book and they have the land. An old Indian once told me that when the missionaries arrived they fell on their knees and prayed. Then they got up, fell on the Indians, and preyed. (Deloria 1988 [1969], 101)

There is no question that countless Native American individuals and communities suffered greatly as a result of encounters and ongoing relations with missionaries and other officials representing the various sects of Christianity.

These abuses are important to bear in mind as part of the legacy of the colonization of Native peoples in North America. It is possible, however, to emphasize a different aspect of the historic relationship between Christianity and Indian people. While in no way dismissing or trivializing the havoc wrought by missionaries and other church officials on Native communities, I would point out that these conditions of abuse and exploitation of Native people by (white) church people did not prevail in every Native community, nor at every historical period. There were more benign processes of Christianization, as well, and it is a mistake to assume that for an American Indian individual to be Christian is necessarily for that person to be assimilated. Nor should one conclude that if a Native community is Christian, with the church serving as a focal point of social life, this necessarily gives evidence of acculturation. Some examples will help illustrate this point.

In her appropriately titled ethnography of the northern Ontario Ojibwe[8] community of Lynx Lake, *Making It Their Own*, Lisa Valentine (1996) describes the way in which the Anglican church has, over a period of many generations, become a key institution, and the Anglican religion has become a meaningful spiritual framework for Lynx Lake Ojibwe. This is not to say, Valentine emphasizes, that they have become acculturated (abandoned the older system in favor of the new), or even that they have syncretized (combined elements of) Anglican beliefs and practices with those of their indigenous culture. Rather, Valentine argues, the Lynx Lake Ojibwe have so thoroughly indigenized Anglicanism—by interpreting its tenets in the context of the Anishinaabe worldview and by using its ritual to celebrate their social and cultural events—that the Anglican church has become integral to the Native identity of Lynx Lake residents. That is, they have taken a foreign system—Anglicanism—and truly made it their own.

Valentine's notion of Native communities indigenizing Christianity and other aspects of non-Native culture is instructive and useful in considering the Indian identity of Anishinaabe people who grew up in the rural Great Lakes–area communities discussed here. While not able to fully make it their own, as the Lynx Lakers did, many Great Lakes–area Anishinaabe communities of the early twentieth century did at least somewhat indigenize Christianity to the extent that it supported their Indian identity more than it conflicted with such an identity. Interviewees' comments about the church in Zhashkooning support this assertion.

Founded in 1889, the church at Zhashkooning, which was of central importance to community life, was described by several interviewees as an Indian church. Although it had been established under the auspices of the Methodist church, it was run solely by the Chippewa people, who made up most, if not all, of the congregation. I was especially struck, while interviewing Rachel Richards, by her bringing up the church, because we had been talking about her mother's indigenous healing practices. In pursuing this topic, her son Tom attempted to induce his mother to say something about the spiritual aspects of her mother's healing practices by asking: "Did she pray for [her patients] as well as give them these different things to drink?" Rachel's response was as follows: "I don't remember my family praying [except] when we'd go to church . . . in Zhashkooning. The Foxes [Chippewa people from a small town in a neighboring county] were the preachers, and they were related to us. They'd come to Zhashkooning, to the church there, and everybody went there" (Jackson, 665). She then explained that the Foxes traveled to Zhashkooning on a regular basis to preach in the Indian church.

When asked by Tom what kind (denomination) of church it was, Rachel, who had later converted to her (non-Native) husband's faith of Catholicism, replied: "They didn't have a Catholic church in those days. . . . We just went to church, and it was all from the Bible. It was all the same, we had only one God" (Jackson, 666). When further pressed by Tom concerning the denomination—"I mean, were they Methodist? Were they Baptist?"—Rachel responded that it was "just the people that was Indians" who ran the church in Zhashkooning. She elaborated: "See, the Foxes [and other Chippewa people] were ministers, and they knew everybody. Then, those ministers would come to our house and we'd go—they'd take us 'cause we didn't have transportation, [and] they had cars. They'd take us to Zhashkooning and everybody met there" (ibid.). In response to being asked if white people went to this church, Rachel said, "No, not hardly; they were mostly all Indians" (ibid.). Finally, she did not recall the Indian preachers ever admonishing the congregation to abandon their indigenous spiritual practices. The significance of this church for the Native people of the area is further illustrated by the fact that even after Rachel's family had moved into the town of Whitfield, they still went to the inconvenience of traveling the ten miles or so out to Zhashkooning to attend this Indian church. This was in spite of the fact that there were at least two churches in Whitfield at the time— one Baptist and the other Methodist—that Rachel's family might have attended.

By the 1940s, the last full decade the Zhashkooning community remained intact, this church no longer existed. I never could find out for certain what had happened to it, but one interviewee said it had been dynamited (presumably by local non-Natives) after drainage ditches had been put in around the Zhashkooning area, thus making the land valuable for farming. The implication was that, since the church was such a central institution in community life, destroying the church was a good way to weaken the community and hasten the departure of the remaining Chippewa families from the area.[9] In any case, regardless of the details of its demise, the Indian Church at Zhashkooning had certainly been an important gathering place for the Chippewa people of the area, and a means of reinforcing, rather than weakening, their sense of Anishinaabe identity.

A similar situation is described by anthropologist James McClurken for the Little Traverse Bay (Michigan) Odawa, for whom the Catholic church was a key community institution. Since as far back as 1820, many Little Traverse Odawa "have identified strongly with the Catholic churches that mark their townsites . . . [and that over time have] . . . become a significant force in maintaining Odawa culture" (1991, 25). Throughout the nineteenth century, Odawa-language Christian prayers and hymns "helped to reinforce the unique Odawa identity," and during the first few decades of the twentieth century, "Indian pageants held as church fund-raisers encouraged the Odawa to continue making and using [traditional indigenous] ceremonial objects" (ibid.). Many of the people I came to know in Riverton who had grown up in that community were devout Catholics, and many of their ties to their home community were in some way related to the church. The great majority of my older interviewees spoke about their home community churches, and their present identity as Christians (either Catholic or Methodist for virtually all Anishinaabe people in the region) in positive terms, and in a way that did not conflict with their Indian identity.

Similarly, the camp meetings, though technically Christian, were in many ways a continuation of nineteenth-century (and earlier) gatherings that Anishinaabe people traditionally held throughout the warmer months of the year.[10] In earlier times, groups that lived in separate areas would travel to a designated location to join together in celebrations that lasted several days, and often included such ceremonials as namings, healings, and inductions into the priesthood of the *Midewiwin* (the Grand Medicine Society). In the fall, ghost suppers, or Feasts of the Dead, were held to remember those who had died during the year. These gatherings allowed occasions for young men and women from different villages or bands to meet and court, with marriages often resulting. Feasting, singing, drumming, and dancing were the typical evening entertainments around the campfire. Thus, the camp meetings of the first half of the twentieth century were very much like those earlier gatherings, allowing families from different cities, towns, rural enclaves, and reservations to visit, for young people to meet and court, and for all to enjoy feasting, singing, and dancing. Most of the specifics of the food, the songs, and the dances had, of course, changed, and Christian prayers and other rituals had been substituted for indigenous spiritual practices, but the basic form and purpose of the gatherings remained essentially the same.

Furthermore, other customs from earlier times continued in many Great Lakes–area Anishinaabe communities well into the twentieth century, often syncretized to some degree with mainstream American holidays such as Thanksgiving or Halloween. Odawa communities have had an especially strong tradition of ghost suppers, right up to the present day. Also, as mentioned earlier, the Birmingham County Indian Association's annual Harvest Dinner, held on the first Saturday in November, is loosely structured as a Feast of the Dead, but also resembles an American Thanksgiving dinner. (Of course, the American Thanksgiving holiday was inspired by an American Indian Feast of the Dead-type ceremonial gathering, so it has now come full circle, with contemporary American Indians taking many of the elements that have come to characterize the Thanksgiving holiday and incorporating them back into their Feast of the Dead tradition.) Finally, Agnes Jones told of a custom still observed in her northern Michigan Chippewa community during the 1920s—a practice called the *jiibay* (spirit or ghost) supper. As Agnes described it: "We used to have it on Halloween and All Souls' Day. . . . There were always two or three families that had a supper, and we'd go from house to house and eat. . . . And Mother always put something out for the *jiibay*—cookies, little pies, candies—for the souls."

Returning to the more overt role of Christianity in the Anishinaabe communities throughout the first half of the twentieth century, one of the Riverton interviewees, Ron Mitchell, described his father's service as an itinerant Methodist preacher during the 1940s. Ron described his involvement with his father's religious work as follows:

> R: My dad was a . . . lay minister for the Methodist Church. He went around preaching at revivals and things like that. And I . . . went along with him [because] I was too little to stay home. They took me with them wherever they went. [So] I got to travel all over for different meetings—Red Lake, Petosky, Manitoulin Island—all over [the Upper Great Lakes region]. And they always talked in Indian. They didn't speak English. . . . Christianity ain't so bad. I mean . . . [there's] a lot of tobacco smoking in the rituals.
>
> D: Did your father still hold some of his traditional spiritual beliefs, or had he completely converted to Christianity?
>
> R: No, he still practiced the old ways.

Of course, in posing the question this way—in suggesting the need to choose between Christian preaching and praying on the one hand and the ceremonial use of tobacco on the other—I was implicitly assuming the very dichotomy that Valentine so effectively critiques, as discussed above. This early interview in Riverton revealed how Anishinaabe people had indigenized Christianity, and how elements of indigenous spirituality had continued to coexist with Christian beliefs and practices in the home communities of my older interviewees and consultants. In fact, this exchange with Ron Mitchell provided a first glimpse into such phenomena.

What is apparent in Ron Mitchell's narrative is that his family was Christian—Methodist—but that it was an indigenized Christianity that peacefully coexisted with various aspects of indigenous spirituality. Ron saw no conflict (presumably because his father exhibited none) between his father being both a Methodist preacher and still practicing the old ways. Ron's description of his father allows more insight into the camp meetings discussed by others, because the "revivals and things like that" Ron referred to were the same gatherings mentioned by others as camp meetings.

Thus, the Christian camp meetings, like the churches, had very much of an Indian feel to them. Many interviewees spoke fondly of these gatherings, saying how much they had enjoyed the opportunity to relax and visit with friends and family who lived in other communities, as well as to exchange important information on political and economic issues affecting Native people. As one older woman described these gatherings: "the Indians would get together . . . in a camp meeting—Indians from all over—and we would see some of our relatives that we didn't see very often." Especially those who had left their childhood community and lived in a (predominantly) non-Native city, town, or rural area would emphasize how good it was to be with other Indian people at the camp meetings, and how comfortable they felt to be with their own kind.

These gatherings, which were common in the Upper Great Lakes region throughout the first half of the twentieth century, began to fade away in the 1960s and have now almost completely disappeared as powwows have arisen to serve some of the same functions. However, in a dynamic similar to that described by Valentine, the "traditional" aspects of contemporary powwows are often not the focal point for the older Anishinaabe people who used to enjoy camp meetings and other gatherings in their home communities. Rather, if they go to powwows at all, the older, rural-raised people are more likely to enjoy sitting off to the side, in the shade, and visiting with friends and family, only venturing into the dance arena for social (as opposed to performance) dances. As Tom Richards put it, there really are two powwows at every powwow—what is taking place in the official dance area, and "what the old people are talking about." Again, the maintenance of interpersonal kinship relations through social networks remains a predominant theme.

In the Anishinaabe communities of the first half of the twentieth century, then, despite the outward appearances of acculturation, there was a certain amount of continuity in the overall way of life with what prevailed in the nineteenth century and earlier. Many of the same basic subsistence practices (hunting, fishing, gathering, and gardening) that had sustained Native people for generations were still practiced. Equally important were the traditional social networks maintained within and across communities as families shared their (often meager) resources and offered assistance to one another. Furthermore, camp meetings carried on the tradition of large, pan-community gatherings, and Christian churches came to serve as places where community members could meet and Indian identities be reinforced and maintained. Finally, despite the prominence of Christian (indigenized or not) forms in these communities, many customs and beliefs of Native spirituality were nevertheless maintained.

However, during the period of time under consideration, such Indian ways were coming to be seen as increasingly ineffective and irrelevant in the context of the staggering hardships faced by these communities. Beyond that, they were even seen by some as an impediment to success in what was fast becoming the only relevant world—that of the dominant (white) society. Surely this is what Charles Lamont's grandmother meant when she exhorted him to go to the Indian school at Mount Pleasant, to work hard, to learn

English, and to "give up [his] Indian ways," thereby enabling him to "make something of [him]self."

There is another set of behaviors, however, that are just as deeply influenced by the traditional Anishinaabe worldview in general and by the power-control belief system in particular. These behaviors remained strong in those early twentieth-century communities and continue into the present-day practices of those who grew up in these communities. They, too, are a part of Indian ways, though far more subtle than those discussed above. I refer to the styles, habits, and manners of social interaction.

TRADITIONAL ANISHINAABE INTERACTION PATTERNS

Relatively early in my research, I interviewed a Chippewa man, Fred Erikson, who had grown up on a reservation in northern Minnesota during the 1940s. The first time Fred ever left his home community was when he went away to college in the mid-1960s. It was a small liberal arts college in central Wisconsin, and Fred was one of only two American Indian students on campus. However, a statewide American Indian Student Organization had recently formed, and after he joined this organization, Fred had the opportunity to meet with other Indian students once a month in Madison. He related the following incident that occurred in the context of this student organization:

> I remember once—our adviser, who was a non-Indian lady, had set something up where we were supposed to interact with some college faculty, business leaders, and church people [to let them know what our special concerns and needs were as Indian students], and she arranged for us to get together at her house. And I remember that none of us [Indian students] said anything. I don't know what the non-Indians were thinking, but I know that what *we* were thinking is that we've never been in this kind of social situation before. For most Indians, when you encounter something new, you wait, and you observe until you see how to react to this situation. So the evening went horribly, in a sense. These poor white people were desperately trying to draw us out, and we didn't know how we were supposed to act! So afterwards, our adviser got us together and coached us. She said, "When someone asks how you're doing, that's just an introduction—they don't really want to *know* how you're doing! And then you're supposed to talk about things you *do*. Not about *who* you are or anything, but things that you *do!*" So then we got back together with the faculty and business and church people again and this time was just as horrible as the last. Because now

all the Indians were telling the non-Indian leaders about our classes, and going to the gym, and what we did on the weekend . . . so we were following our adviser's instructions, but we still didn't get it right—we never really did discuss our needs as Indian students.

Eventually, Fred did "get it right." That is, he mastered the rules that guide social interaction in the dominant society—rules so subtle that the "non-Indian lady" adviser, for all her good intentions, had been hard-pressed to explain to the Native student group what they were doing wrong and how to fix it. This story illustrates how misunderstandings and miscommunications (or no communication) can occur when the participants involved in social situations come from different backgrounds and bring different expectations, presuppositions, and habits of style to the interaction.

In his description of these ill-fated encounters, Fred Erikson gives a hint as to the connection between the Anishinaabe style and the traditional belief system when he says that most Indians encountering something new wait and observe before reacting. This style, which entails not speaking until one has sufficiently listened, fits with the fact that in the Anishinaabe world, where outward appearance does not always match internal reality, one must exercise caution in interactions until reaching a better sense of whom one is dealing with. Of course, the Native students were not literally suspecting that the non-Native leaders might be evil manitous in disguise! Rather, their belief system underlies an interaction style and influences it in subtle ways that are thoroughly incorporated into children's behaviors as they are socialized in the family. Also, since relations in the traditional system are based on kinship, one needs to hold back when meeting a new person, even in a relatively benign situation, to learn the nature of the relationship before one can behave properly.

Other examples of features that characterize Anishinaabe styles of social interaction will help clarify these connections. Such features are often stated by non-Natives in negative terms (as critiqued by Darnell 1988, 70), and while there are limits to this approach, it can provide a reasonable starting point in the process of uncovering more positive values. Thus, I will begin with some of these negatives.

A feature closely related to the reluctance to speak in a new situation or with an unknown person is the aversion to asking direct questions. This is related to the high value placed on personal autonomy in the traditional Anishinaabe worldview, and the corresponding sense that to request something of someone is to risk infringing on that person's autonomy. Again, I have witnessed many instances of such behavior among older Anishinaabe people. One incident that illustrates this style comes from an experience at the Indian Center in Riverton. The staff member who was directing me in what to do, an older Ojibwa man from a reserve in southern Ontario, was talking to me about how helpful it would be if someone were to enter the mailing list into the computer. At first I assumed he must not want me to perform this task. He knew I was there as a volunteer to help in whatever ways I could, and he knew I had computer skills; therefore (I reasoned), if he had wanted me to work on the mailing list, he would have simply asked. Finally, after several instances of his commenting on the problem without asking me to help resolve it, I realized what was probably going on—that he was being indirect so as to allow me the option of not doing the job if I didn't want to. My hunch was borne out when I told him I would be happy to do the work, and he immediately and gratefully accepted my offer.

Another interaction behavior that springs from the desire to protect (one's own and others') autonomy is the avoidance of eye contact during conversation. Since a gaze can be controlling, especially when used by one with more power (for example, a respected elder) on those with less power, it is most polite and respectful to refrain from looking directly at one's interlocutors. I have often observed this phenomenon when interacting with, or observing interactions among, older Anishinaabe people. Especially when people switch over into speaking Ojibwa, as occasionally happens, they alter their positioning in relation to one another ever so slightly so as to be sure to avoid making eye contact.

Finally, there is the disinclination of Anishinaabe people to engage in formal greetings, farewells, and introductions. Such forms are seldom appropriate in a social system that "stresses the ongoing character of relationships through time" (Darnell 1988, 73). It took a while for me to get used to this, but eventually I adjusted. As a result, over time I formed friendships with several of the older Anishinaabe people simply by being at the same events or at the Indian Center when they would stop by. I never introduced myself to these people, nor they to me, but we would start talking a bit when we saw each other, and the conversations gradually got longer and friendlier until we had come to know one another quite well. I knew the other person knew who I was, and the other person knew I knew who he or she was, and it simply did not matter that we had never "met" in the European American way. Similarly, these were not people that I would seek out to make a point of saying hello or goodbye. We would just find ourselves together sometimes and pick up our conversation wherever we had left off the last time.

A final negative rule is not to talk just to fill silences—one should simply allow the silences to occur. This, too, relates to the power-belief system in that one's choice to reflect quietly should be respected and not intruded upon. Perhaps the best illustration of this style comes from a story told by Tom Richards. The setting was a conference for Native American entrepreneurs, but there were quite a few non-Natives in attendance as well. Tom tells of an incident that occurred during a plenary session at the conference:

> One of the traditional Indian people was giving this speech. And he came to a point where he had to reason something out. So, there's like eight hundred people sitting there. And he stops. And he's thinking. And this is going on for about a minute. I knew what was going to happen, and I watched. All the Anglo people were looking around, and bustling, and were [wondering], you know, 'What's wrong?' 'What's happened?' 'Did I miss something?' Just very upset and nervous. But the Indian people knew, 'Hey! He's just thinking!' And there was no problem. (Jackson, 696)

This comfort with silence during what is generally (at least, by European American standards) a speaking situation is a fundamental principle of Anishinaabe social interaction.

As already noted, the foregoing norms of Anishinaabe social interaction are all stated in negative terms: what one does *not* do in conversational settings. But, as Darnell points out, this approach derives from the assumptions of non-Native (white) American/Canadian interaction styles. She describes the problem, and poses an alternative perspective, as follows:

> In general, "speaking" does not receive the same emphasis in the [Anishinaabe] communicative economy that is unquestioned for most whites. A model of pragmatics which grows out of the study of speaking, therefore, requires substantial rethinking before it can state in *positive* terms what organizes [Anishinaabe] interactions if it is not talk. Most simply, the salient issue for Indian persons is co-presence, people being together and acknowledging their so being. (Darnell 1988, 70—emphasis in the original)

This "salient issue" was made explicit in several of my interviews with older Anishinaabe people. For example, Cora Lawson, a woman who grew up in a Miami community in rural northeastern Indiana during the 1920s, told me about how her uncle and grandmother, who lived in another Indian community about fifty miles away, used to come visit the family. Our conversation went as follows:

C: When they came, you'd always know that they were there for a while.

D: And in those days, of course, you probably didn't have telephones.

C: No, you never knew when someone was coming. But when they came, you knew they were gonna stay.

D: So they would just show up one day, and. . . .

C: Stayed there and set there.

D: And when they arrived . . . were there lots of greetings and hugging and [all]? . . . Or were they more reserved?

C: Very much so. They were quiet. As long as you were there, they were happy.

D: So it's not so much a big hug and greeting. It's sort of . . .

C: No, it's that you're there. . . . And they'd sit there for quite awhile, and they maybe wouldn't say anything. Then they'd think of something, and they'd say it. And that's the way it was. It wasn't like people now that think you've got to be talking all the time. No. Not them. (Jackson, 72)

Similarly, a man named Dave Olsen, who had recently retired to his northern Michigan Potawatomi community, told of an old Indian friend who would occasionally come around to visit: "He comes in, sits down in the living room, I sit down in the living room, we smoke, we look around, and after about an hour, he gets up and says, 'Well, it's been nice to see you,' and he leaves! Never said a word the whole time!" It is the behavioral level—that the old man came over, and that he and Dave sat and smoked their pipes together—that counts, not the verbal level.

Another example of behavior taking precedence over talk is the way, among Anishinaabe people, approval "is rarely stated [verbally], being conveyed [instead] by acceptance" (Darnell 1988, 72). As I became attuned to the styles of rural-raised Anishinaabeg, I began to notice examples of this principle in action with regard to their acceptance of me. As mentioned earlier, there were a number of older community members that I never "met," and with whom I was very cautious about interacting. Of course, I was concerned about being accepted by such people, but at first they gave me no indication of what they thought of me. However, with each of these people, a moment came when he or she indicated, behaviorally, that I was accepted. One such incident occurred at the BCIA powwow in the summer of 1994. In the morning, I had been talking with a group of people from the Indian Center when Jack Peters, who had grown up on a Chippewa reservation in Minnesota (and was in his mid-sixties at the time), approached the group. This was someone who "knew me" from having been "co-present" with me on many such occasions, but who had not yet completely acknowledged me. As he joined the group, I noticed there were no more chairs and I got up so he could have mine. A few minutes after I had vacated the chair and gone to sit on the grass nearby, he sat down. Nothing was said between us. That evening, as we were closing up for the day, I was pushing a cart piled with coolers, coffee pots, and other such equipment toward the storage area. Jack Peters saw me struggling along and, taking his place beside me, helped me push the cart to its destination. Again, we did not speak (although I nodded my thanks to him). But the next time we were together, he initiated a conversation with me, and our relationship grew from there.

Similarly, in the Anishinaabe interaction style "criticism of others is accomplished by parable and metaphor rather than directly" (ibid.). A close correlate to this—noticed among rural-raised Anishinaabe people in Riverton—is the reluctance to pass judgment on another person. As mentioned above in the context of the power-control belief system, since one does not know everything about another person, one does not attempt to determine whether that other person's actions make sense, or are right or wrong. This principle was surely at work in the way certain older Anishinaabe people at the Indian Center treated Andrew Williams, the man whose twin brother had died (of neglect, it seems) when he was seven, and who had spent his entire adult life drinking heavily.

As already mentioned, Andrew often stopped by the Indian Center to pick up his mail (since he did not have a home and used the Indian Center's address for important items), or just to sit and have a cup of coffee and perhaps a bite to eat. He was usually in a state of some degree of intoxication, and most of the staff and volunteers at the Center barely tolerated him. However, there were always at least two or three people around who were of the elder cohort and had grown up in rural Anishinaabe communities. These people invariably assisted Andrew in a number of ways. They advanced him money when he ran out before his next check came in, helped him apply for various forms of public assistance, and gave him rides when he needed to get someplace. Occasionally, they even put up the bail money (to be repaid when his next check came in) after he had landed in the drunk tank. While such behavior was condemned by others at the Indian Center as enabling (in the terminology of Alcoholics Anonymous and other such twelve-step programs), the Anishinaabe people who helped Andrew in these ways were simply following their own rules of social interaction. From their perspective, you help a community member who is in need (to quote Nancy Miller: "If you have it, you share"), and you do not judge him because you have no way of knowing why he behaves as he does—it's just his way. In turn, Andrew followed the same rules—he always reciprocated these kindnesses when his next check came, taking those who had helped him out to dinner, bringing them small gifts, and donating money to the fund drives the Indian Center would hold from time to time.

In these ways—in establishing and reinforcing co-presence primarily through behaviors rather than through words—older, rural-raised Anishinaabe people in Riverton maintained important relationships that allowed for mutual assistance while at the same time preserving the autonomy of the parties involved. In their characteristically Indian way, rooted in the conduct prescriptions and proscriptions of *Anishinaabe bimaadiziwin*, which in turn are based on the Anishinaabe power-control belief system, these elder-generation urban Indian people constantly expressed their Indianness through the embodied behaviors of their daily social interactions.

THE COMMUNITY

As mentioned previously, it was not immediately apparent to me that some of the people involved with Riverton's official Indian institutions had these different styles, and even less apparent that there was a type of Indianness inherent in such behaviors. Since these behavioral styles are subtle, and since the Indianness of those who choose to convey their identity more overtly through a corpus of symbols is so much more accessible, it took some time before I became fully aware of the differences in styles. It took more time yet for me to understand that such styles correlate with a general category of Indian people in Riverton—those who grew up in rural Anishinaabe communities during the first half of the twentieth century. However, there were clues early on that an important segment of Riverton's Native American population was, for the most part, not represented in the official institutions. One of the most significant clues was a certain use of the term "the community" by people associated with the official institutions.

The first time I heard "the community" used this way was at a board meeting of the Birmingham County Indian Association. The discussion had turned to the powwow committee and the possibility that it would break away to become a separate entity, no longer under the auspices of the BCIA. (This is part of the background factionalism that culminated in the confrontation at the 1994 annual meeting of the BCIA.) People were concerned that "the community," which generally supported the powwow but had become alienated from the Association, would completely abandon the BCIA if it no longer produced the annual powwow. This assertion struck a nerve, and a heated discussion proceeded in a way that made clear they all knew who or what was being referred to by the term "the community." They may have differed as to what they thought of the community, whether or not they cared about the opinions of the community, what they thought it most likely the community would do, but they all seemed to be in (tacit) agreement as to the identity of the community.

I had no idea what the referent to this term might be. It could not be "the American Indian community" in its official sense, because the BCIA was not only supported by but was the primary institution of that community, almost by definition. It also did not make sense that it would be the larger "Riverton (or Birmingham County) community," because again, to the extent that Native Americans were supported by the general population and the agencies and offices of the Riverton area, it was through the BCIA that such support was given. The BCIA was not only the most prominent "game in town," it was virtually the only organization that purported to represent the American Indian population of Birmingham County (and the outlying counties, as well). So what could this community be that supported the powwow, but did not support the Association? And why did it matter so much?

Gradually over the next several months, as I paid close attention to usage of this term, I learned that when "the community" was used in this way, it referred to the families headed by the same general category of people I have been referring to throughout this book as "elder-generation" and/or "rural-raised" Anishinaabeg. That is, it refers to families in which the elder generation had grown up on reservations or in off-reservation Indian communities around the Upper Great Lakes region during the first half of the twentieth century, and who had migrated to Riverton around midcentury, usually for jobs in the automotive factories.

It was this segment of the urban community that not only maintained what ties they could with their home communities, but also forged close bonds with extended family and others from their home reservations who were in the city. And it was those in the elder generation of these families that founded the Birmingham County Indian Association and the Riverton University AISO, and that was involved in the early years of the Indian Education Program, although they later became alienated and drifted away from these official institutions. And yet, this community also still maintained an interest in the BCIA (and the other institutions), and was curious to know what kinds of changes might be afoot now that so many new Indians had become active in the Association. A few community people had remained quite active in the BCIA over the years (for example, Joe Niles, Ron Mitchell, and to a lesser extent, Jack Peters). Others left for many years but had come back into active participation (in many cases because their grown children had become involved and had encouraged them to return). The majority, however, had remained only peripherally involved all along, coming to large events, but not participating in the day-to-day operations. Finally, there were those who rarely if ever attended even the large events, such as the powwow or the Harvest Dinner, and yet who remained interested enough to want to stay on the mailing list and to keep up with the latest changes in personnel, policy, and so on.

Shortly after the board meeting at which I first became aware of how the term "the community" was being used, I began noticing something. Occasionally someone, or two or three people together, would show up at a board meeting or powwow committee meeting of the BCIA, or at other BCIA-sponsored events. Usually the BCIA board or committee members did not know these people; if anyone knew them it would be older board or committee members—those who were also affiliated with the community. These mysterious visitors were themselves older, and they always sat quietly in the back, arms folded across their chests in the characteristic "Indian" manner, carefully observing, never introducing themselves (unless called upon to do so by someone with the interactive style of the mainstream culture), not overtly participating in the proceedings. When the meeting or event was over, they would simply get up and leave. These people, I eventually learned, were members of the community who, while not interested in being active participants in the BCIA, did want to learn about what was going on in the Association.

The more these community members learned about how the powwow was being produced during the early 1990s—by those newer to their Indian identity and without connections to extended Indian families—the less they liked it. According to these elder Anishinaabeg, basic values modeled on proper kinship behavior—like gracious hospitality and looking out for one's own—had given way to a concern for profits. Thus, instead of hosting the dancers properly, with a dinner, the powwow committee had simply given them meal tickets to be redeemed by the traders selling food. Instead of making sure local Anishinaabe artists were given a fair chance to sell their wares, priority was given to outsiders (many of them non-Natives, according to community people) who could afford to pay more to rent a space at the powwow. Another development that was angering community members was the increasingly bold manner in which the new Indians were telling them what to do, and how to do things. I was witness to, or was told about, a number of incidents in which a rural-raised Anishinaabe elder was "corrected" in some aspect of ceremony or ritual by someone who was much younger, who had grown up in the city, and who was relatively new to his or her Native American identity.

The resentment and alienation felt by community members, both the elder generation and their grown children, toward the younger, new Indians was often stated in terms of race. For example, Joe Niles confided that: "a lot of the [community people] don't want anything to do with the Indian Center anymore because the board of directors is too white"; furthermore, he continued, "now our *dancers* are starting to be white!" Similar comments have already been quoted by the urban-raised Anishinaabeg at the 1994 annual meeting, and by earlier interviewees talking about why Indian people who had originally been active in the Indian institutions of Riverton had left. However, these references to people and events being white (and therefore not Indian) are better seen as a sort of shorthand for something else than as a focus on race per se. It is the family connections that clearly count more than anything else to these older people: someone is Indian if he or she is a member of a family that is known as Indian—this, in turn, is determined by that family's connection to a home community (and thus to all the values, behaviors, styles of interaction, and so on, that are engendered in such communities). And while this usually coincides with "race" in that those who have such affiliations will most likely have relatively "higher blood quantums" than those who do not, and are therefore more likely to "look Indian," there are certain exceptions that are quite telling with regard to the criteria that are actually at work.

Perhaps the most dramatic illustration of such an exception from the mid-1990s is the case of a young man, Kevin Alexander, who had no "Indian blood" whatsoever—he was of entirely European American ancestry. Yet he had been adopted and raised by an Odawa family who were highly regarded as one of the leading Anishinaabe families in Riverton, and Kevin was completely accepted by the community as Indian. Kevin had become a powwow dancer, and part of his regalia included eagle feathers. While it is illegal for most residents of the United States to own eagle feathers (eagles being an endangered species), Native Americans are allowed (with certain restrictions) to own them for ceremonial purposes, under freedom of religion legislation. A woman named Marcy, a "quarter-blood" who did hold a tribal card but who had very little connection to her home reservation and who was not at all affiliated with the community in Riverton, learned about Kevin. She was quite outraged when she discovered that this "white man" was "posing" as a Native American, dancing in pow-wows in full regalia. As a political act, she took it upon herself to report him to the federal agents who oversee such matters, and Kevin was arrested and jailed for illegal possession of eagle feathers. In response, the community rallied in his support, not only in Riverton but throughout the state, to help pay for his defense when the case came to trial. Meanwhile Marcy, who had categorized Kevin on the basis of "race" and thought she was acting on behalf of "her people," was quickly ostracized by the community she had sought to impress and support. She did not understand that Anishinaabe people most often base their loyalties on family and community affiliations—that is, on the kinship-based social networks they have built and maintained over the years through shared values and patterns of social interaction—and not on such technicalities as "race."

This, then, is the ultimate criterion for Indianness as (tacitly) defined by the elder generation of Anishinaabe people. Sometimes tribal affiliation is invoked (i.e., Indian cards); sometimes ancestry, or blood quantum, is emphasized; occasionally phenotype takes precedence (as in the phrase: "It's good to see so many brown faces in the crowd"). But the ultimate bottom line seems to be family connection, which entails affiliation with a nonurban Indian community that in turn ensures knowing how to behave properly in the Indian way. It is this criterion that defines the Riverton Anishinaabe community—an apt phrase, since it is social relations (and more specifically, kinship relations) that really count, far more than genetic heritage, phenotype, or even tribal affiliation.

These extended family groups formed the core of urban Anishinaabe social life: they held "cedar circles," organized work parties to help improve one another's homes, bowled together, and so on. Finally, just as in the early days of the BCIA, during the mid-1990s family groups still held spaghetti suppers, potlucks, and other such parties and gatherings to give their members a chance to socialize with one another and with members of the other Anishinaabe families. One such event was Pete Chimingan's annual ghost supper, which I attended in the fall of 1995.

PETE CHIMINGAN'S GHOST SUPPER

Pete Chimingan is a retired autoworker who left his Ottawa home community in the 1940s to look for employment in Riverton. His family has been prominent in its home community for generations, and Pete was among those whose social gatherings during the 1950s eventually become formalized into the Birmingham County Indian Association. Though his participation had waned over the years, Pete maintained some ties with the BCIA and other official institutions in the Riverton area. Furthermore, he remained closely associated with his Ottawa home community and continued his family's annual ghost supper tradition in Riverton, with members of his extended family who still lived in the home community coming down each year to help out.

The event had been held in the same place for many years. Pete, a proud veteran of World War II, rented the VFW hall on Riverton's north side. In the Indian tradition, Pete and his family provided the meat (roast beef and turkey), the beverages, and all the tableware, with side dishes being offered by the guests. The official hours were from 2:00 P.M. to 10:00 P.M. When I arrived at about 2:30, several of Pete's female relatives from the home community were busy in the kitchen getting things underway, and guests were just starting to arrive. (That is, they were operating according to "Indian time"—see Philips 1989 [1974].) Pete greeted me warmly and was eager to show me the decorations and explain their significance. Hanging from the ceiling throughout the hall were streamers that alternated three flags—American, German, and "Indian." These, Pete explained, were the nationalities of the (deceased) family members being honored that day. He then took me over to a wall on which banners had been taped up that gave the names of all family members who were being remembered. After we had visited a bit, Pete had to leave to greet newly arriving guests, and I joined some of my friends from the Indian Center who were seated at one of the tables. From this vantage point, I looked around the room to see who was there.

Most surprising was the number of people there I had never seen before. I had been volunteering at the Indian Center, serving on the powwow committee, and attending virtually every official American Indian event in Riverton for nearly two years, and yet this was almost an entirely new crowd to me. However, when Joe Niles, with whom I was sitting, began naming people who were there, I recognized nearly all the last names as those of prominent Anishinaabe families active in the BCIA and other official institutions during the 1950s, 1960s, and early 1970s. Many were older couples, some had their grown children with them, and a few had brought along grandchildren. For the most part, they displayed none of the symbolic markers of Indian appearance favored by those newer to that identity, yet they exhibited all the behavioral markers of Indianness. People were sitting in characteristic postures and positions relative to one another and talking quietly in small groupings. A generally relaxed and congenial atmosphere pervaded the hall.

At 3:00 o'clock, Pete called for everyone's attention and said it was time to eat, but first he wanted to introduce his "elder"—an uncle from his home community—to give the blessing. We all stood, and the uncle gave a Christian prayer, beseeching the Lord to bless this gathering—those who had died as well as the living—thanking Him for the bountiful food, and asking Him to watch over us all to ensure our safe return home that evening. The entire blessing was in English without the use of a single word of Native language or even of English terms such as "Creator" that are often used by Native Americans in traditional ceremonial contexts. Yet the content and tone were decidedly Anishinaabe. When the blessing was completed, Pete invited us to line up and help ourselves to the many dishes crowded onto the buffet table.

The group I sat with during dinner included people who were all about the same age (fifties and sixties) and were all from reservations and other Indian home communities around the Upper Great Lakes, and talk soon turned to stories of growing up in these communities. Everyone had a humorous outhouse story to tell; all remembered having only two sets of clothing (from the Sears catalog) during the school year—one to wear while the other was being washed; all recalled how their parents would trace their feet on cardboard to send in for the right shoe size. In the summer they went barefoot, and the previous year's Sears catalog was relegated to the outhouse to be used as toilet paper! There was obviously a deep camaraderie evoked by these stories, but it was not the deprivation of their rural poverty per se that provided the common ground. Rather, these reminiscences, told with warmth and wry humor, established among the participants a bond of shared experience, invoking their parents and other loved ones (now dead), and holding far more sweetness than bitterness.

Next, the conversation turned to the "Indian bar scene" of the 1970s, and again everyone had a humorous story to tell of their drinking escapades, many of which related to the Indian conferences that my companions had participated in during that time. While those who were telling such stories either did not drink at all anymore, or did so only rarely and in moderation, they recalled their old drinking days with obvious fondness. For example, one man told of being in a strange city for an Indian Education Program conference, and going out with fellow conference attendees in search of an Indian bar. After going to a number of establishments that were clearly not Indian bars, they finally found a little out-of-the-way place that had only a few (white) people in it. The man telling the story explained, "Since there were more of us than there were of them, we decided to *make* it an Indian bar!" All laughed in appreciation, obviously enjoying how this group of "skins" had gotten the best of the situation. Again, there was a solidarity being established and strengthened through these interactions. The stories were about camaraderie among Indians (that is, the drinking being described was incidental to the social aspect and the fact that they were Indians doing these things together). In sharing these stories many years later, they created a camaraderie among themselves in the present situation. Not only were their experiences of the past shared ones, but so also was the manner in which the stories were told—the rhythm, the body language, the quiet, gentle humor. As I looked around the room, I could see many small groupings like the one I was in, all engaging in similar conversations as they enjoyed their dinner together—conversations that reinforced connection, solidarity, and shared identity through subtle gestures and postures as much as through the actual topics discussed.

By 6:00 o'clock, everyone had finished eating and it was time for dancing. We were treated to the musical stylings of the Swingin' Troubadours, who turned out to be two older men of Polish descent playing accordion and drums (enhanced by a synthesizer-type sound system), and who proceeded to regale us with polka music! Meanwhile, the Chimingan family had started serving beer to those who were interested (coffee and punch for others), and things got quite festive and lively. Pete led off the first dance with his wife, and many other couples joined in. These folks were clearly no strangers to the polka! Some were quite skilled, and all were obviously enjoying themselves. As the evening progressed, classic rock-and-roll tunes such as "Rock Around the Clock" (to a slightly polka beat) were added to the repertoire, bringing more of the (relatively) younger people—those under fifty—out onto the dance floor to do the twist and other old favorites. Finally, late in the evening, some contemporary country and western songs gave those under thirty a chance to demonstrate their skill at line dancing.

While some people left early—right after dinner or shortly after the music started—most stayed until the end, and many ended up dancing to at least a few of the numbers. Meanwhile, when Pete wasn't dancing or visiting with guests, he circulated with his camcorder and—all smiles—recorded the festivities for posterity. Then, promptly at 10:00 o'clock, the band stopped, the lights went on, and Pete thanked everyone for coming and bid us goodnight. People retrieved their empty dishes from the buffet table and stopped by to thank Pete and say goodbye to his wife.[11] Then we drifted out into the parking lot, and with small groups dispersing as people headed for their separate cars, soft laughter punctuated the stillness of the warm autumn night.

Driving home, I thought about all the extended kinship networks and communities that had come together, overlapped, and interacted that evening. At a general and abstract level, the Catholic church was invoked (through the blessing), as well as all three "nations" whose flags festooned the hall (American, German, and Indian), and generations of Ottawa people whose tradition was being upheld by the act of having a ghost supper. More specifically, there were families currently living in Riverton whose home community was the same as Pete's—this category accounted for most of the guests. But there were others as well: a few Riverton Anishinaabe families from other home communities; those associated with the BCIA (with or without home communities); members of the Chimingan family who still lived in the home community; and finally, members of the Chimingan family who had died. All were present, all were members of the community formed for that occasion, and all participated in the semiotic reinforcement of a certain kind of Indianness that can only exist when those with a shared Anishinaabe background and behavioral style gather, paraphrasing Darnell, to be together and to acknowledge their so being.

Conclusion

A Matter of Community

▼ ▼ ▼

People get mixed up when they talk about Indian
culture. They think powwows, dancing, and beadwork
are Indian culture. But our way of life is [our]
culture....[It's] our way of raising children,
our way of dealing with each other.

—*Wuanetta Dominic*[1]

I began this book by explaining that when I first went to Riverton, my intent had been to study the role that home communities
play in the lives of Native Americans in that city's urban Indian community. I recounted how this plan had been thwarted during my first
year in the field as I became increasingly uncertain about whom I
ought to count as American Indian—and by the fact that many of
those most active in the city's American Indian institutions had no
home communities. Finally, I described how the issue of identity had
"found me" at the Birmingham County Indian Association's 1994
annual meeting, as I witnessed differently positioned segments of the
BCIA membership contesting each other's Indianness. Consequently,
I set aside the home communities topic and began gearing my research toward investigating issues of American Indian identity.

As should be clear by now, in pursuing the question of identity I
did in fact end up investigating the role of home communities after
all. The more attuned I became to the nature of the Indian identity
of those who had grown up in Anishinaabe communities, the more I
found their particular kind of (subtle) Indianness to be rooted in
those communities. Even the urban-raised Anishinaabe people—
those brought up in the city by parents who had migrated from
rural areas at midcentury—were profoundly influenced, directly or

indirectly, by their parents' home communities. In fact, the criterion used throughout this book for distinguishing what I find to be the three salient categories of American Indian people in Riverton has been the nature of their ties (or lack thereof) to rural Indian home communities. I have emphasized the differences in ethnic identity between those who grew up in such communities (the original Anishinaabe migrants) and those who grew up in the city, but with parents who had spent their youth in rural Indian communities (the "paper Indians"). These two groups constitute the adult members of the Anishinaabe families that form the core of Riverton's Native American community. They can be distinguished, in turn, from a third group that grew up in the city in families with no ties to nonurban Indian communities (and who have not been a primary focus of the current work). Thus, the home communities of the elder generation of Riverton's Indian community came to have central ethnographic significance in this book.

There are other communities as well that have shaped and constrained the identities of the urban Indian people profiled above. These several communities are not mutually exclusive—on the contrary, they can be thought of as nested within a series of levels that vary with regard to how abstractly or concretely they manifest themselves in peoples' daily lives, with each "higher level" creating a context that contributes to the reconfiguring of the "lower levels." These communities are the transnational corporate community; the Upper Great Lakes region; the city of Riverton; the official urban Indian institutions; and the extended Anishinaabe families.

Working down from abstract to concrete, the first of these levels is the transnational corporate community, in which profits are sought for company stockholders and executives by moving production operations to parts of the world where such costs are cheap. This strategy has had a devastating impact on the economy of the Upper Great Lakes region, which once thrived on the success of its local automotive plants, and now is struggling to find products and services to fill the void as automotive companies move their operations out of the area. The city of Riverton exemplifies these trends, having suffered through extremely difficult times when the American Automotive Corporation began to close its plants there in the 1970s and 1980s, and the city has not yet found the means to recover its former prosperity.

As mentioned earlier, one result of Riverton's political-economic history—a history shared by many midsized and smaller cities in the Upper Great Lakes region—is that its urban Indian population is configured according to the following correlation between residence of origin and age: nearly all those who grew up in rural Indian communities were born before 1940 and therefore were in their late fifties or older at the time of this study (mid-1990s); and nearly all those who grew up in the city were born after 1940 and therefore were in their thirties, forties, and early fifties at the time. The converse also holds: those in the elder generation (born prior to 1940) were not originally from the city, but rather had grown up in rural Indian communities and had migrated to Riverton as young adults; and virtually all those in the middle-aged and younger generations (born after 1940) had grown up in the city, with varying degrees of connection (including no connection) to their parents' and grandparents' home communities.

This structure is not found in the largest Upper Great Lakes–area cities such as Chicago, Minneapolis, Milwaukee, Indianapolis, Detroit, and Cleveland. While some larger cities in the region suffered economic recessions—during the 1970s and early 1980s—more severe than those experienced by similar-sized cities elsewhere in North America, their economies remained sufficiently diverse and stable to allow them to continue to draw new job seekers from various quarters, including the Indian reservations of the region. Thus, in these larger Upper Great Lakes urban centers, one is likely to find younger Indian people who grew up on reservations and have only recently migrated to the city. Moreover, since most of the largest cities had more jobs to offer earlier in the twentieth century than did smaller cities such as Riverton, they attracted considerably more Native American migrants prior to 1940 than did the smaller cities. Therefore, the largest cities are far more likely than Riverton to include in their American Indian populations people who are over age sixty and who grew up in the city. Due to their location in the same region, the larger Upper Great Lakes–area cities share many features with their midsized and smaller counterparts.[2] Still, the American Indian populations of these larger cities do not show the structure that characterizes Riverton's Indian community, in which older age correlates with having grown up in a rural Indian community, and (relatively) younger age correlates with having grown up in the city.

This layered structure has, in turn, shaped the development over time of Riverton's urban Indian institutions. As the rural-raised Anishinaabeg grew older, they became increasingly alienated by the different climate created by younger Indian people, virtually none of whom had experienced growing up in a rural Indian community. This was in part a "cohort effect"—those born prior to 1940 experienced certain kinds of conditions and events in their life cycle that differed considerably from the experiences of younger people.[3] These disparities have been further exaggerated in Riverton by the rural/urban distinction that characterizes the backgrounds of the different generations.

Finally, there is the significance of family as a criterion that has served to further polarize the urban Indian community in Riverton. Kinship is the key organizing principle of the traditional Anishinaabe world, and family ties have remained a strong source of Native identity over the many decades of hardship and deprivation, despite the acculturation and assimilation projects of church and state, and the disruptions of large-scale urban migrations. As Gerald Vizenor, a self-described "cross-blood" of Anishinaabe heritage, points out:

> Tribal people [in the past] used the word Anishinaabeg to refer to the people of the woodland who spoke the same language. The collective name was not an abstract concept of personal identities or national ideologies. Tribal *families* were the basic political and economic units in the woodland and the first source of personal identities. (Vizenor 1984, 13, emphasis added)

This deep identification of Indianness with one's family and of (extended) family with Indianness still holds, I would argue, for Anishinaabe people in contemporary Riverton. Despite the very real differences that divide those of the elderly rural-raised generation from their urban-raised children and grandchildren, the heart of the matter remains—they are family. And, while many in the elder generation had sought, to one extent or another, to loosen their ties to extended families in their home communities, most had at the same time taken care to keep some kind of connection to their Anishinaabe kin and hence to their Indianness. It is this family connection—this "first source of personal [Indian] identity"—that serves to unite the two generations of Native people studied in this work and allows them to transcend many of their differences.

On the other hand, members of the urban-raised generation tend to express their Native American identity with markers that rural-raised elders for the most part shun. Many urban-raised American Indians have long hair and wear Native American styles of jewelry and clothing, and they seek out Native spiritual and cultural practices such as sweat lodges, drumming, and powwow dancing. Moreover, it is urban-raised people, both with and without Anishinaabe family and community ties, who became active in Riverton's official Native American institutions as the older rural-raised folks began drifting away. But, as the incident at the BCIA's annual meeting so dramatically revealed, when tensions mounted in the community, those urban-raised people who were members of Anishinaabe extended families ultimately chose to identify with and support their elders in confronting the more aggressive of the urban-raised "wannabes" who lacked such family ties.

Each of the levels of community that has been considered—the global economy, the Upper Great Lakes region, the city of Riverton, the official urban Indian institutions, the informal community of Anishinaabe families in Riverton, and the rural Anishinaabe communities in which the original migrants grew up—has its own character and personality. As a semiotic system, constantly being created, reproduced, and transformed over time by the signing activities of the selves that comprise it, each community both reflects and shapes the identities of its members. Thus, the character of Riverton became prosperous and optimistic along with the prosperity and optimism of its citizens, who then subsequently became discouraged and frustrated as the larger community got left behind in the American Automotive Corporation's pursuit of higher profits in the global economy. Similarly, the Birmingham County Indian Association, Riverton's Indian Education Programs, and Riverton University's American Indian Student Organization went through distinct changes in character, from informal social clubs to institutions with a much more cultural and political focus, as their personnel and constituencies changed over the years. Finally, the rural Anishinaabe communities of the late nineteenth and early twentieth centuries transformed their character quite dramatically in response to the brutal forces of acculturation, poverty, racism, and proletarianization to which they were subjected. Those who lived in these communities in turn experienced alterations in their own daily conduct and cultural practices as a result of these pressures. At the same time, however, the communities retained certain key aspects of their Anishinaabe identity, as their members continued to interact in characteristic patterns.

When considered from a semiotic perspective, these changes and continuities in both communities and individuals are recognizable, ultimately, as processes of identity construction and transformation. The static and enduring markers most readily associated in the popular imagination with Native Americans can be appreciated from an objective point of view as "instrumentally" useful, or from a subjective perspective as "affectively" meaningful—and surely they are both. But the changing dynamics of the many relevant communities do not lend themselves to such dichotomous classifications, nor do the far more subtle behavior patterns that characterize the Indianness of those (especially the elders) in the Anishinaabe families. This last point is particularly difficult to grasp when the links between identity and community and their endurance through time are not appreciated. An illustration of an approach that does not fully recognize the power of such links comes from the work of Appadurai.

In confronting conditions of postmodernity and the "corresponding dilemmas of perspective and representation that all ethnographers must confront," Appadurai (1991, 191) focuses on the question of group identity. He notes that the challenge of attempting to analyze issues of group identity in the contemporary world is that social groups are "no longer familiar anthropological objects, insofar as [they] . . . are no longer tightly territorialized, spatially bounded, historically unselfconscious, or culturally homogeneous" (ibid.). The construct Appadurai proposes for studying such entities is that of the "ethnoscape"—"the landscape of persons who make up the shifting world in which we live: tourists, immigrants, refugees, exiles, guest-workers, and other moving groups and persons" (ibid., 192). This term, he suggests, can be substituted for "earlier 'wholes' such as villages, communities, and localities" (ibid., 209) to better illuminate the realities of people's lives in the late twentieth century.

In countering the outdated notion of "wholes," Appadurai explores how, given the realities of mass media and the global marketing of products, imagination has come to play a new role in social identity as people can envision a larger set of "possible lives" (ibid., 198). The challenge, then, is to "figure out a way in which the role of imagination in social life can be described in a new sort of ethnography that is not so resolutely localizing" (ibid., 199). It is toward this goal that the construct of the "ethnoscape"—a "landscape of group identity" (ibid., 191)—can be deployed, as it incorporates imagination as well as "reality," and transcends the bounds of fixed localities.

While I appreciate that Appadurai, along with several other anthropologists,[4] seeks alternatives to the classic Redfieldian ideal of the geographically bounded, homogenous, harmonious, traditional community, I would suggest that he goes too far in abandoning this construct. Appadurai states that in the process of investigating the "pasts" of the "constructed lives" of those inhabiting various global ethnoscapes, "we need to be careful not to suppose that as we work backward in these imagined lives, we will hit some local, cultural bedrock, constituted of a closed set of reproductive practices, untouched by rumors of the world at large" (ibid., 208).

This admonition is well taken when we consider the ethnic identity of those in Riverton who were not aware of their (partial) American Indian ancestry until they were well into their adult lives, and who self-consciously choose to represent themselves as Native American within the context of the city's formal urban Indian institutions. These "newer Indians" certainly have every right to pursue the truth of a heritage that is part of their family lineage. But I would suggest, following Appadurai, that it is unrealistic in these cases to "suppose that as we work backward in these imagined lives, we will hit some local, cultural bedrock. "

The situation changes dramatically, however, when we turn to consider the Indianness of those who grew up in rural Anishinaabe communities during the first half of the twentieth century. As I have worked backward from this segment of Riverton's Indian community, a "local, cultural bedrock" is exactly what I have found. And while not "closed" and certainly not "untouched by rumors of the world at large," it most definitely is "constituted of a . . . set of reproductive practices"—namely, the features of belief and habit that underlie characteristic Anishinaabe interaction patterns. Furthermore, these features of interaction style are deeply and historically rooted, via cultural constructs such as power, control, responsibility, and autonomy, in traditional Anishinaabe social structure, economic practices, and life ways.

The failure, on the part of Appadurai and other anthropologists of postmodernity, to recognize the essential connection between community (in its more or less traditional sense) and identity implies an underlying failure to appreciate the fact that the self is ultimately socially and materially constituted—a notion that is central to a semiotic view of the self.[5]

IDENTITY AS *COMMUNITY*

Let us consider one final time the confrontation that occurred at the 1994 annual meeting of the BCIA, and especially the climax of that encounter, when the members of the Anishinaabe families held up their Indian cards as the ultimate assertion of their claim to an Indian identity. The regular habits that characterized their style of interacting with one another, as they enjoyed each others' company at the potluck dinner preceding the meeting, were suddenly disrupted as increasingly vociferous and aggressive challenges to Indian identity erupted between the factions. The shock of the confrontation reverberated throughout the Anishinaabe group—the cluster of families seated together on the left side of the room—and they responded, one by one, forcefully and dramatically, by holding small cards up in the air. This was not a series of simple acts by single individuals. Rather, it was a wave of protest by a group—a semiotic gesture—defined by its collective nature; that is, even the first individual to hold up a card knew that the power of the gesture lay in the certainty that others in the group could, and would, do the same, and that those in the other faction across the room could, and would, not. At the same time, this gesture had its meaning not at the subjective level of "interests, desires and intentions," but rather in the quintessentially objective *act* of holding up the card. This act was spontaneous and unique to the moment, engendered in that particular time and place where the Native American identity of those in the Anishinaabe families was being challenged by certain people in a certain way. Habit gave way to a singular act, which gained force as it was replicated and repeated by one person after another holding up an Indian card.

The significance of those cards—based ironically on the European American notion of race, yet ultimately indexical of far deeper historical, political, and economic realities—has been analyzed in the course of writing this book. The cards point to home communities where the brute actualities of racism, poverty, and oppression were experienced. But in addition, these same communities were places where an intensity and a density of social and material interactions engendered and reinforced certain sets of ideas, beliefs, attitudes, values, presuppositions, styles, postures, and patterns of behavior, which in turn embodied a uniquely Anishinaabe worldview. Moreover, these processes continue to recur in the present in the form of habits of daily interaction that continually evoke and reinforce a certain level and kind of Indianness among those who have grown up in such communities.

When these habits that characterize the Anishinaabe way of interacting are not challenged or intruded upon in any way, when those interacting are all in sync with one another, the identity that is constituted through such interactions remains for the most part tacit. This is the case at the level of *belief,* as in the conversations between Tom Richards and his mother and aunts. In the comfort of their intimate family interaction, stories of bearwalking and other such forms of medicine were told with impunity, and with humor. No disclaimers were called for, no explanations or apologies were necessary. Everyone involved in the interaction knew all about this sort of medicine and what it could do, and that shared understanding was taken for granted.

Similarly, *actions* can also have that taken-for-granted quality among those who share the same general worldview and experience— Nancy Miller, for example, witnessing her mother-in-law giving small pouches of tobacco to older Anishinaabe people at large social gatherings. The elder Mrs. Miller acted without fanfare, without explanation. It was an unpretentious act that would have been noteworthy only in its absence; it was simply what one did.

Finally, an example of shared *emotional* response, or sensibility, comes from the conversations at Pete Chimingan's ghost supper. As middle-aged and older Anishinaabe men reminisced on such topics as their childhood experiences growing up poor on reservations, and their exploits on the Indian bar scene of the 1970s, it was the response to these stories that created solidarity among the participants as much as the fact of the experiences themselves. Narrated events that might have struck others as sad, or inappropriate, or shameful, were responded to by those in this conversational group with the humor that was intended. This gentle, ironic humor, grounded in shared life circumstances and fond remembrances of family members long dead, reinforced the Anishinaabe identity that was formed through such experience. In this, as in the other instances recounted above, the Indian identity is in the habits—whether of belief, action, or sensibility—that the participants take for granted.

However, when these habits are questioned, challenged, or thwarted, as happens when those who hold them interact with those who do not, they become matters of confusion. If such encounters occur often enough, the habits become matters of conscious reflection and, therefore, at least partially under one's control. An Ojibwa friend now in his sixties, who grew up on a reserve in Ontario, told me about how uncomfortable he had been interacting with white people during the first few years he lived off the reserve, when he was in his twenties. He had finally realized that it was because they looked at him while speaking, much more than they were "supposed to." Once he became consciously aware of this difference, he was able to get used to it and accept it; but to this day, when he gets together with his brother (who also has lived off the reserve during all his adult life), and especially when they start speaking Ojibwa, their postures and bodily orientations shift ever so slightly, and they gaze off past each other while speaking in the "proper Anishinaabe way."

This process—of taking habits for granted, then having those habits challenged or disrupted, and finally becoming fully conscious of the differences involved—can be another source of strengthening and reinforcing Indian identity among Anishinaabe people. The more they recognize their otherness vis à vis the dominant (white) culture, the more they can use references to their uniquely Indian traits as a means of intensifying their sense of in-group solidarity while at the same time gently poking fun at those in the dominant culture. The story told by Tom Richards about the Native conference speaker who paused too long (by non-Native standards) to collect his thoughts captures the distress of the Anglo people compared to the relaxed comfort of the Indian people in the audience. This kind of contrast— the double vision of understanding both what the speaker was doing and why the non-Natives found it upsetting—can only be appreciated by someone who has experienced the shock of confronting a style different from that of one's own cultural group. The contrast between the two cultural traditions—Anglo and Indian—highlighted the characteristic role of silence in Anishinaabe interactions, and Tom Richards's experience with both traditions allowed him to recognize what was happening and to find it amusing. In settings where the norm is the Indian style, such as the rural Anishinaabe communities of the first half of the twentieth century, there would not be much occasion for reflection on the silences that punctuate Anishinaabe conversational interactions, because without a contrasting style, the Anishinaabe style would remain invisible.

Conversely, when confronted by a different style but not recognizing it as such, one cannot help but interpret the variation by the rules of one's own style. This phenomenon, I would suggest, might have been at least partially at work when the urban-raised children of those who grew up in Anishinaabe communities tried to interpret the silences (and cryptic statements, partial answers to questions, etc.) of their parents. Certainly much of their portrayal rings true—that these rural-raised Anishinaabe parents had been ashamed of their past and had tried to put it behind them, had their demons to contend with, and so on. But, there might also have been a clash of styles operating in these interactions. That is, given the high level of exposure to the style of the dominant culture throughout their lives, the urban-raised Anishinaabeg might have—in reflecting on their childhood experience—interpreted certain silences as pathological when in fact they were culturally appropriate for Anishinaabe people. In contrast to the accounts of urban-raised people, Cora Lawson's description of her grandmother's visits shows no hint that she experienced any negative reaction to her grandmother's reserved and quiet manner, nor any feelings of rejection or neglect that such reticence might evoke in the context of social interactions in the dominant society; it was simply the Indian way. That is, to some extent the perlocutionary force (the effect on the listener) of these silences must be kept separate from the illucutionary force (the intention of the sender of the message) in attempting to determine their meaning.

However interpreted by their urban-raised children and others who interact with them, it is the characteristic Anishinaabe habits, postures, attitudes, beliefs, conversational styles, and interaction patterns that constitute a crucial dimension of the American Indian identity of those who grew up in Anishinaabe communities during the first half of the twentieth century. This is not to say, however, that those who did not grow up in such communities cannot have an authentic American Indian identity. Those who are aware of some American Indian heritage in their family background—even if they have only learned of it as adults—can find genuine meaning in learning about the traditions associated with that heritage, and in joining together with others who share those interests in communities such as those provided by Riverton's official institutions. Similarly, those who grew up in the city with parents who had migrated from home reservations can recover elements of ethnic identity in learning about and participating in the cultural traditions their parents could not or would not share with them when they were children.

Yet a distinction must be made between the first group—those whose parents had no home community ties—and the second group, whose parents did have such ties. The latter group—the first generation of urban-raised Anishinaabeg—were also, throughout their childhood years, members of Indian communities of the sort that coalesced and dispersed as their Indian parents included them in visits with extended family, gatherings of Anishinaabe families in Riverton, or trips to home reservations. Their narratives indicate that they view these sporadic encounters—encounters that immersed them in the density of behavioral patterning that uniquely characterizes Anishinaabe social interactions—in poignant counterpoint to their parents' isolated silences, and to the evasions and denials their parent maintained about their own Indianness. These lived experiences, too, constitute Indian identity. And a semiotic perspective on the self—that is, a notion of the symbolic construction of the self that involves communities as well as individuals, that operates both above and below the level of conscious awareness, that embodies both material and ideational forces, and that acknowledges the role of time and change—allows for all these various processes and expressions of Indian identity to be recognized and appreciated.

I would suggest that such a semiotic notion of the self is highly compatible with the traditional Anishinaabe worldview. In the Anishinaabe world, individuals are not separate fixed entities, but rather are constantly being constituted through kinship relations and leadership roles that shift with the social context. Furthermore, despite the respect for autonomy, in the world of *Anishinaabe bimaadiziwin,* each person is dependent on and responsible for other beings, both human and nonhuman. The community is a palpable and familiar entity that continues over time and that comprises persons of various orders and states of being—human and other-than-human, living, dead and not-yet-born, and so on. Finally, it is behavior, not appearance, that ultimately establishes one's identity—thus, social interaction is at the heart of an Anishinaabe sense of self.

Wuanetta Dominic, as quoted above, seeks to specify a level and kind of Indian culture that cannot necessarily be captured in such obvious and accessible forms as powwows, dancing, and beadwork. In this book, I have sought to contribute to such a specification from the standpoint of Indian identity. Such an identity *can* be expressed in powwows, dancing, and beadwork, but these representational forms are not the only place Indian identity can be found, nor even the most important place. This identity also resides in a characteristic "way of life, . . . way of raising children, . . . [and] way of dealing with [one another]" (Dominic) that can only be engendered within the "local, cultural bedrock" of the "reproductive practices" that are emergent in the face-to-face encounters of an on-the-ground community (Appadurai 1991, 208). These are the practices that shaped the Indianness of the elder, rural-raised generation of urban Anishinaabeg and that manifested themselves during the visits and gatherings in which their urban-raised children participated. And these are the practices that reemerge and are reinforced when these families gather together, whether in the relatively bounded traditional space of a home community, or in the dispersed and fluctuating "ethnoscape" of the present-day American Indian community in Riverton.

Elder generation Anishinaabe people—those who grew up in the home communities of the early twentieth century—do not often seek their Indianness, nor do they usually express it in self-conscious ways. What they do—daily, subtly, with grace and gentle humor—is live it.

Appendix

Anishinaabe People Quoted in Text

Name	Tribal/ Cultural Affiliation	Childhood Home	Approximate age at time of interview
Benson, Jake	Ottawa	Riverton* (Indian community in Lower Michigan)	Late Forties
Butler, Sue-Ellen	Ojibwa	Riverton (Southern Ontario reserve)	Early Thirties
Chimingan, Pete	Ottawa	Ottawa reservation about 300 miles from Riverton	(Not interviewed— mid-70s at time of ghost supper)
Duncan, Michelle	Odawa	Riverton (Reservation in Lower Michigan)	Mid-Forties
Erikson, Fred	Chippewa	Northern Minnesota reservation	Mid-Fifties
Evans, Rob	Chippewa	Minneapolis, Minn. (Minnesota reservation)	Early Thirties
Gardner, Walter	Chippewa	Small city in Minnesota	Late Forties
Gonzales, Carlos	Mexican (Ojibwa wife)	Riverton	Mid-Forties
Great-Uncle Hank (Walter Gardner's great-uncle)	Chippewa	Minnesota reservation	(Not interviewed— died around 1960 at about age 70)
Harmon, Larry	Ojibwa	Riverton (Southern Ontario reserve)	Mid-Forties
Hartwick, Yolanda	Chippewa	City near Riverton (Chippewa reservation)	Late Sixties
Jones, Agnes	Chippewa	Michigan's Western Upper Peninsula	Early Seventies
Lamont, Charles	Chippewa	Lake Superior island Chippewa community	Mid-Eighties
Lawson, Cora	Miami	Rural area in Northern Indiana	Late Seventies
Miller, Nancy (Bob's wife)	Non-Native	Whitfield	Early Fifties
Miller, Bob	Chippewa	Whitfield's "Indian Town" /Zhashkooning	Late Fifties
Mitchell, Ron	Menominee	Wisconsin reservation	Late Fifties

Name	Tribal/ Cultural Affiliation	Childhood Home	Approximate age at time of interview
Morgan, Doris	Potawatomi	Riverton (Northern Indiana Potawatomi community)	Mid-Forties
Nelson, Sharon	Chippewa	Rural area near Riverton	Early Fifties
Niles, Joe	Chippewa	Wisconsin reservation	Early Sixties
Parker, Jeff	Ojibwa	Reserve in Ontario	Late Forties
Peters, Jack	Chippewa	Minnesota reservation	Mid-Seventies
Richards, Tom	Chippewa	Riverton	Early Fifties
Richards, Rachel (Tom's mother)	Chippewa	Whitfield	Mid-Eighties
Aunt Margaret (Tom's aunt; Rachel's sister)	Chippewa	Whitfield's "Indian Town" /Zhashkooning	Early Sixties when recorded in the mid-1970s
Great-Aunt Grace (Rachel's aunt, Tom's great-aunt)	Chippewa	Whitfield's "Indian Town" /Zhashkooning	Early Eighties when recorded in the mid-1970s
Smith, Rosemary	Chippewa	Riverton (rural area near Riverton)	Mid-Thirties
Williams, Andrew	Odawa	Reservation in Lower Michigan	Late Forties
Wilson, Greg	Chippewa	Riverton (reservation in Michigan's UP)	Early Thirties

* Parenthetical statements indicate where family is from originally.

Notes

1. The lack of direct participation on the part of the elders should not be taken, however, to indicate their lack of any role in the confrontation. Their mere presence served as crucial validation for their more assertive children. I am grateful to Regna Darnell for pointing this out.

2. "Indian card" is an informal term for a card documenting enrollment as a member of a federally recognized tribe.

3. This usage of "indexical" was established by C. S. Peirce and has been widely adopted by semioticians. In Peirce's system, there are three main types of signs, distinguished according to the nature of their relationship to the object for which they stand: icons are related to their objects through resemblance; symbols through habit; and indexes through connection—being close to, pointing toward, or in acual physical contact with the object. Thus, an "indexical sign" is one that functions as an index, conveying meaning through connection.

4. Although Peirce himself preferred "semeiotic" (see Daniel 1996, 213, note 3 in Introduction, for an explanation of why Peirce used this idiosyncratic form), I conform here to the conventional spelling.

5. For an extended discussion of Peirce's notion of the sign and its implications for cultural analysis, see Daniel (1984), 12–56.

6. While other writers have not explicitly drawn on the philosophy of C. S. Peirce in discussion American Indian identity, several authors of recent works on American Indian identity issues have taken a perspective similar to that taken here in that they have emphasized such features as social interaction, community norms, behavior patterns, and discourse (for examples, see Braroe 1975, O'Nell 1996, Hensel 1996, and Harmon 1999).

7. For an excellent analysis of the rise of such pan-Indian, or "supratribal," identities starting in the 1960s and of their significance to contemporary Native American identity politics, see Nagel (1996).

CHAPTER 1

1. While I will continue to refer to "Riverton" or "the Riverton area" as a sort of shorthand, the more appropriate unit of analysis with regard to most of this discussion is Birmingham County, which includes Riverton and six or seven small suburban cities. The city and its suburbs have always been interdependent in such a way as to form one greater urban area.

2. These quotes are all taken from an article in the January 8, 1995, edition of the local "Riverton" newspaper. To maintain the anonymity of the community, I am unable to cite the actual newspaper or journalist's name.

3. This line of reasoning is inspired by Leslie Sklair's (1991) discussion of the global system, in which she points out that the most important factor in determining whether an individual, group, or community will be rich or poor, will prosper or suffer, is not their geographical location (a first-world as opposed to a third-world nation), but rather their "transnational class position." Similarly, in her discussion of regional politics in the context of the global economy, Ann Roell Markusen (1985) points out that in "regions of exit" (regions that are losing large, formerly prosperous industries), of which Birmingham County is certainly one, the workers and local businesses tend to align against what Markusen calls "transregional corporations."

4. See Rafert (1996) for a full ethnohistorical report on the Miami of Indiana and their communities.

5. This is by no means always the case, however. Some reservations in the region do not have casinos and other businesses, or if they do, the profits are needed simply to provide basic infrastructure and social services to reservation residents. For example, a February 1999 report on National Public Radio's *All Things Considered* program told of the extreme burdens created for hard-pressed tribal governments when urban residents leave deindustrializing Upper Great Lakes cities to return to their home reservations. The report focused on the Red Lake Chippewa of northern Minnesota and the difficulties they have had in trying to accommodate increasing numbers of returning (formerly) urban tribal members in an economy that is already strained trying to meet the needs of reservation residents.

6. See Weibel-Orlando (1991) for examples from Los Angeles's American Indian community, Straus and Arndt (1999) for illustrations from the Native community in Chicago, and Danziger (1991) for examples from Detroit's Native American Communities.

CHAPTER 2

1. Also, this policy was opposed by traditionalists in many tribal communities because of its insistence on Western-style governments that were closely linked to the Bureau of Indian Affairs (BIA). As Nagel (1996) points out, this issue remains salient in present-day tribal communities where "close links between tribal governments and the much-maligned BIA remain a source of tension on most reservations and has contributed to the factionalization of tribal ethnicity" (31).

2. The 1830s policy represented the federal government's concerted effort to address the "Indian problem." American Indian communities were forcibly removed from their homelands and sent to live in Oklahoma (originally all "Indian Territory"), Kansas, or other areas west of the Mississippi. The most well-known event of this period is the Trail of Tears of the Cherokee and other Southeast Indian tribes.

3. The phenomenon of "Black Indian" communities—the result of intermarriage between Native Americans and African Americans, especially in the South—has not been written about much. However, some information on this topic can be found in Katz (1986). Also, see Lewis 2000 for an exploration of identity issues among people of mixed African and Indian descent in Mexico who are perceived by outsiders as blacks, or black Indians, but who see themselves as Afromexicans.

4. See Josephy (1985 [1971]) and Nagel (1996) for detailed descriptions and in-depth analyses of this era in American Indian political activism.

5. John Trudell is an American Indian (Santee Sioux) artist, poet, activist, and self-proclaimed "warrior" who first gained notoriety as spokesman for the occupation of Alcatraz Island in 1969 and later served as national chairperson of the American Indian Movement, from 1973 to 1979. He continues to address Native American political issues in his poetry and public talks.

6. Vernon Bellecourt, from the White Earth Chippewa Reservation in Minnesota, is also a long-time activist with AIM and other American Indian groups, starting with his involvement in the Wounded Knee occupation of 1973. His talk at Riverton University was titled "The U.S. Constitution: Five Hundred Years of Guaranteed Racism and Oppression."

7. This documentary film, produced by Robert Redford, gives a portrayal (sympathetic to the Native Americans) of the events leading up to the arrest and subsequent conviction of AIM activist Leonard Peltier; it also reviews more recently revealed evidence that greatly damages, if not entirely destroys, the government's case against Peltier.

CHAPTER 3

1. At least until the 1950s, American Indians on the island were barred from being buried in the white cemetery, and therefore had to have their own separate cemetery. This was the case in many communities throughout the Upper Great Lakes region, and these old Indian graveyards still dot the countryside.

2. It is important to keep in mind that during this historical period, it was not just American Indian communities, but rather all rural communities in the Upper Great Lakes region and surrounding areas that lacked basic utilities. It was not until the 1930s that electricity and other amenities were made available in these areas. And, when electricity did finally come, American Indian communities were rarely, if ever, included.

3. The fact that Charles reports being able to "talk Indian" to the new students is consistent with what Alice Littlefield reports about a change in policy that took place at the Mount Pleasant Indian School (and other Indian schools) in the 1920s. Prior to that time, Native language use was strictly forbidden under any circumstances, and students were severely punished for "talking Indian." However, after about 1920, these punishments for Native language occurred only rarely. Littlefield speculates that the change was due less to enlightened policy than to the reality that increasing numbers of children

already knew English when they arrived at the school, and the Native language simply did not pose the threat it once had (Littlefield 1996, 121).

4. Despite differences in specifics of timing and implementation, the U.S. and Canadian governments developed very similar laws and policies with regard to Native peoples.

5. I use "appeared" here intentionally in the sense that appearances can be deceiving. In Chapter 5, I discuss how people who went to these boarding schools *did*, in fact, maintain their Indian identity and pass it along to their children in important, though subtle, ways.

6. This was consistent with many other points in the interview where Walter explicitly framed certain incidents in political terms.

7. I specify the first half of the twentieth century here because my purpose is to describe the circumstances under which Riverton's elderly cohort of Anishnaabe people grew up. I do not mean to imply that pressures on American Indians to assimilate and acculturate, as well as overt and subtle forms of racism against them, have not continued into the second half of the twentieth century and up to the present day. In fact, anti-Indian racial prejudice and acts of harassment and brutality arising from such prejudice have increased recently as Native Americans have experienced successes in regaining treaty-guaranteed rights to hunting, fishing, and gathering, as well as financial gains through casinos and other tribally owned businesses.

8. Again, this is not to say that rural—or for that matter, urban—poverty has been eradicated for American Indians. To the contrary, American Indians continue to rank lowest in virtually every category of economic and educational attainment, and highest in virtually every category of social and health problem. My point is simply that relative rates of poverty have been generally decreasing in Indian communities since about the middle of the twentieth century.

9. Although non-Native spouses and parents are an important presence in Riverton's urban Indian community, my research did not focus on them, and an analysis of their roles and perspectives are beyond the scope of this study.

CHAPTER 4

1. As stated in the introduction, I will not be focusing on this group, but rather on the contrasts between the two generations of Anishinaabe families—those born in the 1920s, 1930s, and early 1940s and raised in rural Anishinnabe communities, and those born in the later 1940s, 1950s, and 1960s and raised in Riverton. The third group—those who grew up in Riverton with no connection to an American Indian extended family or home community—serve my study more as a backdrop against which to better perceive the two generations of Anishinaabe families than as a focus of analysis in its own right.

2. This progressive trend in the literatures of philosophy, the humanities and the social sciences privileges language as an active and interactive process rather than as a collection of static texts, an abstract formal system, or a transparent window on "reality." In this view, language does not simply *de-*

scribe the world but rather has the power to *constitute* the (social) world, and even to *transform* it. The social world, in turn, is seen as "localized in concrete, publicly accessible signs, the most important of which are actually occurring instances of discourse" (Urban 1991, 1). Anthropological analyses that adopt this perspective comprise varied and wide-ranging literature; what these works share is the premise that speaking is a powerful force in the reproduction and transformation of social identities. In this way, they are highly compatible with the semiotic notion of identity on which I draw throughout this book, and it is within this general perspective that I ground my analysis of the narratives I collected among American Indians in Riverton.

3. Two other ethnographic works that, while not devoted to the topic of silence, do explore its manifestations in some detail, are Philips (1989 [1974]) and Darnell (1989 [1974]). Note that four out of the five ethnographic works mentioned deal with American Indian communities, and that the fifth, while about Quakers rather than American Indians, is by a Native Americanist anthropologist. Since so little work has been done outside Native North America on silence, it is difficult to know whether Native Americans "use" silence more than other cultures, or whether the Native Americanist intellectual tradition in anthropology has fostered such studies more than other traditions have, or both.

4. Throughout this chapter, I draw primarily on only four cases, with occasional references to a fifth. While this is a very small number in terms of sampling, I am attempting in this chapter to convey the experience of my interviewees as richly and vividly as possible. Thus, I have chosen to explore a few cases in depth rather than a greater number more superficially. I have selected these particular cases because they provide exceptionally good illustrations of themes that emerge, echo, rebound, and recur throughout the narratives of virtually everyone I talked with, both formally and informally, who was of this cohort of city-raised Anishinaabe people in Riverton. That is, I have sought "cases that represent the typical with atypical clarity" (Rosenwald 1988, 2) and can only hope I have met with some measure of success.

5. Greg was one of only two people I met in Riverton who preferred the term "Indigenous" to Indian, American Indian, or even Native American.

6. Greg's grandfather is referring to money owed to Upper Great Lakes–area tribes as the result of a 1972 ruling by the Indian Claims Commission (set up in 1948 to address tribal claims of inadequate compensation for land ceded to the federal government) that awarded the tribes $10 million to compensate for the amount they were underpaid by an 1836 treaty. The money was not paid out, however, because the tribes could not agree on a distribution plan. Finally, an agreement was made and the money paid in 1997—by which time it had grown to $17 million due to interest accrued. This was about three and one half years after I interviewed Greg.

7. Of course, the response described here is by no means universal. Because my fieldwork was based in American Indian institutions and social circles, I had little opportunity to meet those in this same category—the first-generation urban-raised Anishnaabeg—who had chosen not to pursue a more

overt American Indian/Anishinaabe identity through involvement with such organizations. I became aware there were many such people, since quite a few of my interviewees, friends, and acquaintances told me of siblings who seemed content to identify as whites, and who had little interest in Native American political and cultural issues.

8. This point was made by Joan Weibel-Orlando in her discussant's remarks for the panel "Being Indian in the City: Reflections on Urban Indian Identity and Community" at the 1996 annual meeting of the American Anthropological Association in San Francisco, where I gave the paper "Urban Indian Identity and the Power of Silence," which forms the core of this chapter.

9. Since more recent waves of immigration are predominantly composed of people of color from various parts of the world, the "racial" aspect should be similar for these newer immigrants to that of American Indians.

10. Since the parents were the generation that founded the BCIA and participated in those early potlucks, spaghetti suppers, bowling leagues, and so on, some urban-raised children had exposure to these urban Indian gatherings.

11. Actually, language was the one overt ethnicity marker that was sometimes present in these interactions. In addition to Michelle Duncan's comment about sometimes hearing her father "talk in a funny language" when they'd go to visit certain families, quite a few others in the urban-raised generation report hearing parents, grandparents and/or older relatives "talking Indian" when they were together with other Native-speaking people. However, the great majority of the time, these urban-raised Indian people heard their parents speak only English.

CHAPTER 5

1. This is the same family with eleven children who had to hitchhike in the summer to sell their handmade baskets in tourist areas and to pick cherries in faraway orchards.

2. A similar observation was made by Tom Richards with regard to Native Americans. He told me that, in his opinion, American Indian business people would tend to "go broke unless they had a *Chimookmaan* (Ojibwa word for non-Native/white American) collecting the bills and handling the complaints. Because [if an Indian were doing it], he'd just say, 'Oh, no, just keep it.' . . . Because [the way Indians are raised], everybody shares everything" (Jackson, 701).

3. In constructing this general portrait of the traditional Anishinaabe world, I have drawn on a variety of sources—chief among them are the following: Landes (1937, 1938, 1969); Hallowell (1955, 1992); Overholt and Callicott (1982); Brown and Brightman (1988); Darnell (1989 [1974], 1988); Black (1977a, 1977b); Black-Rogers (1988); and Smith (1995).

4. In this section, I use the discredited "ethnographic present" tense purposely. My point here will be to convey some sense of a generally "indigenous" (though not necessarily "pristine"/pre-contact) worldview and belief system, without regard to exactly which individuals/communities in which

times and places are/were living in such a world, and to what extent this worldview prevails/prevailed as conditions have changed. This "outside of time and space" Anishinaabe world will serve as a framework for understanding the Indian ways already discussed in this chapter, and as a point of departure from which to consider, later in this chapter, other specific beliefs and behaviors of contemporary Anishinaabe people. That is, the specificity of time, place, and person—or history, political economy, and agency—that the "ethnographic present" suspends (and for which it has been rightly criticized) will soon be reinstated.

5. There is no necessary correlation between malevolent spiritual beings and bad medicine, on the one hand, and benevolent spiritual practices and good medicine, on the other hand. Rather, an Anishinaabe man or woman can obtain spiritual power by developing a relationship with any powerful other-than-human person: it is then up to that man or woman to use his or her power "for the good" or "for the bad" (see quote from Ron Mitchell, below).

6. I quote from this tape with permission of Tom Richards. All three of the women relatives he recorded are now deceased.

7. Cleland is writing specifically about Catholic missionaries in the Upper Great Lakes region during the seventeenth and eighteenth centuries, but his point holds for most Christian denominations and most parts of North America.

8. This spelling, like "Ojibway," is a Canadian variation on "Ojibwa."

9. If this is, in fact, what happened, it makes for a poignant and ironic counterpoint to what happened to the Ottawa community at Burt Lake, Michigan, in the early 1900s. There, the Ottawa peoples' homes were destroyed by land-hungry whites, while the one building left standing was the church.

10. For a discussion of the emergence in the early 1800s of camp meetings among another Northeast Woodlands Indian people—the Iroquois—see Wallace (1972), 26.

11. This custom is, of course, more in keeping with the non-Native, white, interaction style.

CONCLUSION

1. Wuanetta Dominic (her real name) was an Ottawa born into the Grand Traverse Ottawa community near Petosky, Michigan, in 1921 and lived there most of her life. Along with her husband, Robert Dominic (also Grand Traverse Ottawa), Mrs. Dominic worked tirelessly on behalf of her own community and for American Indian people throughout the Upper Great Lakes region. In 1948, the Dominics founded the Northern Michigan Ottawa Association to press for settlement of claims in connection with the sale of Native land during the treaty era—the "Indian money" that Greg Wilson's grandfather was so bitter about having not yet received. The quote used above is taken from an article about Wuanetta Dominic that appeared in the *Detroit News Magazine* (Dammann 1979, 3).

2. For a detailed consideration of these shared features, see Teaford (1993).

3. For an exploration of the significance of cohort in understanding a particular elderly population, see Jackson and Chapleski 2000.

4. Examples include: Sherry Ortner's (1997) ethnography of her high school graduating class, in which she identifies various types of "postcommunities"; and Roger Rouses's (1991) study of Mexican immigrants to California's Silicon Valley in which he emphasizes the importance of "transnational migrant circuits" as the most relevant social spaces for his subjects.

5. While the notion of the self as socially and materially constituted is central to a semiotic view, this insight is overtly recognized in different degrees by researchers who employ a semiotic perspective. Among anthropologists in the Boasian tradition, two primary early proponents of such an approach were Edward Sapir (1985 [1949]) and A. Irving Hallowell (1955). This general tradition, in combination with other strands in American social science, has continued up to the present in the work of Native Americanist anthropologists such as Mary Black-Rogers, Regna Darnell, and Lisa Valentine, whose work I drew on in chapter 5. Another tradition that defines the self as essentially social in nature and that focuses on behavior as constitutive of the self has come to be known as the "symbolic interactionism" school of sociology; this approach was pioneered by George Herbert Mead (1962 [1934]), C. H. Cooley (1922), and Harry Stack Sullivan (1953), and was carried forward and further developed by Herbert Blumer (1969) and Erving Goffman (1959), among others. Recent studies of American Indian identity that further either or both of these traditions include: Braroe (1975); Foster (1991); Philips (1989 [1974]); O'Nell (1996); Hensel (1996); and Harmon (1998). I choose to rely primarily on C. S. Peirce's formulation of the semiotic self because it is, in my opinion, the most thoroughly elaborated, well integrated and far-reaching among such approaches, and therefore the most fruitful in its applications.

Bibliography

Ablon, Joan
    1964   Relocated American Indians in the San Francisco Bay Area: Social
            Interactions and Indian Identity. *Human Organization* 23:
            296–304.
Appadurai, Arjun
    1991   Global Ethnoscapes: Notes and Queries for a Transnational An-
            thropology. In *Recapturing Anthropology: Working in the Present.*
            Edited by Robin Fox. Sante Fe: School of American Research Press.
Austin, John
    1962   *How to do Things with Words.* Cambridge: Harvard University
            Press.
Bakhtin, Mikhail
    1981   *The Dialogic Imagination.* Austin: University of Austin Press.
Barth, Frederik
    1969   Introduction to *Ethnic Groups and Boundaries: The Social Organiza-
            tion of Cultural Difference.* Edited by Frederick Barth. Boston: Lit-
            tle, Brown.
Basso, Keith
    1979   *Portraits of 'the Whiteman': Linguistic Play and Cultural Symbols
            Among the Western Apache.* Cambridge: Cambridge University Press.
    1990   "To Give Up On Words": Silence in Western Apache Culture. In
            *Western Apache Language and Culture: Essays in Linguistic Anthro-
            pology.* Tucson: University of Arizona Press.
Bauman, Richard
    1977   *Verbal Art as Performance.* Prospect Heights, Ill.: Waveland Press.
    1983   *"Let Your Words Be Few": Symbolism of Speaking and Silence Among
            Seventeenth-Century Quakers.* Cambridge England and New York:
            Cambridge University Press.
Bauman, R., and J. Sherzer, eds.
    1989 [1974]   *Explorations in the Ethnography of Speaking.* 2d ed. Cam-
            bridge: Cambridge University Press.
Becker, Alton
    1984   Biography of a Sentence: A Burmese Proverb. In *Text, Play, and Story:
            The Construction and Reconstruction of Self and Society.* Edited by
            Edward L. Bruner. Washington, D.C.: American Ethnological Society.
Behar, Ruth
    1993   *Translated Woman: Crossing the Border with Esperanza's Story.*
            Boston: Beacon Press.

Black, Mary
   1977a Ojibwa Power Belief System. In *The Anthropology of Power: Ethnographic Studies from Asia, Oceania, and the New World*. Edited by Raymond D. Fogelson and Richard N. Adams. New York: Academic Press.
   1977b Ojibwa Taxonomy and Percept Ambiguity. *Ethos* 5(1): 90–118.
Black-Rogers, Mary
   1988   Ojibwa Power Interactions: Creating Contexts for "Respectful Talk." In *Native North American Interaction Patterns*. Edited by Regna Darnell and Michael K. Foster. Hull, Quebec: Canadian Museum of Civilization, National Museums of Canada.
Blu, Karen I.
   1980   *The Lumbee Problem: The Making of an American Indian People*. Cambridge: Cambridge University Press.
Blumer, Herbert
   1969   *Symbolic Interactionism: perspective and method*. Edgewood Cliffs, N.J.: Prentice-Hall
Bourdieu, Pierre
   1991   *Language and Symbolic Power*. Edited by John B. Thompson, translated by Gino Raymond and Matthew Adamson. Cambridge: Harvard University Press.
Braroe, Neils Winter
   1975   *Indian and White: Self-Image and Interaction in a Canadian Plains Community*. Palo Alto: Stanford University Press.
BraveHeart, Maria Yellow Horse, and Lemyra M. DeBruyn
   1998   The American Indian Holocaust: Healing Historical Unresolved Grief. *American Indian and Alaska Native Mental Health Research Journal* 8, no 2.
Brown, Jennifer S. H., and Robert Brightman
   1988   *"The Orders of the Dreamed": George Nelson on Cree and Northern Ojibwa Religion and Myth, 1823*. St. Paul: Minnesota Historical Society Press.
Bruner, Edward
   1957   Differential Cultural Change. *Items* (Social Science Research Council): 2(1).
Churchill, Ward
   1996   Review of *Issues in Native American Cultural Identity*. *American Indian Culture and Research Journal* 20(3): 206–11.
Cleland, Charles E.
   1992   *Rites of Conquest: The History and Culture of Michigan's Native Americans*. Ann Arbor: University of Michigan Press.
Clifton, James
   1989   Alternative Identities and Cultural Frontiers. In *Being and Becoming Indian: Biographical Studies of North American Frontiers*. Edited by James Clifton. Chicago: Dorsey Press.
——, ed.
   1990   *The Invented Indian: Cultural Fictions and Government Policies*. New Brunswick: Transaction Publishers.

Cohen, Abner
  1974   Introduction to *Urban Ethnicity*. Edited by Abner Cohen. London: Tavistock

Colapietro, Vincent M.
  1989   *Peirce's Approach to the Self: A Semiotic Perspective on Human Subjectivity*. Albany: State University of New York Press.

Cooley, C. H.
  1922   *Human Nature and the Social Order*. New York: Scribner's. Corrington, Robert S.
  1993   *An Introduction to C. S. Peirce: Philosopher, Semiotician, and Ecstatic Naturalist*. Lanham, Md.: Rowman & Littleman.

Dammann, Sara Gay
  1979   What is an Indian? *Detroit News Magazine*, 4 November. pp.33-36

Daniel, E. Valentine
  1984   *Fluid Signs: Being a Person the Tamil Way*. Berkeley: University of California Press.
  1996   *Charred Lullabies: Chapters in an Anthropology of Violence*. Princeton, N.J.: Princeton University Press.

Danziger, Edmund Jefferson, Jr.
  1979   *The Chippewas of Lake Superior*. Norman: University of Oklahoma Press.
  1991   *Survival and Regeneration: Detroit's American Indian Community*. Detroit: Wayne State University Press.

Darnell, Regna
  1988   The Implications of Cree Interactional Etiquette. In *Native North American Interaction Patterns*. Edited by Regna Darnell and Michael K. Foster. Hull, Quebec: National Museums of Canada.
  1989 [1974]   Correlates of Cree Narrative Performance. In *Explorations in the Ethnography of Speaking*. Edited by Richard Bauman and Joel Sherzer. Cambridge: Cambridge University Press.

Darnell, Regna, and Michael K. Foster, eds.
  1988   *Native American Interaction Patterns*. Hull, Quebec: Canadian Museum of Civilization, National Museums of Canada.

Deloria, Vine, Jr.
  1988 [1969]   Missionaries and the Religious Vacuum. In *Custer Died For Your Sins: An Indian Manifesto*. Norman: University of Oklahoma Press.

Derrida, Jacques
  1982   Difference. In *Margins of Philosophy*. Translated by Alan Bass. Chicago: University of Chicago Press.

Fogelson, Raymond D.
  1998   Perspectives on Native American Identity. In *Studying Native America: Problems and Prospects*. Edited by Russell Thornton. Madison: University of Wisconsin Press.

Foley, Douglas
  1996   *The Heartland Chronicles*. Philadelphia: University of Pennsylvania Press.

Foster, Morris W.
  1991   *Being Comanche: A Social History of an American Indian Community.* Tucson: University of Arizona Press.
Foucault, Michel
  1972   *The Archaeology of Knowledge.* Translated by A. M. Sheridan Smith. New York: Harper Colophon.
  1973   *The Order of Things: An Archaeology of the Human Sciences.* New York: Random House, Vintage.
  1979   *Discipline and Punish: The Birth of the Prison.* Translated by Alan Sheridan. New York: Random House, Vintage.
  1980   Introduction to *The History of Sexuality.* Vol. 1. Translated by Robert Hurley. New York: Random House, Vintage.
Freud, Sigmund
  1914   Remembering, Repeating, and Working Through. Vol. 12 of *Standard Edition: Complete Psychological Works of Sigmund Freud.* Edited by James Strachey. London: Hogarth Press.
Friedlander, Judith
  1975   *Being Indian in Hueyapan: A Study of Forced Identity in Contemporary Mexico.* New York: St. Martin's Press.
Gal, Susan
  1991   Between Speech and Silence. In *Gender at the Crossroads of Knowledge.* Edited by Micaela di Leonardo. Berkeley: University of California Press.
Glazer, Nathan, and Daniel Moynihan
  1975   Introduction to *Ethnicity: Theory and Experience.* Edited by Nathan Glazer and Daniel Moynihan. Cambridge: Harvard University Press.
Goffman, Erving
  1959   *The Presentation of Self in Everyday Life.* New York: Doubleday, Anchor Books.
Gonzales, Angela
  1998   The (Re)Articulation of American Indian Identity: Maintaining Boundaries and Regulating Access to Ethnically Tied Resources. *American Indian Culture and Research Journal* 22(4): 199–225.
Green, Michael, ed.
  1995   *Issues in Native American Cultural Identity.* New York: P. Lang.
Greenspan, Henry
  1992   Lives as Texts: Symptoms as Modes of Recounting in the Life Histories of Holocaust Survivors. In *Storied Lives: The Cultural Politics of Self-Understanding.* Edited by George C. Rosenwald and Richard L. Ochberg. New Haven: Yale University Press.
Hallowell, A. Irving
  1955   *Culture and Experience.* Philadelphia: University of Pennsylvania Press.
  1992   *The Ojibwa of Berens River, Manitoba: Ethnography into History.* Edited by Jennifer S. H. Brown. New York: Harcourt Brace.

Hansen, Marcus Lee
 1987 [1938] *The Problem of the Third-Generation Immigrant.* Rock Island,
  Ill.: Swenson Swedish Immmigration Research Center.
Harmon, Alexandra
 1999 *Indians in the Making: Ethnic Relations and Indian Identities Around
  Puget Sound.* Berkeley: University of California Press.
Hensel, Chase
 1996 *Telling Our Selves: Ethnicity and Discourse in Southeastern Alaska.*
  New York: Oxford University Press.
Herskovitz, Melville J.
 1958 *Acculturation: The Study of Culture Contact.* Glouster, Mass.: Peter
  Smith Publishing.
Hill, Richard Child, and Joe R. Faegin
 1987 Detroit and Houston: Two Cities in Global Perspective. In *The
  Capitalist City: Global Restructuring and Community Politics.* Edited
  by Michael Peter Smith and Joe R. Faegin. Oxford: Basil Blackwell.
Hobsbawm, Eric, and Terence Ranger
 1983 *The Invention of Tradition.* Cambridge: Cambridge University
  Press.
Hymes, Dell, and John Gumperz
 1972 *Directions in Sociolinguistics: The Ethnography of Communication.*
  New York: Holt, Rinehart, and Winston.
Irwin, M. H., and S. Roll
 1995 The Psychological Impact of Sexual Abuse of Native American
  Boarding School Children. *Journal of the American Academy of
  Psycho-Analysis* 23(3): 461–73.
Jackson, Deborah Davis
 1996 "Transcripts of the Intergenerational Family Interview Oral His-
  tory Project." Edited by Crisce Bierwert. Sponsored by Confeder-
  ated Swan Creek and Black River Ojibwa Tribes.
Jackson, Deborah Davis, and Elizabeth E. Chapleski
 2000 Not Traditional, Not Assimilated: Elderly American Indians and
  the Notion of "Cohort." *Journal of Cross-Cultural Gerontology* 15:
  229–59
Jameson, Fredric
 1991 *Postmodernism, or, The Cultural Logic of Late Capitalism.* Durham:
  Duke University Press.
Johnston, Basil
 1988 *Indian School Days.* Toronto: Key Porter Books.
Josephy, Alvin M.
 1985 [1971] *Red Power: The American Indians' Fight for Freedom.* Lincoln:
  University of Nebraska Press.
Katz, William Loren
 1986 *Black Indians: A Hidden Heritage.* New York: Athenaeum.
Knack, Martha C., and Alice Littlefield
 1996 Native American Labor: Retrieving History, Rethinking Theory. In

    Native Americans and Wage Labor: Ethnohistorical Perspectives. Norman: University of Oklahoma Press.

LaDuke, Winona

  1999 *All Our Kin: Native Struggles for Land and Life.* Cambridge: South End Press.

Landes, Ruth

  1937 *Ojibwa Sociology.* New York: Columbia University Press.

  1938 *Ojibwa Religion and the Midewiwin.* Madison: University of Wisconsin Press.

  1969 *The Ojibwa Woman.* New York: AMS Press.

Landsman, Gail

  1988 *Sovereignty and Symbol: Indian-White Conflict at Ganienkeh.* Albuquerque: University of New Mexico Press.

Lewis, Laura A.

  2000 Blacks, Black Indians, Afromexicans. *American Ethnologist* 27(4): 898–926.

Linton, Ralph

  1940 *Acculturation in Seven American Indian Tribes.* New York: Appleton-Century.

Littlefield, Alice

  1993 "Learning to Labor": Native American Education in the United States, 1880–1930. In *The Political Economy of North American Indians.* Edited by John H. Moore. Norman: University of Oklahoma Press.

  1996 Indian Education and the World of Work in Michigan, 1893–1933. In *Native Americans and Wage Labor: Ethnohistorical Perspectives.* Edited by Alice Littlefield and Martha C. Knack. Norman: University of Oklahoma Press.

Lobo, Susan

  1998 Is Urban a Person or a Place? Characteristics of Urban Indian Country. *American Indian Culture and Research Journal* 22(4): 89–102.

Lurie, Nancy

  1971 The Contemporary American Indian Scene. In *North American Indians in Historical Perspective.* Edited by Eleanor Burke Leacock and Nancy Oestreich Lurie. New York: Random House.

Mannheim, Bruce

  1991 *The Language of the Inka Since the European Invasion.* Austin: University of Texas Press.

Markusen, Ann Roell

  1985 *Profit Cycles, Oligopoly, and Regional Development.* Cambridge: MIT Press.

McClurken, James

  1991 *Gah-Baeh-Jhagwah-Buk (The Way it Happened): A Visual Culture History of the Little Traverse Bay Bands of Odawa.* East Lansing: Michigan State University Press.

1996   Wage Labor in Two Michigan Ottawa Communities. In *Native Americans and Wage Labor: Ethnohistorical Perspectives.* Edited by Alice Littlefield and Martha C. Knack. Norman: University of Oklahoma Press.

McDonnell, Janet A.

1991   *The Dispossession of the American Indian, 1887–1934.* Bloomington: University of Indiana Press.

Mead, George Herbert

1962 [1934]   *Mind, Self, and Society: From the Standpoint of a Social Behaviorist.* Chicago: University of Chicago Press.

Nagel, Joane

1996   *American Indian Ethnic Renewal.* New York: Oxford University Press.

Native American Task Force

1990   *Empowering Native People* (Report to the Michigan State Department of Social Services). Harris, Mich.: Hannahville Printing.

Nelson, Daniel

1995   *Farm and Factory: Workers in the Midwest, 1880–1990.* Bloomington: Indiana University Press.

Noriega, J.

1992   American Indian Education in the United States: Indoctrination for Subordination to Colonialism. In *The State of Native America: Genocide, Colonization, Resistance.* Edited by M.A. Jaines. Boston: South End.

O'Nell, Theresa D.

1996   *Disciplined Hearts: History, Identity, and Depression in an American Indian Community.* Berkeley: University of California Press.

Ortner, Sherry

1997   Fieldwork in the Postcommunity. *Anthropology and Humanism* 22(1) (June): 61–80

Overholt, Thomas W., and J. Baird Callicott

1982   *"Clothed-in-Fur" and Other Tales: An Introduction to an Ojibwa World View.* Lanham, Md.: University Press of America.

Paquin, Ron, with Robert Doherty

1992   *Not First in Nobody's Heart: The Life Story of a Contemporary Chippewa.* St. Ignace, Mich.: RJP Press.

Peirce, Charles Sanders

1932   *Collected Papers.* Vols. 1–6. Edited by C. Hartshorne and P. Weiss. Cambridge: Harvard University Press.

1958   *Collected Papers.* Vols. 7–8. Edited by Auther Burks. Cambridge: Harvard University Press.

1955   The Principles of Phenomenology. In *Philosophical Writings of Peirce.* Edited by Justus Buchler. New York: Dover Publications.

Philips, Susan U.

1989 [1974]   Warm Springs "Indian Time": How the Regulation of Participation Affects the Progress of Events. In *Explorations in the*

Ethnography of Speaking. Edited by Richard Bauman and Joel Sherzer. Cambridge: University of Cambridge Press.

Rafert, Stewart
1996 *The Miami Indians of Indiana: A Persistent People, 1654–1994*. Indianapolis: Indiana Historical Society.

Redfield, Robert, Ralph Linton, and Melville Herskovitz
1936 Outline for the Study of Acculturation. *American Anthropologist* 38: 149–52.

Romanucci-Ross, Lola, and George DeVos
1995 Preface: 1995. In *Ethnic Identity: Creation, Conflict, and Accommodation*. Edited by Lola Romanucci-Ross and George DeVos. Walnut Creek, Calif.: Altamira Press.

Rosenwald, George C.
1988 A Theory of Multiple-Case Research. *Journal of Personality* 56(1): 239–64.

Rouse, Roger
1991 Mexican Migration and the Social Space of Postmoderism. *Diaspora* 1(1): 8–23.

Sapir, Edward
1985 [1949] *Edward Sapir: Selected Writings in Language, Culture, and Personality*. Edited by David G. Mandelbaum. Berkeley: University of California Press.

Sassen, Saskia
1991 *The Global City: New York, London, Tokyo*. Princeton, N.J.: Princeton University Press.
1994 *Cities in a World Economy*. Thousand Oaks, Calif.: Sage Press, Pine Forge.

Sherzer, Joel
1983 *Kuna Ways of Speaking: An Ethnographic Perspective*. Austin: University of Texas Press.

Sklair, Leslie
1991 *Sociology of the Global System*. New York: Harvester, Wheatsheaf.

Smith, Theresa S.
1995 *The Island of the Anishinaabeg: Thunderers and Water Monsters in the Traditional Ojibwa Life-World*. Moscow: University of Idaho Press.

Sorkin, Alan
1978 *The Urban American Indian*. Lexington, Mass: D.C. Heath & Company.

Stack, Carol B.
1974 *All Our Kin: Strategies for Survival in a Black Community*. New York: Harper & Row.

Straus, Terry, and Grant P. Arndt, eds.
1999 *Native Chicago*. Chicago: McNaughton and Gunn.

Sullivan, Harry Stack
1953 *The Interpersonal Theory of Psychiatry*. New York: Norton.

Tax, Sol
    1978   The Impact of Urbanization on American Indians. *Annals of the American Academy of Political and Social Science* 436: 121–36.
Teaford, Jon C.
    1994   *Cities of the Heartland: The Rise and Fall of the Industrial Midwest.* Bloomington: Indiana University Press.
Urban, Greg
    1991   *A Discourse-Centered Approach to Culture: Native South American Myths and Rituals.* Austin: University of Texas Press.
Valentine, Lisa
    1996   *Making It Their Own: Severn Ojibwe Communicative Practices.* Toronto: University of Toronto Press.
Vizenor, Gerald
    1984   *The People Named Chippewa: Narrative Stories.* Minneapolis: University of Minnesota Press.
Wallace, Anthony F. C.
    1972   *The Death and Rebirth of the Seneca.* New York: Vintage Books
Weibel-Orlando, Joan
    1991   *Indian Country, L.A.: Maintaining Ethnic Community in Complex Society.* Urbana: University of Illinois Press.
Wittgenstein, Ludwig
    1953   *Philosophical Investigations.* New York: Macmillan.
Whorf, Benjamin
    1956   A Linguistic Consideration of Thinking in Primitive Communities. In *Language, Thought, and Reality: Selected Writings of Benjamin Lee Whorf.* Edited by J. B. Carroll. Cambridge: MIT Press.

Index

Ablon, Joan, 76
acculturation, 74–75, 84, 116, 127, 134, 139, 158, 159, 172n.7
Alcatrez Island, occupation of, 49, 171n.5
alcohol abuse, 58, 67, 104–5; and fetal alcohol syndrome, 73; and child abuse, 67; and domestic violence, 67
Alexander, Kevin, 149–50
allotment, 61–62, 84, 86; as legislated by the Dawes Severalty Act of 1887, 33
American Automotive Corporation, ix, 20, 22–25, 28–29, 39, 42, 55, 91, 156, 159
American Indian Movement, 49, 171n.5,n.6,n.7
American Indian Student Organization at Riverton University (formally the Native American Student Organization), x, xi, 27, 32, 43, 49–51, 96, 100, 115, 147, 159
Anishinaabe/Anishinaabeg, defined, x; families in Riverton, xi, 3–6, 16–18, 26, 27–31, 36–41, 48–49, 51, 53–54, 56–57, 61, 67, 76–77, 80, 82–84, 86–89, 99–100, 107–8, 110, 113, 115, 172n.1; traditional beliefs and practices of, 106–8, 116, 118–19, 121–33; language use, 4, 57, 59, 60, 76, 92, 104, 126, 136, 142, 171n.3, 174n.11
Anishinaabe bimaadiziiwin, 122, 124, 128, 146, 165
Appadurai, Arjun, 159–61, 166
Arndt, Grant, 170n.6

assimilation, 10, 33–34, 51, 74–77, 84, 87, 110–11, 114, 158, 172n.7
automotive industry, x, 19–26, 134
Aztec, 51

Barth, Frederik, 6–7, 10, 75
baskets, traditional Chippewa, 66, 95–96, 117, 174n.1
Basso, Keith, 93
Bauman, Richard, 93
bearwalking and other forms of "bad medicine," 123, 127–33, 162
Becker, Alton, 93
Behar, Ruth, 82
Bellecourt, Vernon, 51, 171n.6
Benson, Jake, 93–95, 97–98, 101, 104–5, 107
Birmingham County, ix, 3–4, 20, 21–25, 27–29, 31–32, 39, 41–44, 50–51, 137, 147, 169n.1,n.3
Birmingham County Indian Association (BICA), xi, 3–6, 16–18, 27, 30, 32, 36–43, 49–51, 68, 81, 91, 100–101, 115, 144, 146–48, 150–51, 154, 155, 158, 159, 161, 174n.10; annual meeting of, 3–6, 12–14, 16
Black, Mary. *See* Black-Rogers, Mary
"Black Indians," 47, 171n.3
Black-Rogers, Mary, 93, 123–24, 176n.5
blood quantum, 14, 44, 149
Blu, Karen, 10
Blumer, Herbert, 176n.5
Braroe, Neils Winter, 10, 169n.6, 176n.5
Brightman, Robert, 174n.3
Brown, Jennifer S.H., 174n.3